OPERATING WITH
POSITIVE IMPACT

How
to navigate
ESG
complexity

Axel Smits
Jochen Vincke

Lannoo
Campus

Photo credits:
iStock (pp. 16, 23, 30, 34-35, 45, 47, 51, 69, 88, 96-97, 131, 134, 153, 155, 161, 176, 180, 188 and 197) and Adobe Stock (p. 55)

ISBN 978 94 014 9817 3
D/2023/45/448
NUR 800

Second edition, 2024

LannooCampus Publishers
Vaartkom 41 box 01.02   P.O. Box 23202
3000 Leuven   1100 DS Amsterdam
Belgium   Netherlands
www.lannoocampus.com

Table of contents

How to operate with positive impact — 97

Foreword

Our world is seriously out of balance. The climate is off kilter, biodiversity is being reduced at an alarming rate, a number of vital eco-systems are endangered. Growing inequalities threaten our social cohesion, and increasing migratory flows put pressure on our societies and on our political systems.

Clearly, many situations, trends and behaviours that this generation is facing are unsustainable. What is unsustainable will, by definition, come to an end. The question, however, is whether we will be able to course-correct in time and avoid the most negative outcomes, or whether we will face a very hard landing. The jury is still out.

Unfortunately, there are no easy answers. There are no quick fixes or all-encompassing solutions. In order to change our trajectory before it is too late to avoid ever more catastrophic consequences, the conjunction of many efforts is required. It will take the combination of far-sighted political will, smart regulation, massive technological innovation as well as behavioural changes both at the individual, corporate and collective level. It will not do to shift the burden of adaptation and of intergenerational solidarity on someone else. We are all in this together.

The conscience thereof is growing. Following a number of pretty stark warnings which the media and the scientific community have brought to us in graphic clarity, we have seen some more hopeful developments. There is a growing understanding of the need for a more sustainable development.

An increasing number of citizens, especially in the younger generations, are actually changing their behaviours. Politicians are enacting more decisive legislation and redirecting funding, led by the European Union and recently also by the United States. International cooperation is making slow but steady progress. Innovation driven by academia and the business world is bringing new solutions more rapidly than many had thought possible. And many businesses are actually re-inventing their strategy and re-examining their modus operandi.

But, to date, all of this is not going fast enough. We need to act with more fortitude and steadfastness. This is also true for the business world.

Personally, I am convinced that corporations should take the sustainability concerns to heart if only out of pure (long-term) self-interest. It is companies that take see sustainability concerns and constraints earlier than others, and act on them, that will have the more resilient business models. It is companies that perceive sustainability-related opportunities earlier than their competitors, that will innovate faster and create new sources of competitive advantage. And it is companies that will take sustainability as a true priority (rather than as a communications imperative) that will attract the best talent.

But this belief is not universally shared in the corporate world. There are front-runners, but also laggards, sceptics and more opportunistically orientated actors.

This is why the ESG concept has been created. Originally driven by a number by a number of front-running corporations, academic thought leaders, consultants and by financial players promoting socially responsible investments, it is now increasingly being embraced by governments and standard-setters.

This formalisation of ESG frameworks and reporting standards has the great merit of forcing the laggards to address their issues more forthrightly and to help level the playing field for the more advanced companies. It carries some risks of bureaucratic overkill and box-ticking though. Therefore, it is crucial that we all work towards thoughtful, clear and eventually globally harmonised standards.

In any case, it appears that the notion of ESG is here to stay. The EU has made it a centrepiece of its regulatory strategy. In the United States it has recently been caught up in the culture wars, but also there the long-term trend appears to be inescapable. The rest of the world is moving ahead at various speeds, but it will be gradually pulled in as European and North American companies are forced to take more responsibility for their global supply chains.

This book is therefore a very timely overview of this rapidly evolving and complex subject matter. It is practical, precise and comprehensive, and I hope it can bring very concrete insights and inspiration to many in the corporate world.

Navigating the ESG complexity is now a priority for all of us.

Thomas Leysen
Chairman Umicore

A word from the editors

Environmental, social and governance (ESG) considerations are becoming increasingly vital in the corporate world today. Businesses are realising the importance of not only achieving profitability, but also having a positive impact on society and the environment. As companies grow more aware of the negative consequences of their operations on society and the planet, taking a sustainable approach helps mitigate these impacts and creates a more equitable and resilient future.

Aside from being socially and environmentally responsible, companies that prioritise ESG considerations also tend to experience better financial outcomes. Studies by McKinsey[1,2,3] show that companies with strong ESG performance are more likely to have stable earnings and are considered less risky investments. A strong ESG proposition can drive value creation in different ways: top-line growth (e.g. attracting more customers, better access to resources, brand spillover), cost reductions (e.g. lower energy costs), productivity uplift (e.g. improved employee motivation, talent attraction and retention), and investment and asset optimisation (e.g. enhanced investment returns, improved access to capital).

It therefore makes a lot of sense for companies to invest in a more sustainable operating model; one that takes into account the best interests of all of its stakeholders and not merely those of its shareholders. Even if some movements – in particular in the US – seem to disagree with focusing on ESG for the benefit of all stakeholders.

A lot has been written about ESG and its related topics, but we felt that what was missing was a roadmap not only providing insights into the various elements to consider, but also showing how to achieve a more sustainable business strategy. We hope this book provides that roadmap.

Operating with Positive Impact is a practical guide, based on decades of practical experience, written to help companies develop both a clear vision and a roadmap of what they can actually do to achieve greater positive impact. We hope it can guide and inspire you to identify areas for improvement and implement concrete actions to steer your business towards greater positive impact. We start with some basic insights to provide a broad understanding of ESG from a business perspective, from high-level concepts and principles to more specific details. We then dive into what companies (will) need to do in terms of strategy, reporting, transforming their operating model, etc., and what should be considered when engaging in M&A transactions.

We hope that this book will help companies that are seeking to make a more positive contribution to the impact economy. First, to assess and understand their current situation when it comes to their ecological, social and governance footprint. And secondly, to define their own transformation roadmap to achieve greater sustainability.

Axel Smits & Jochen Vincke

Editors

Axel Smits

Since 2016, Axel has been Chairman and Senior Partner at PwC Belgium, a network firm with a revenue of €400 million and around 2,400 employees.

Before assuming his current position, he was head of both PwC's Belgian Tax and Legal practice, and its EMEA Tax and Legal network.

In addition to his roles as Chairman and Senior Partner, Axel remains active as a client partner within the Belgian firm. He is also a member of the PwC Europe Board.

A lawyer by training, with additional degrees in taxation, accounting and finance, Axel is a chartered tax consultant.

For the first 20 years of his career, starting in 1990 with the predecessor firm Coopers & Lybrand, Axel was a chartered tax consultant with a particular focus on international tax planning. He served clients across the globe and was very active both as a speaker and as a writer of articles and books in his area of expertise. Topics included intellectual property as well as substance in international tax planning. Later on, while continuing to serve clients, Axel took on various management positions in the Belgian and EMEA firms, leading up to his current position.

Jochen Vincke

Jochen Vincke is Management Consulting Partner at PwC, coordinating services in the field of ESG, and consulting leader for PwC's EMEA industrial manufacturing industry practice. He is also a member of the Board of FlandersMAKE, a strategic research centre for the manufacturing industry, with over 750 researchers.

Jochen's ambition is to help drive a new industrial model that makes an overall net positive contribution to society; a model built on innovation, data, customer proximity, and short and circular supply chains.

After graduating as bio-engineer in environmental sciences, Jochen studied business economics and attained an MBA from Vlerick Business School. He is certified Master Black Belt in Lean Six Sigma.

Jochen has extensive experience in industry, including the food and beverage, chemical, steel processing, pharmaceutical and process industries. He has worked with ESG matters throughout his career, from developing corporate social responsibility (CSR) policies, to coaching and training, and business transformation consultancy.

Authors

Antoine Manderlier

Antoine is a manager in the operations team at PwC Belgium, with 11 years' experience in planning and running operations transformations. He has significant expertise in energy transition strategy for industries, with a track record in hard-to-abate sectors.

Bart Wyns

Bart has over 15 years' experience in grants and incentives specifically related to topics linked to sustainability, environment and climate. Since the 2019 EU Green Deal, Bart has been closely following and tracking all environment- and climate-related incentives, within the EU and globally.

Christoph Vanderstricht

Christoph has over 30 years' experience in the areas of ESG, M&A, governance, risk and compliance, and circular economy and sustainable value chains, across more than 43 countries. He has helped build PwC's ESG strategy and transformation business, having carried out more than 80 end-to-end circular and sustainable supply chain transformation projects for companies, industries and governments at country and international level. He has served as expert consultant for the EU, the OECD, UNECE and UNEP.

Colin Metzler

Colin has 10 years' experience closely following the evolution of European and global sustainability reporting regulations. His expertise is in guiding companies to build robust sustainability strategies and effective reporting processes. His insights are reflected in several thought leaderships where he has worked with leading sustainability reporting standard-setters.

Florian Jacques

Florian is a Senior Manager in PwC Belgium's Risk Assurance practice, focusing on sustainability advisory engagements. He supports his clients in developing their sustainability strategy as well as performing ESG due diligence in transactions.

Dennis Beel

Dennis Beel has specialised for 27 years in transforming companies from A to Z. He focuses on how to evolve capabilities (organisation, process, system, people, governance) in line with new strategic demands, from concept all the way through to running in 'the new normal'.

Dries Catteceur

Dries is a Manager in PwC Belgium's Technology Consulting practice, focused on integrating ESG into organisations through innovative technologies. By leveraging technology, he aims at empowering companies to embed sustainable practices and drive positive change.

Els Empereur

Els is a partner at PWC Legal and has more than 30 years' experience in environmental and public law. From this deep knowledge of the existing environmental regulations, she is well placed to stay on top of the rapidly expanding legal landscape and to advise her clients on all sustainability issues. This goes well beyond ticking boxes, because the legal function is a critical player in meeting ESG goals, and in creating sustained outcomes that drive value and fuel growth, whilst strengthening our environment and societies.

Sien Eylenbosch

With 10 years' experience in the sustainability field, Sien is specialised in sustainability reporting and assisting companies in identifying what sustainability means to them, how they can compose a solid sustainability strategy and how to become compliant with non-financial reporting regulations. She has a proven track record in leading sustainability assurance projects.

Ben Colson

Ben is a Director in PwC Belgium's Risk Consulting practice, with over 15 years' experience, specialising in governance, risk and compliance. He helps clients with establishing governance and operating models to comply with good corporate governance standards and regulatory obligations.

Marc Daelman

Marc Daelman is a Partner at PwC Belgium, specialising in Sustainability Assurance and Advisory Services, with over 30 years' experience. With a particular focus on ESG matters, he leads the Sustainability Assurance and Reporting Services of PwC Belgium and actively engages with research groups and associations in Belgium addressing corporate social responsibility and sustainable development. Marc manages a portfolio of national and international clients on sustainability from strategy, through execution, reporting and assurance.

Peter Opsomer

Peter is a Deals Partner at PwC Belgium. In addition to his responsibility for carve-outs and integrations and corporate accounts, he also looks after the link between due diligence and ESG specialists, moving the needle for ESG compliance-focused due diligence work towards creating a value bridge for clients.

Thomas De Cuyper

Thomas has 20+ years' experience in assurance and in the implementation of financial and internal control frameworks. He leverages this expertise to support his clients in implementing audit-proof ESG reporting frameworks. Thomas closely monitors the new EU regulations related to ESG reporting and helps clients in the transition towards a CSRD-compliant reporting of their non-financial information, as well as the technological solutions that can support this.

Tom Wallyn

Tom has over 20 years' experience in grants and incentives specifically related to topics linked to innovation, environment and sustainability. He focuses on implementing sustainable tax strategies and application of available tax incentives, in the EU and globally.

Julie Dejonckheere

Julie has 12 years' experience in operations, particularly operational excellence, across various industries. Today she focuses on sustainable supply chain management, CSRD and strategic sustainable transformation. She drives and coordinates several internal and external programmes regarding sustainability at PwC Belgium and Europe.

Jessica De Bels

Jessica has been a lawyer in social and employment law since 2014. As a senior managing associate at PwC Legal, she takes on a wide variety of social and employment law files. She deals with questions on individual and collective labour law, (international) restructurings and reorganisations, individual and collective dismissal, reward, social due diligence, social inspections, the new way of working and ESG (sustainable workforce).

Pierre Queritet

Corporate and M&A lawyer Pierre is co-lead lawyer at PwC Legal, where he advises corporations operating cross-border on corporate legal matters in transactions and reorganisations, including governance modelling, director liability, and rights and obligations of shareholders. He focuses on the specific role of legal counsels for ESG (CSRD/CS3D) in their companies.

Contributors

Hadrien Bosly

Hadrien, a lawyer since 2020, obtained an LL.M degree from University California Los Angeles where he specialised in international environmental law. His professional focus is on environmental law and regulatory matters at PwC Legal.

Ellen Cortvriend

Ellen is a Partner in the Indirect Tax Technology team in Belgium, with over 15 years' experience in EU VAT, e-invoicing, e-archiving and e-reporting requirements. She heads PwC's global Centre of Excellence on e-invoicing and e-reporting requirements.

Hanne Droesbeke

Hanne is Senior Manager in the PwC Belgium Corporate Tax group. She provides corporate tax services for multinationals and Belgium-based groups. As part of the central R&D team, Hanne has relevant experience in R&D tax incentives.

Marie Huret

As Associate at PwC Legal's Employment Law department since 2022, Marie advises clients on Belgian and global employment law, and on regulations related to social security (HR-oriented viewpoints on terminations, reorganisations, M&A activities, ESG matters and social inspections).

Samar Héchaimé

Samar is a Director at PwC Belgium, enabling clients to achieve strategic sustainable transformation. She is a multidisciplinary strategic leader with 25+ years' international experience across sectors. She relentlessly shapes long-term, value driven impact through system thinking, innovation, behavioural sciences and creativity, to design and implement sustainable, equitably diverse, renewable, valuable social and societal centric transformations.

Sander Van Driessche

Also an Associate at PwC Legal's Employment Law department since 2022, Sander advises clients on Belgian and international employment law and social security legislation. Specific topics are (collective and individual) dismissals, restructurings and M&A projects from an HR perspective, ESG matters and social inspections.

Quinten Smits

Quinten is a Senior Associate in the PwC Legal corporate and M&A practice where he provides legal assistance to various (inter)national companies and SMEs. He mainly focuses on M&A, (cross-border) legal restructurings, business contracts and corporate compliance including all ESG-related matters.

Lisa Vandorpe

Lisa, a lawyer with 5 years' experience in national and international labour and social security tax law, works with large and medium sized companies in different industrial sectors. At PwC Legal, she has built expertise in company restructurings and M&A, cross-border transactions, and information and consultation procedures. She also advises companies on flexible reward and ESG matters, and on day-to-day HR.

Miriam Pozza

Miriam is a Deals Partner at PwC Canada and leads the ESG Deals practice globally and across Canada. She has over 30 years' experience advising clients on leading the deals process to transaction close. As ESG Leader, she ensures that ESG factors are incorporated into investment decisions, to determine risks and opportunities in clients' acquisitions and capital investments.

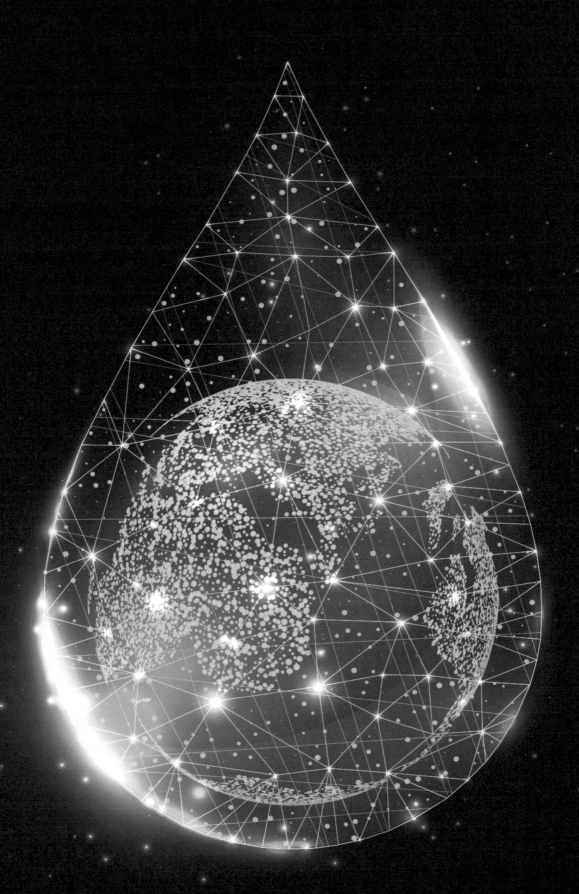

Understanding ESG

A primer on ESG and sustainability

01. Perspectives on today's world

02. A brief history of ESG

03. E for Environmental

04. S for Social

05. G for Governance

06. From ESG to SDG

07. From SDG to circular economy

Part 1 of Operating with Positive Impact focuses on the basics of evolving towards a more sustainable business operating model. Starting from our perspective on the world we live in today, we explain the concept of ESG, the introduction of the UN's SDGs and the movement towards a more circular economy.

Terminology

The terms 'sustainability' and 'ESG' can be confusing. 'Sustainability' has been defined in a thousand ways... Unless it's specifically defined, the only way to discern the meaning is to be guided by the context. It can mean:

- long-term economic/financial health and viability (of a company, operation, activity, etc.)
- [eco]system longevity
- survival of the human (or other) species
- survival of the planet
- all of the above.

The term ESG – environmental, social and governance – is defined in detail in Chapters 3, 4 and 5. More broadly speaking, 'ESG' is a relatively new umbrella word that's increasingly replacing or being used interchangeably with 'sustainability'.[4] We frequently use it like that in this book (e.g., ESG reporting ≅ sustainability reporting).

See the Appendix for a glossary of other terms and abbreviations used in this book.

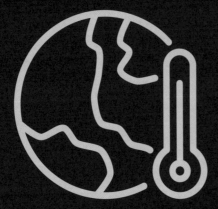

01.
Perspectives on today's world

Key takeaways

1. We are living in a world of increasing imbalance, with an uneven distribution of wealth, food and labour.

2. Nature is showing us that it can no longer cope with how we are mistreating our planet, while people are showing that they will no longer tolerate inequality.

3. It's time to move towards an 'impact economy' where sustainability is achieved through improving balance.

4. We all have a role to play in striving for positive impact.

The growing imbalance

These are interesting times. We live in a world of complete abundance. Never have technology, medicine and science in general been so advanced, never has there been so much wealth, and never have we been able to leverage so much of our planet's natural resources. Yet we do not seem to master this abundance very well: our resources are not well distributed.

For example, although there is ample food on our planet, we are unable to distribute it evenly. Too many people are still dying from hunger today, while there are more deaths from eating too much than from not eating enough.

Although there has always been a natural tension between supply and demand, we see an important imbalance occurring today. To fuel economic growth – and to mitigate the impact of any potential demand crisis – money was kept artificially cheap, resulting in levels of consumption which supply has been unable to keep up with. Suppliers are investing heavily to increase supply but it will take time to catch up. **Supply chains are also stressed when players strategically manipulate resources for speculative or other purposes.** From this perspective, the recent inflation and thus interest rate rise is not a bad thing, as it allows a certain cooling off to the benefit of our planet's resources.

The supply and demand challenges don't just affect goods. The labour market is also under pressure. In the developed world, a combination of factors – such as an ageing population, record high resignations and burnouts, skills mismatches, and the like – continues to drive the imbalance between supply and demand in the labour market. Companies in all sectors face recruitment difficulties that neither the large migration flows of recent years nor the work-from-anywhere trend have been able to resolve, yet many people do not have access to employment.

Another worrying imbalance is that between equity and debt. Because money was cheap, individuals and companies took on debts at levels exceeding what they could normally afford. Given the supply gap, prices went up dramatically, triggering in turn record high inflation numbers. To combat inflation, central banks have been increasing interest rates, which results in a much higher lending cost. Does that mean there is not enough equity in the world? No. But the record levels of consumption in recent decades have led to an extreme concentration of wealth, resulting in the equity sitting with the few while the ever-increasing debt sits with the many. And there are increasing signals that those who are or perceive themselves to be disadvantaged are no longer prepared to sit back and allow 'the rich get richer while the poor get poorer'.

And then there's the imbalance between what we take from our planet and how we nourish it. Climate change is a clear demonstration that there are limits to the abuse nature can take without adverse consequences. We have destroyed massive areas of forest, depleted natural energy resources (oil and gas), polluted the air, water and soil, and much more, in order to accommodate the needs of a population now exceeding eight billion. We have witnessed the abnormal rise of natural disasters in recent years. We have become dependent on finite resources such as oil and gas. And we have witnessed severe economic fall-out when war and otherwise disrupted supply chains were brought into the mix.

The rising tension

We have come to a culmination point where all these imbalances seem to reinforce each other. Where we proceed from crisis to crisis. We lived through the largest health crisis in a century, and before that was over we faced war in Europe and a resulting energy crisis, which in turn triggered high inflation and an economic downturn. And through all of this, every day one or more regions across the planet has to contend with some extreme weather event or natural disaster.

Some individuals have the resilience to cope with this level of uncertainty. Many do not. Covid-19, in particular, resulted in people rethinking their lives; many took major decisions, such as to resign from their jobs, with or without an alternative, change careers, change location... Others were simply no longer able to keep going and burned out.

The danger is that the tension caused by these imbalances results in social unrest and eventually

violence. It's only normal that everyone on the planet wants a decent standard of living for themselves and their families — something that will be increasingly difficult with a population of eight billion. If more and more people are unable to pay their debts or no longer have access to affordable housing, energy or food, then we may see behaviours we have not seen before. We may see otherwise good people resort to violence to get what they need.

Things. Must. Change.

We can no longer continue to kick the can down the road. We cannot continue to think that by simply printing more money all of our problems will go away. And yet this has been the answer of governments across the world to deal with many of today's challenges. We need fundamental behavioural change by both companies and individuals. Otherwise, the combination of today's imbalances will only drive us further apart.

For our very survival, we need to come together more than ever before, and use all the wisdom and human resources available to reimagine our collective futures.

The importance of communication — and hope

In case of fire, an accelerant will make things much worse, making it gradually impossible to extinguish. Yet this is what we see today when it comes to the storytelling around all these challenging events. It seems easier to bring messages of despair than to give people hope and the necessary confidence and energy to solve the problems that are upon us.

Whether it's about geopolitical tension, record high inflation, bankrupt governments, climate change, the energy crisis, inequality or social unrest, the news we read and hear about paints a very gloomy picture. Bad news travels faster and sells more but it rarely provides us with a solution.

Let's be clear. We are not naïve. And yes, all of these problems are very real. But we will not solve them by complaining that they exist. The biggest challenge today is not that we've got a lot of problems, but rather that they need a longer term vision and a detailed roadmap to solve them.

Unfortunately, this longer term perspective towards a more sustainable future is what's lacking in today's politics. Short-termism dominates and has opened the doors for extremist political parties to win support. People are struggling to get by today and they need a solution now, not ten years from now. But these extremist parties do not offer a real solution. Their strategy is to blame others and focus on what sets us apart. Divide to conquer. This is likely to only increase the tension that's already there, and result in further impoverishment and a higher likelihood of violence.

Considered at scale, this will only end up in wars, which will benefit neither our planet nor its inhabitants.

Restoring the balance

We believe that despair gets us nowhere. And in our opinion **there is a solution: to move towards an 'impact economy'.** An economy where sustainability is achieved through improving balance: balance between what we give and what we take, between the interests of the individual and of the collective, between those who have a lot and those who have less, between what's good for our planet and what works for its inhabitants. An economy that provides equal opportunities, irrespective of background or persuasion.

In a world thus balanced, a real estate developer, for example, would accept a somewhat reduced return to allow for affordable housing. Investors would require a societal return rather than just a purely financial return.

But for the required changes to have a sizable, significant impact, we need to dream BIG. And this is where the EU Green Deal[5] and the US Inflation Reduction Act (IRA)[6] offer hope. Big ambitions aimed at a more sustainable longer term future.

The EU Green Deal aims to set the EU on the path to a green transition, with the ultimate goal of reaching climate neutrality by 2050, by addressing environmental issues such as climate change, biodiversity loss, ozone depletion, water pollution, urban stress, waste production and more. The US Inflation Reduction Act offers funding, programmes and incentives to accelerate the transition to a clean energy economy.

Globalisation has brought us many benefits, even though we may be pushing its limits these days. Disrupted supply chains demonstrate how we have become overly dependent on faraway economies, and geopolitical tension is driving many to start 'thinking local' once more. Yes, we have pushed too much for low cost manufacturing and wilfully ignored the downsides, such as dependency and the negative impact of long distance logistics on our environment.

But we do not need to go to the other extreme either; we should not lose the advantages of access to global and diverse perspectives, of building connections that span the globe, helping us to nurture mutual understanding of each other's cultures.

In an increasingly digital world, it would be hard to imagine a more locally restricted digital economy. The internet has given us the opportunity to interact with others no matter the physical distance. The rise of the metaverse will further strengthen this ability to do business globally and take away some of the barriers encountered in the physical world.

For physical goods, we need to find new solutions: to think both 'global' and 'local', combining global delivery with more localised supply chains that reduce dependency and environmental impact.

While staying open to global opportunities, we will also need to rediscover the importance of our local communities. We will need to show more empathy for those around us, and accept that not everyone is able to move at the same pace.

We all have a role to play

It is upon all of us – indeed it's a moral duty – to leave the world behind in a better shape than we found it, to strive for a positive impact. Each one of us has something to contribute, no matter who we are or what our talents are. We should make the most of those talents. As for the cynics who will say that individual initiatives will not result in big changes, consider the proverb: if you think you are too small to make a difference, try sleeping with a mosquito in your room.

Aside from individual efforts, governments and companies can of course drive change at a larger scale if they so will. But rather than governments spending taxpayers' money on their own initiatives, they should focus on driving the right actions by their constituents, be they individuals or companies. Governments should offer an inspiring vision and create a framework that stimulates everyone to do their part — and demands an effort from everyone. Those who have a lot should be made to understand that they have a responsibility to accept a somewhat lower return and take on a positive role in society, whereas those who have little should be made to understand that their efforts also matter.

There is ever-increasing pressure on business to align its policies, actions and lobbying strength with its sustainability/ESG goals. And for individual companies to, as the saying goes, 'put their money where their mouth is'.

We believe that companies can contribute hugely to resolving some of today's most pressing issues. Even if companies are sometimes seen as part of the problem, the Edelman Trust Barometer[7] indicates that people still see companies as more likely to be successful in solving problems than governments, which continue to lose the trust of their constituents. Given their broad societal reach, most companies are a great ecosystem within which to test potential areas of progress, as they deal with a vast array of environmental, social and governance issues.

We have come to a point where action can no longer be optional. Considering the imbalance and increased tension we described earlier, the only alternative is to end up with a world where we will all be worse off.

In this book, we explore how to build a more sustainable business, starting with an outline of the meaning, role and importance of environmental, social and governance – ESG – factors.

02.
A brief history of ESG

The underlying ideas of ESG (environmental, social, governance) have been around for a very long time. The social challenges around labour and inequality have been part of social discourse for centuries. And the climate debate has been ongoing for more than fifty years.

Throughout the 20th century, we witnessed campaigns pressuring companies into fairer, more sustainable business practices. How well they worked is a matter of debate, but they certainly tried.[8]

Examples include efforts to stop the exploitation of workers, or the funding of wars or oppressive regimes like apartheid, and the introduction of corporate governance codes — legal 'rulebooks' telling companies how to manage themselves.

Events like these demonstrated that governments, investors and consumers recognised the power of corporate entities to shape the world around them. Over time, this power came under more and more scrutiny.[9]

Needless to say, the UN has played an important role in the fight against climate change, notably via its annual Conferences of the Parties (COPs). The first was in Berlin in 1995 and it continues to date.

But it wasn't until 2004 that the UN coined the much broader term 'ESG', in its report entitled 'Who cares wins'.[10] The report leaned heavily on all business stakeholders to embrace ESG principles in their strategies.

Ever since, people have been caring increasingly about climate change, mutual respect and diversity in the workplace, to name just a few. Two decades have passed, during which governments have embraced the ideas in their public policy and passed significant legislation to update their laws to reflect ESG principles.

Annual conferences such as the COP have kept and continue to keep the flame burning, emphasising the need for immediate action, especially around climate change. As we will illustrate further in this book, unfortunately – although growing – the sense of urgency is not yet ubiquitous, so the risk remains that we will not be able to stop global warming on time. Which in turn means that the focus may gradually shift towards dealing with its consequences (adaptation), rather than preventing it (mitigation).

Growing sense of urgency

Today, ESG has found its place in our priorities for dealing with the global challenges we all face.

But how concerned are business leaders? Well, it varies. Results from a global survey of CEOs[11] suggest that today's business leaders are conscious that we are living through extraordinary times, with five broad megatrends – climate change, technological disruption, demographic shifts, a fracturing world and social instability – reshaping the business environment. Although none of these forces is new, their scope, impact and interdependence are growing, with varied magnitude across industries and geographies.

How business leaders respond inevitably depends on how directly their own business is affected by these trends. For example, the survey found that:

"CEOs who feel most exposed to climate change are more likely to take action to address it. This kind of reactive approach is understandable – when your house is in the path of a forest fire, you reach for the hose – but it creates risks of its own. Combating climate change requires a coordinated, long-term plan. It won't be solved if the only companies working on it are those that face immediate financial impact. We also don't know how much the actions that are being undertaken most frequently – decarbonisation initiatives, along with efforts to innovate climate-friendly products and services – will move the needle, particularly in the near term, which, in light of emissions already in the atmosphere, promises continued warming under virtually every scenario."

In Chapters 3, 4 and 5, we outline the meaning of E, S and G and describe their current status and direction. Our purpose is to highlight the urgency of addressing ESG matters — not just by those companies directly affected in the short term, but by all of us, collectively and individually. In Part 2 of this book we provide insights and practical guidance on how to do so.

03.
E for environmental

Key takeaways

1. 'E for environmental' often focuses mainly on global warming, addressing issues linked to the increase of greenhouse gases (GHG).

2. Global industrialisation has resulted in soaring carbon dioxide (CO_2) emission rates.

3. CO_2 concentration has been unequivocally linked to global warming.

4. We need an 11-times faster decarbonisation rate to reach the Paris Agreement ambition of limiting global warming to 1.5°C.

5. Transitioning to renewable energy sources and carbon capture, utilisation and storage are the principal paths to reducing GHGs.

6. E is not limited to emissions: issues concerning our natural capital also include biodiversity loss, resource scarcity, land and water pollution, deforestation and more.

7. Some planetary boundaries or tipping points may already have been breached.

What's behind the 'E'?

Although 'ESG' is a whole concept, with the three aspects – environment, social and governance – being largely interdependent, the 'E', environment, generally dominates the discourse.

This is understandable in view of the sheer scale of the problems that are encompassed by this one word (or letter!).

Humans have always faced environmental problems. Practices that have had negative impacts on wildlife habitats and human cultures have occurred for millennia, from cutting down huge swathes of forest to hunting animal species to extinction. In the past centuries, air or water pollution due to human activities was often a source of major concern as cities expanded. Across the world, both agricultural and industrial practices have resulted in harmful effects on land and people; this is nothing new.

In the 1970s, concern for the environment began to grow. But widespread public alarm about envi-

ronmental issues is relatively recent. Since the turn of this century, that alarm has been turning into something resembling panic. Much of that is focused on the most pressing of our environmental issues: climate change.

In the past decades, it has become impossible to ignore signs of climate change, no matter where in the world you are.

While extreme weather events have always occurred, they are happening with a frequency and intensity that are not 'normal' (Figure 1). Such events are not just frightening, but also expensive and potentially dangerous in the longer term. They cause massive damage to property and communities, sometimes leading to population displacement and social unrest. As a result, it has become nearly impossible to deny that our activities – notably emissions of greenhouse gases (GHG) – are causing global warming and climate change. There are still some who deny climate change or its impact, but their numbers are dwindling.

Figure 1 – World map of some extreme weather events that occurred in one month, June 2022[12]

GLOBAL AVERAGE TEMPERATURE
June 2022 average global surface temperature was the sixth highest for June since global records began in 1880.

CONTIGUOUS U.S.
Heavy rain and melting snowpack resulted in severe flooding in parts of southern Montana on June 13, forcing the evacuation and temporary closure of Yellowstone National Park and surrounding towns.

TROPICAL STORM ALEX
Alex was the Atlantic's first named storm of the season. Before becoming a named storm, it caused flash flooding in western Cuba and southern Florida.

NORWAY
Tromsø, Norway's largest city above the Arctic Circle, set a new temperature record for June, beating the previous record set in 1974.

EUROPE
Europe had its second-hottest June on record.

ARCTIC SEA ICE EXTENT
The Arctic had its 10th-smallest June sea ice extent in the 44-year record.

ASIA
Asia had its second-hottest June on record.

JAPAN
A heat wave scorched Japan in the middle of its rainy season. This June marked the worst documented streak of hot weather in June since 1875.

MEXICO
Monterrey, Mexico, suffered a weeks-long water shortage due to persistent drought and high rates of surface water evaporation. The region has been in a state of emergency since February.

SOUTH AMERICA
Much of South America experienced near- to cooler-than-average June temperatures. As a whole, it had its coolest June since 2016.

AFRICA
Africa had its 10th-warmest June (tied with 1999) on record.

GLOBAL CYCLONE ACTIVITY
Globally, five named storms formed, which is near-average June cyclone activity. Only one storm (Bias) reached tropical cyclone strength.

ANTARCTIC SEA ICE EXTENT
Sea ice extent in Antarctica hit a record low for the month of June.

CHINA
Severe flooding forced thousands to evacuate parts of southern China. Some locations were hit by the heaviest downpours in 60 years.

NEW ZEALAND
New Zealand had its eighth-warmest June on record.

The climate emergency: global warming

Climate change is not the only environmental issue we face, as we will discuss below, but it's potentially the most urgent, as the impact of global warming becomes ever more obvious.

Figure 2 – Visualisation of global mean temperature increase since pre-industrial times[13]

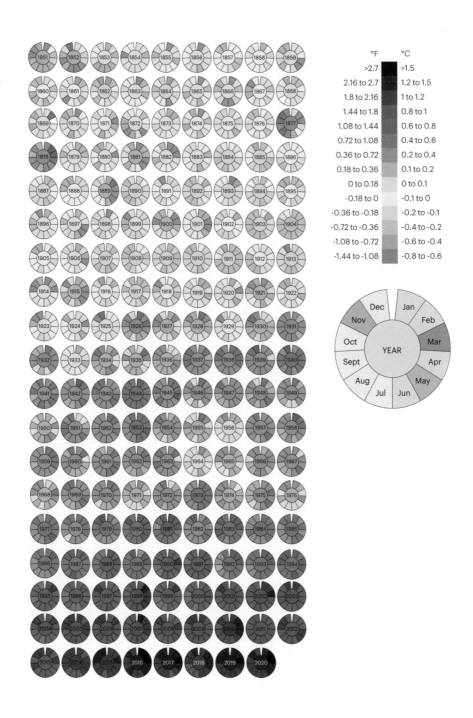

In recognition of the dangers of global warming for our climate and planet, in 2015 the large majority of countries came together under the Paris Agreement, announcing a shared goal to limit global warming to 1.5°C above pre-industrial levels.

The Agreement sets long-term goals to guide all nations to:[14]

- substantially reduce global GHG emissions to hold the increase in the global average temperature to well below 2°C above pre-industrial levels and pursue efforts to limit the temperature increase to 1.5°C above pre-industrial levels
- review countries' commitments every five years
- provide financing to developing countries to mitigate climate change, strengthen resilience and enhance abilities to adapt to climate impacts.

The Agreement is a legally binding international treaty since 4 November 2016. Today, 194 Parties (193 States plus the European Union) have joined the Paris Agreement.

Progress can be seen all around us in terms of decarbonisation. But it's insufficient. Our decarbonisation rate should be 11 times faster than it has been these last 2 years if we are to reach the Paris Agreement ambitions (Figure 3).[15]

Figure 3 – Net Zero Economy Index 2022. Source: PwC

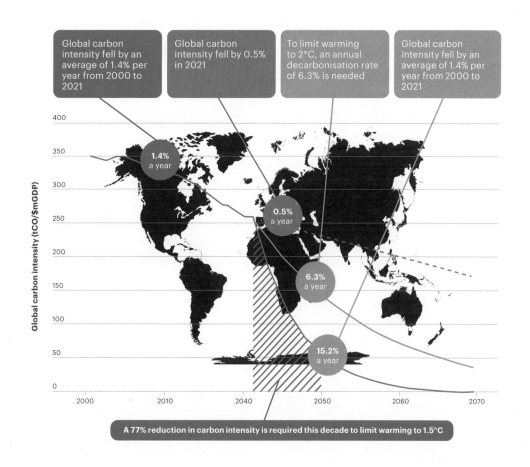

GHG emissions

Science has clearly demonstrated that global warming is very real. Its causes are complex. However, the latest Assessment report from the UN Intergovernmental Panel on Climate Change (IPCC)[16] highlights that global warming is primarily related to increased CO_2 emissions due to human activity.

Industrialisation was fuelled by electricity and fossil fuel use; the western world has a lot to be grateful for thanks to the use of these resources. It's often argued that we cannot now expect less wealthy countries to progress and grow without using cheap natural resources such as gas and oil. And that more-advanced economies have a moral obligation to support and invest in those countries to support their growth while taking climate impact into consideration.

Since World War II, globalisation and global trade have increased. Supply chains became longer and more complex as production shifted to lowest-wage countries. This made our industries more susceptible to events such as Covid-19 and led to the emissions levels seen today. The future probably holds more local-for-local supply chains that have a smaller carbon footprint,[17] but are connected by a digital backbone.

GHG categories

Greenhouse gas emissions all fall under one of three categories, referred to as Scope 1, Scope 2 and Scope 3. This classification system was developed by the Greenhouse Gas Protocol[18] as part of its standards, tools and online training developed to help countries, cities and companies track progress towards their climate goals (Figure 4).[19]

- Scope 1 covers direct emissions that a company generates through operating the assets it owns or controls (running buildings, driving vehicles, powering machinery...).
- Scope 2 covers indirect emissions: those created by the production of the energy the company buys for power, heating and cooling.
- Scope 3 covers everything else: both upstream and downstream indirect emissions. It includes emissions due to the use or disposal of their products by their customers and users further down the value chain, right to the end of the product's life cycle, or emissions produced by suppliers that make the products the company uses.

Scope 3 (indirect) emissions are the largest, and most difficult to measure and tackle, as they include all GHG emissions both upstream and downstream in the value chain.

Figure 4 – Overview of sources of Scope 1, 2 and 3 emissions across the value chain[20]

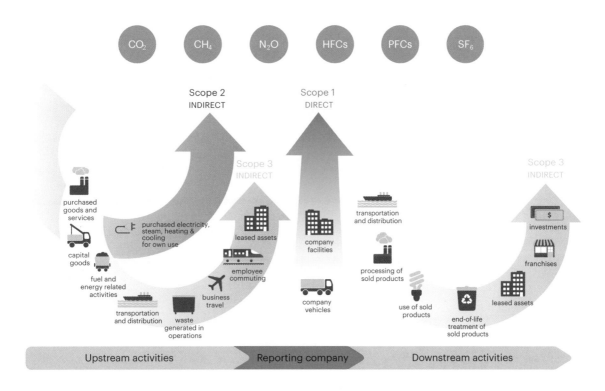

Emissions resulting from industrialisation

Mapping global temperature against carbon dioxide emissions indicates a disturbing correlation (Figure 5).

Concentrations of CO_2 in the atmosphere have risen more than 40% from around 290 parts per million (PPM) in 1800 to over 410 PPM today, while average global temperatures have risen by 1.1%.

Figure 5 – Correlation between global temperatures and carbon dioxide concentration[21]

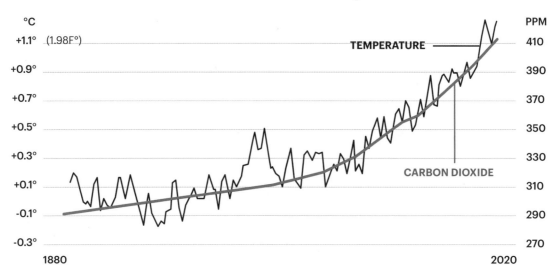

GLOBAL TEMPERATURE & CO$_2$

Global temperature anomalies averaged and adjusted to early industrial baseline (1881-1910)
Global annual average carbon dioxide
Source: NASA GISS, NO. NCEI, ESRL

CO_2 is the worst offender in terms of global warming, but it's not the only culprit. As Figure 6 indicates, in the past two decades other gases have also contributed to GHG emissions from human activities. Methane, for example, has a significant impact. Methane emissions are primarily linked to meat production. The race to reduce emissions needs to focus on all the sources.

However, CO_2 emissions from the use of fossil fuels cause more GHG emissions than the other sources combined, which explains the huge focus of legislators and corporations on reducing the use of fossil fuels.

Global net anthropogenic emissions have continued to rise across all major groups of GHGs.

Figure 6 – Global net anthropogenic GHG emissions[22]

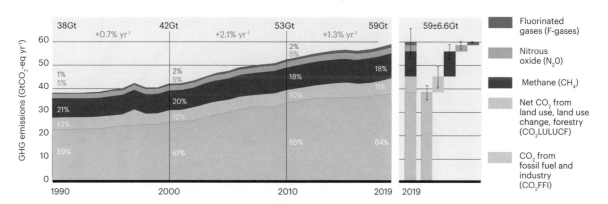

a. Global net anthropogenic GHG emissions 1990-2019)

b. Global anthropogenic GHG emissions and uncertainties by gas — relative to 1990

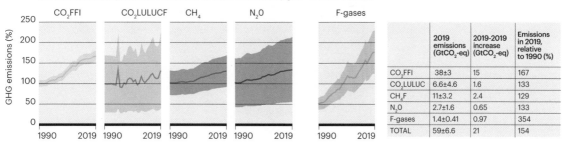

	2019 emissions (GtCO$_2$-eq)	2019-2019 increase (GtCO$_2$-eq)	Emissions in 2019, relative to 1990 (%)
CO$_2$FFI	38±3	15	167
CO$_2$LULUC	6.6±4.6	1.6	133
CH$_4$F	11±3.2	2.4	129
N$_2$O	2.7±1.6	0.65	133
F-gases	1.4±0.41	0.97	354
TOTAL	59±6.6	21	154

The solid line indicates central estimate of emissions trends. The shaded area indicates the uncertainty range.

GHG emissions by industry sector

Figure 7 – Global greenhouse gas emissions by sector. Graphic shows emissions in 2016. Global GHG emissions were 49.4 billion tonnes CO_2e.[23]

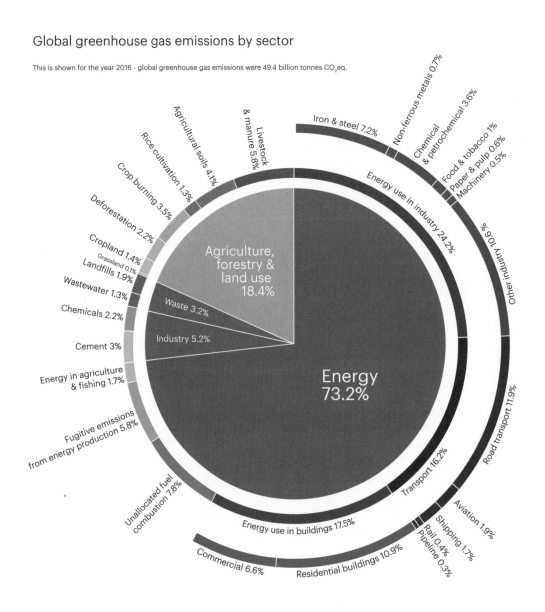

Global greenhouse gas emissions by sector

This is shown for the year 2016 - global greenhouse gas emissions were 49.4 billion tonnes CO_2eq.

Before we can figure out the most effective ways to reduce GHG emissions, we need to understand where they come from.

Most human activities contribute to GHG emissions, as illustrated in Figure 7. The predominant source – almost three-quarters – is from energy, including energy use in buildings, transportation and industry. Reducing GHG emissions significantly in these sectors will clearly deliver the greatest results.

Figure 7 also helps challenge assumptions and, perhaps, misperceptions. When faced with accusations in relation to our own (personal or corporate) responsibility for global warming, we are all good at pointing a finger to place the blame elsewhere. This graphic helps to put our assumptions into perspective. GHG emissions come from many different activities in different sectors — and many are closely interrelated or even interdependent.

Tackling GHG emissions

Finding the best ways to reduce GHG is undoubtedly complex. For example, it has been argued that reducing meat consumption would cause an increase in GHG emissions from the cultivation of rice and other crops. One needs to explore at what point does such a potential trade-off become beneficial or detrimental in terms of overall GHG emissions? In 2021, such a study was published. It concluded that *"Global greenhouse gas emissions from animal-based foods are twice those of plant-based foods"*.[24]

It further concluded that of the global GHG emissions from the production of food, 57% corresponds to the production of animal-based food (including livestock feed), 29% to plant-based foods and 14% to other utilisations. Rice and beef were the largest contributing plant- and animal-based commodities. A quarter of global GHG emissions in the food industry result from beef production alone, while 12% result from rice production.

More importantly, any legislation or business transformation would need to take into account complete food systems including processing, packaging, transport, retail and waste.

One of the primary methods being used to reduce GHGs is carbon capture, utilisation and storage (CCUS).

Carbon capture, utilisation and storage
CCUS is a set of technologies and practices aimed at mitigating CO_2 emissions from industrial processes and power generation. CCUS offers a promising pathway for reducing greenhouse gas emissions while enabling continued use of fossil fuels and supporting the transition to a low-carbon economy.

Carbon capture	Carbon utilisation	Carbon storage*
Capture of CO_2 emissions from various sources, such as power plants, industrial facilities, and even directly from the atmosphere. Typically employs technologies such as post-combustion capture, pre-combustion capture or oxyfuel combustion, which separate CO_2 from flue gases or exhaust streams. Captured CO_2 can then be transported for further utilisation or storage.	Conversion of captured CO_2 into valuable products or chemicals, creating economic opportunities while reducing CO_2 emissions. Encompasses a wide range of applications, including the production of chemicals, building materials, plastics and fuels. Carbon utilisation not only reduces GHGs but also provides a circular economy approach to carbon management.	Injection of captured CO_2 deep underground into geological formations, such as depleted oil and gas reservoirs, saline aquifers or coal seams. This permanently isolates CO_2 from the atmosphere, preventing its release and subsequent contribution to climate change. *Also known as carbon sequestration

CCUS technologies offer multiple benefits in the fight against climate change. They provide an opportunity to capture and store significant amounts of CO_2 emissions, reducing the carbon footprint of energy-intensive industries and fossil fuel-based power generation. Additionally, carbon utilisation transforms CO_2 from a waste product into a valuable resource, promoting the circular economy and driving innovation in various sectors.

However, challenges remain in the widespread deployment of CCUS. These include high costs, technical complexities, infrastructure require-ments and public acceptance. Overcoming these challenges requires continued research and development, and supportive policies to incen-tivise investment and foster collaboration among industry, governments and research institutions.

All of this illustrates the importance of not jumping to the perhaps 'obvious' solutions when looking to make positive changes, but of making decisions based on solid data, factual information and analysis of complete value chains, as well as forecasts of consequences.

Transition to renewable energy

Instead of, or in parallel with carbon capture, utilisation and storage, GHG emissions can be reduced by transitioning to alternative, renewable energy sources. This of course comes at a cost.

Combustion fuels — Natural gas and grey hydrogen are the most cost-effective today (Table 1), but the situation is expected to change fast as regulations put an ever-increasing price on CO_2 emissions, and as technology improvements make sustainable fuels more affordable. **It's expected that by 2030, blue and green hydrogen will be cost competitive with natural gas** (See also: Figure 10, p. 46).

Electricity generation — Renewable energy is more local and is highly variable in price (Table 2). For example, hydropower is cheaper in Norway than in Belgium.

Table 1 – Current costs (range) of gas, biomethane and hydrogen.[25]

Combustion fuel	Production cost [€/MWh]	Transport cost [€/MWh]	Total cost [€/MWh]
Natural gas	23	19	42
Biomethane	81		81
Green hydrogen	90-240	15-210	105-450
Blue hydrogen	45-75	15-210	60-288
Grey hydrogen	30-60	15-210	45-270
Turquoise hydrogen	45-60	15-210	60-270
Pink hydrogen	69-75	15-210	84-288

Table 2 – Current costs for alternative electricity generation processes.[26]

Electricity generation process	Production cost [€/MWh]
Reference price for 2023	113
Wind onshore	60
Hydropower	75
Nuclear electricity	75
Wind offshore	85
Solar panels	100
Concentrated solar power (CSP)	180

In the EU, renewable electricity is already cost competitive with or even cheaper than conventional sources. However, one of the main challenges that persists is the intermittency and availability of renewable resources. Unlike fossil fuels, which can provide consistent power generation, the availability of solar and wind resources is subject to natural fluctuations. Addressing this challenge requires further advancements in energy storage technologies, grid flexibility, and the integration of complementary renewable energy sources.

A primer on energy sources and emissions

Understanding the intricacies of energy sources and their impact is essential for making informed decisions regarding sustainability and environmental impact. The decisions we make regarding energy sources and consumption have far-reaching consequences, not only for our planet but also for businesses and economies worldwide. **By integrating the relationship between energy choices and CO_2 emissions into decision making, executives can actively participate in mitigating climate change**, fulfilling their corporate social responsibility, and aligning with global sustainability goals.

Fossil fuels

Fossil fuels have been the dominant sources of energy for centuries. However, the extensive use of fossil fuels, notably coal, oil and natural gas, has resulted in significant environmental and climate damage due to releases of GHGs and other pollutants.

Coal
Coal, a carbon-rich sedimentary rock, has historically played a crucial role in electricity generation and industrial processes. While coal reserves are abundant in many parts of the world, its extraction and combustion release substantial amounts of CO_2 as well as other harmful pollutants such as sulphur dioxide (SO_2) and nitrogen oxides (NO_x). These emissions contribute to air pollution, respiratory diseases and global climate change. In recent years, the declining use of coal has been driven by environmental concerns and the increasing competitiveness of renewable energy sources.

Oil
Oil, also known as petroleum, is a versatile fossil fuel used in transportation, heating and various industrial processes. Burning oil releases CO_2 and other pollutants, and its extraction and transportation pose risks to ecosystems, including the potential for oil spills. Moreover, oil reserves are geographically concentrated, leading to geopolitical tensions and economic vulnerabilities in regions heavily dependent on oil imports. The transition towards cleaner energy alternatives and electric transportation is gradually reducing the demand for oil.

Natural gas
Natural gas, composed mainly of methane (CH_4), has gained prominence as a relatively cleaner fossil fuel with lower CO_2 emissions compared to coal and oil. It is primarily used for electricity generation, heating, and industrial processes. Natural gas reserves are abundant and widely distributed globally. However, methane, a potent greenhouse gas, can leak during extraction, transportation, and storage, contributing to climate change. Technological advancements in methane detection and capture are crucial to minimise emissions from natural gas operations. As the energy landscape evolves, natural gas is being scrutinised as a transitional fuel, with renewable energy sources gaining prominence as long-term solutions.

Fossil fuel consumption

Fossil fuel consumption has been steadily rising since the early 19th century. The current forecast expects fossil fuel demand to peak around 2025 and then steadily decrease as society transitions to sustainable energy sources. Coal demand is expected to decrease at the fastest rate, as it's the most carbon-intensive source of energy in use today.

Figure 8 – Global fossil fuel consumption: global primary energy consumption by fossil fuel source.[27]

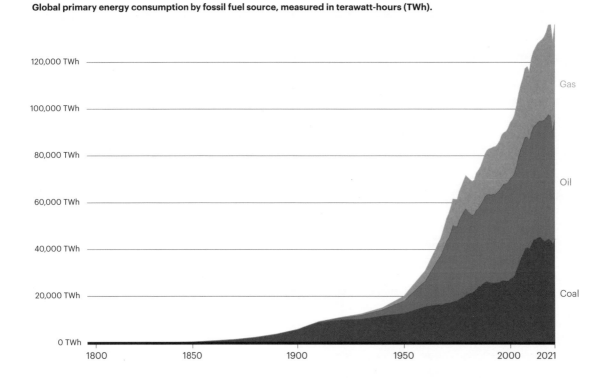

Global primary energy consumption by fossil fuel source, measured in terawatt-hours (TWh).

Nuclear power

Nuclear power plants generate electricity through a process called nuclear fission. Nuclear power plants provide a low-carbon energy option, but they also pose challenges related to waste management, safety concerns and public perception.

Renewable energy sources

Renewable energy sources are more sustainable alternatives to fossil fuels: they are naturally replenished and have a lower environmental impact. They play a crucial role in mitigating climate change and reducing GHGs.

Solar energy

Solar energy is sunlight converted into electricity through photovoltaic (PV) cells or concentrated solar power (CSP) systems. PV cells directly convert sunlight into electricity, while CSP systems use mirrors or lenses to concentrate sunlight and produce heat, which is then converted into electricity. Solar energy is abundant, widely available and emits zero GHGs during electricity generation. It is used for residential, commercial and industrial applications, ranging from rooftop solar panels to large-scale solar power plants.

Wind energy

Wind energy is harnessed through wind turbines that convert the kinetic energy of the wind into electricity. As the wind blows, the rotating blades of the turbines spin a generator, producing electricity. Wind power is a rapidly growing source of renewable energy due to its vast availability and relatively low environmental impact. Wind farms can be installed on land or offshore, and they produce clean electricity without emitting GHGs. Energy generation is dependent on suitable wind conditions and requires careful site selection.

Hydroelectric power

Hydroelectric power is generated by harnessing the energy of moving water, typically in rivers or [ocean] tidal dams. Water flows through turbines, which rotate and generate electricity. Hydroelectric power is one of the oldest forms of renewable energy and a significant source of electricity worldwide. It is a reliable and flexible source, capable of providing base-load power. However, hydroelectric projects can have environmental impacts, including habitat disruption, alteration of river ecosystems, and displacement of communities.

Geothermal energy

Geothermal energy uses heat from within the Earth's crust to generate electricity or provide heating and cooling. It is obtained through geothermal power plants that tap into underground reservoirs of hot water or steam, or from local installations to power individual buildings. Geothermal power is a constant and reliable source of energy with minimal environmental impact and GHGs. Extraction of geothermal energy from the grounds does lead to a release of GHGs (hydrogen sulphide, carbon dioxide, methane and ammonia), but the amount of gas released is significantly lower than with fossil fuels. Generation of large amounts of geothermal energy is geographically limited to areas with active geothermal resources.

Biomass energy

Biomass energy is derived from organic materials, such as wood, organic residues or dedicated energy crops. It can be used directly for heating and cooking or converted into biogas, bioethanol or biodiesel for electricity generation and transportation.

Biomass is considered a renewable energy source because the carbon released during its combustion is offset by the carbon absorbed by plants during their growth. Biomethane can even be considered carbon-negative when compared with letting organic waste decompose and emit methane in the atmosphere, by capturing the emitted methane to burn it. However, careful sourcing and sustainable management of biomass resources are essential to ensure its environmental benefits and to prevent deforestation or food security concerns.

Figure 9 – Anaerobic digestion process to produce biogas and biomethane[28]

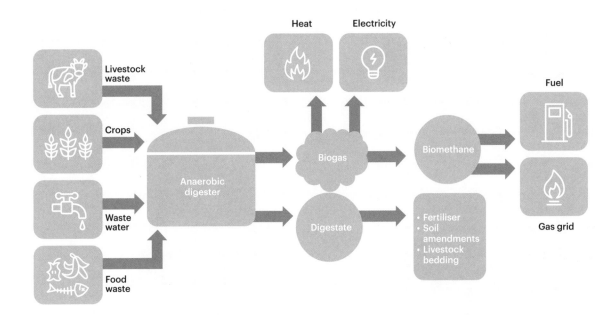

Hydrogen

Hydrogen is an energy carrier, or vector, rather than a direct source of energy.[29] When we talk about hydrogen as an energy source, it's a shorthand for a process (see p.47). Hydrogen is the most abundant element in the universe, but in its pure form, it's not readily available and must be extracted from various sources.

Hydrogen has gained increasing attention in recent years due to its potential as a versatile and clean alternative to traditional fossil fuels. There are two main ways to produce hydrogen: steam methane reforming (SMR) and water electrolysis.

Hydrogen is classified into an intricate colour system, ranging from black to green, that defines its production method (Figure 10).

Hydrogen holds promise as a sustainable energy solution: its combustion produces only water vapour, making it a zero-emissions fuel. Moreover, hydrogen can be utilised across various sectors, including transportation, power generation and industrial processes.

However, widespread adoption of hydrogen as an energy source is challenging. First, because hydrogen production is currently energy intensive, costly and often relies on fossil fuels. Secondly, establishing an extensive hydrogen infrastructure, including production, storage and distribution networks, requires substantial investment and coordination among various stakeholders. Producing affordable, low-carbon hydrogen at scale will require significant infrastructure investments and technological improvements.

Figure 10 – Main hydrogen colours

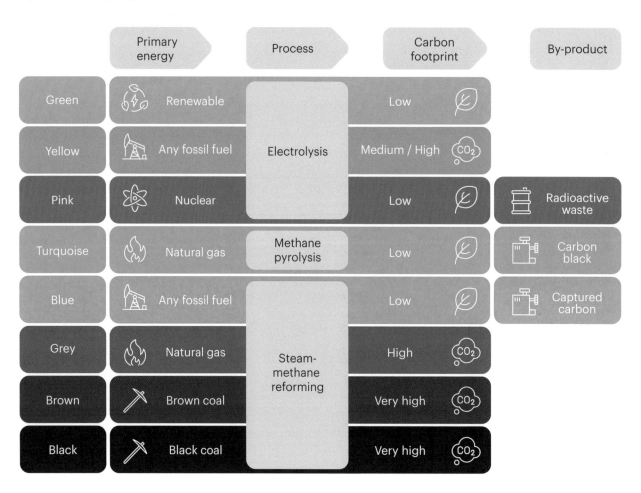

Hydrogen production

Steam methane reforming is a process commonly used to produce hydrogen from natural gas, which is primarily composed of methane (CH_4). It involves a series of chemical reactions that convert methane and steam (H_2O) into hydrogen gas and carbon dioxide (CO_2). The process typically takes place at high temperatures (700–1,000°C) and requires a catalyst to facilitate the reactions.

Steam methane reforming is a well-established and commercially viable method for large-scale hydrogen production, as it can efficiently utilise existing natural gas infrastructures. However, it results in the release of CO_2. To mitigate its environmental impact, SMR can be combined with carbon capture and storage technologies.

Water electrolysis involves the splitting of water molecules (H_2O) into hydrogen gas (H_2) and oxygen gas (O_2) using an electrical current. The process typically requires three main components: an electrolyser, a source of electricity and water.

One of the significant benefits of water electrolysis is that it can utilise renewable electricity sources, such as solar or wind power, enabling the production of green hydrogen with zero carbon emissions. The process can be energy-intensive, and the overall efficiency depends on factors such as the quality of the electrolyser and the source of electricity.

Today, there are also experimental initiatives to produce hydrogen in 'ultra-green' systems, such as photosynthesis-based processes using light instead of electricity.

Trends in renewable energy generation

Over the past century or so, hydroelectric power generation was the dominant form of renewable energy, as shown in Figure 11.[30] Today, its potential for growth is limited by the availability of suitable areas and by its impact on local communities and the environment. Wind and solar energy are the fastest growing types of renewable energy; this growth is expected to continue for the foreseeable future.

Figure 11 – Renewable energy generation worldwide. Note: 'Other renewables' refers to renewable sources including geothermal, biomass, waste, wave and tidal. Traditional biomass is not included.[31]

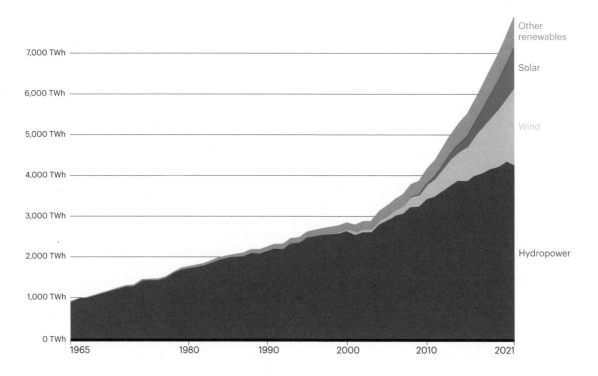

Renewable energy generation, World

E for ecosystem

The E in ESG stands for environmental, meaning everything that surrounds us. But environmental sustainability is not just about the environment. It's about the interconnections and interactions between the environment and the living organisms within it — the ecosystem.

Changes in the air we breathe and the atmosphere that envelops our planet are top of mind when we think of environment and climate change. Understandably so: the emissions sent into the atmosphere from human activities are the primary root cause of rapid climate change. But **healthy ecosystems are just as important as a stable climate.** Ecosystems provide the air we breathe, the food we eat and the water we drink. And they help us absorb and store carbon.

Natural capital

Unfortunately, atmospheric emissions are very far from being the only thing threatening our ecosystem. There are equally significant environmental threats to land and oceans, animals (including humans!) and habitats.

Worldwide, the destruction of nature is occurring at an unprecedented pace. Urban sprawl, intensive agriculture, pollution, invasive species and climate change are exerting immense pressure on ecosystems and the valuable services they provide. Our natural capital – i.e., the stock of natural resources, including geology, soils, air, water and all living organisms – is in alarming decline. In Europe, more than 80% of natural habitats are in poor condition.

To properly assess the sustainability of human activities, we need to take a holistic view of their impact on our natural capital.

Since 2009, scientists have come together under the auspices of the Stockholm Resilience Centre[32] (Stockholm University) to study and quantify these threats to our natural capital, defining them within a regularly updated framework of nine planetary boundaries.

The nine planetary boundaries

Figure 12 – The nine planetary boundaries[33]

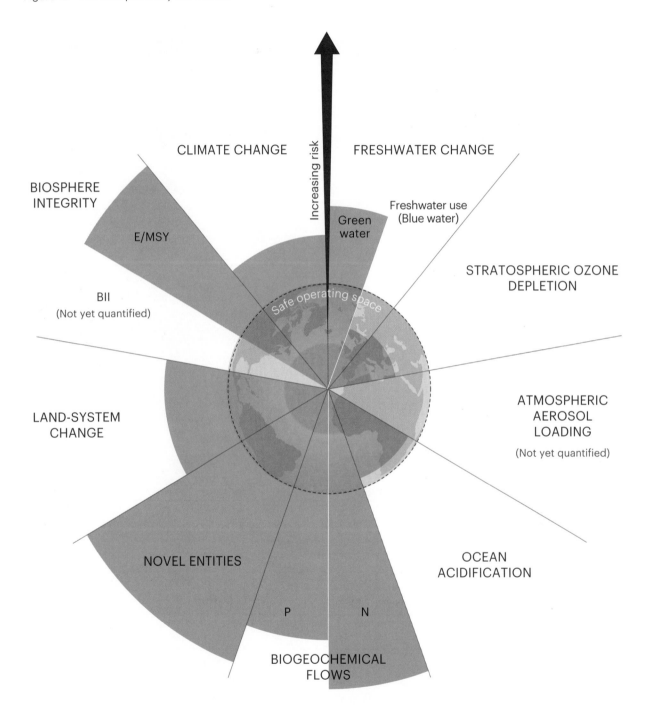

'Planetary boundaries' is a concept presenting a set of nine limited zones within which humanity can continue to develop and thrive for generations to come. Figure 12 is an illustration of where we currently stand with respect to each boundary, with the green area representing a 'safe' zone and the yellow-to-orange areas signifying increasing levels of risk.

Outside the green zone is where we have already gone beyond what's considered a safe operating space. Each of the boundaries incorporates a zone of uncertainty (the orange area around the green area). This zone signifies gaps and/or weaknesses in the current scientific knowledge including uncertainties about how the Earth system functions and how resilient it is to changes within this boundary. The further one gets beyond the safe zone, the higher the probability of a change to the functioning of the Earth system. And the higher the risk of consequences such as diversity loss, human suffering, massive human migration, socio-political upheaval and regime shifts.

Everything connects

The nine planetary boundaries are intimately interconnected. For example:

- CO_2 emissions contribute significantly to ocean acidification. Seawater absorbs CO_2 from the atmosphere. Once dissolved, CO_2 lowers the pH, making the water more acidic.
- There is increasing evidence that ratios between elements in the environment – shown in Figure 12 as the biogeochemical flows of phosphorus (P) and nitrogen (N) – may have impacts on land and ocean biodiversity. Note that these P and N levels are almost entirely from fertilisers applied to croplands, from just a few agricultural regions that have very high P and N application rates.
- Novel entities are new substances, new forms of existing substances and modified life forms introduced into the environment by human activities. They have potential to impact any of the boundaries. For example, CFCs (chlorofluorocarbons) were once considered harmless but had dramatic effects on the stratospheric ozone layer. Today, heavy metals, nanoparticles, micro-plastics or genetically modified organisms are just some examples of substances increasingly being mobilised in industry but whose long-term impacts on the planetary boundaries are not yet clear.
- Land-system changes impact the climate and biosphere integrity (i.e. loss of biodiversity). For example, cutting down tropical forests to create croplands creates changes in evapotranspiration (the interchange of water between soil and the atmosphere) and destroys animal habitats.

What does 'E for environmental' mean for companies?

Companies bear the brunt of responsibility

The World Economic Forum (WEF) has pointed out in their Global Risk Report that climate change is of the highest importance in terms of risk for human life,[34] but what does it mean exactly for corporations? And what of the other planetary boundaries?

There's no question that it is corporations and organisations – not individuals – who have the greatest impact on the planetary boundaries, and therefore bear the weight of responsibility for finding solutions. Individuals can do their part, from recycling plastics to using less-pollutant means of transport, but the data clearly shows that individual contributions to environmental impacts are miniscule compared to corporate – particularly industrial – impacts.

That said, individuals have potentially enormous power to influence corporations. We can stop eating meat, buy local, switch to energy companies providing green energy, and – to put it simply – buy less stuff. We could reuse, reduce, recycle. And a growing number of people are doing so. But such decisions are often reserved for the better-off, and are more a matter of lifestyle than far-reaching socio-economic change.

However, such behavioural changes do illustrate the increasing social pressures on companies to 'clean up their act'. Governments are adding further pressure through legislative and regulatory initiatives to drive improved industrial operations and corporate practices.

What can companies do?

Each company needs to develop their own ESG plan, including a transition roadmap focusing on emissions, pollutants and other factors within the planetary boundaries scope. But it's not all about individual companies and individual initiatives. Real change will also depend on governments, such as actions to promote renewable energy sources, and prohibitive measures such as carbon taxation. One of the more important mechanisms is the Carbon Border Adjustment Mechanism (CBAM)[35] in the EU as part of the EU Green Deal. Under the CBAM, EU importers will have to buy carbon certificates corresponding to the carbon price that would have been paid, had the goods been produced under the EU's carbon pricing rules.[36]

Chapter 12 – The legal framework for ESG provides a detailed overview of the relevant legislation.

As a company, it's not only financial value creation that determines successful survival in the long term. To be truly sustainable, a company needs to be both financially viable and protect all key stakeholders' interests, not just those of the shareholders.

Getting all key stakeholders on your radar, successfully interacting with them and gaining their approval, is often referred to as a social licence to operate (SLO). It indicates the acceptance of a company as part of society when it not only creates financial value but does so while sustainably making use of social and natural capital.

Achieving this is not restricted to environmental measures to protect our ecosystem. Social and governance factors also play vital roles, as outlined in the next two chapters.

04.
S for social

Key takeaways

1. The S in ESG is about companies' responsible and sustainable behaviour with respect to society, not just its own employees and value chain.

2. It is challenging to actually – and accurately – measure and report social performance and impact.

3. Everywhere in the world, there is increasing scrutiny of the social impact of corporate activities.

4. The social side of ESG requires standardisation and quantification in order to allow for proper reporting.

What's behind the 'S'?

Usually, when people talk or write about ESG, they focus almost completely on the environmental (E) element. This focus results in the E being best documented, easiest to measure and getting most of the attention. And yet, if you consider the 17 SDGs the UN defined in 2015, 8 out of 17 relate more to the social (S) part of ESG, whereas 7 explicitly deal with the E (see *Chapter 6 – From ESG to SDG*).

These goals tackle fundamental concerns: poverty, hunger, health, education, equality, work and economics, peace and justice.

Figure 13 – The UN Sustainable Development Goals

Is this focus on E because our planet is more important than its people? Is it because without our planet, people cannot survive, or because people are the cause of our planet's problems? More likely, it's because the environmental challenges are easier to define and easier to measure.

And yet you would expect things to be the other way around. Attention for how we should deal with our planet only picked up in the second half of the 20th century, whereas social challenges such as poverty, inequality, health, work, etc. have been a matter of attention for the past 2000 years. Sadly, after all this time, they are still very real and therefore deserve to be addressed under the ESG umbrella. But contrary to the E in ESG, far less work has been done on both defining and measuring the S.

Towards a definition of the S

The S in ESG is about companies' responsible and sustainable behaviour in society. In essence, it's very much about how to improve corporate social performance. But what does that social performance entail?

In general, the S covers items such as:

- workforce health, well-being and safety
- human capital development
- diversity and inclusion
- equal pay and opportunity
- employee engagement and retention
- talent attraction and training
- respect for privacy and data security
- etc.

Most of the focus on social performance is related to the company's relationship with its employees. But the field of S is wider than just employees and the local community: to more accurately assess the social impact of a company, the S should be much more comprehensive. People are central to the success of organisations, their value chain and society. The way companies **consider how people are treated across the value chain** is therefore rightly under increasing scrutiny.

Beyond employees

Figure 14 – Social impact: who is affected by an organisation's policies, operations, products and services?

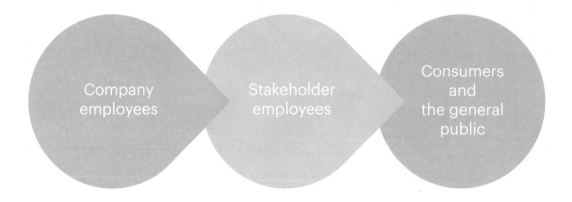

Properly measuring social impact goes beyond merely how a company's treating its own people and how they in turn treat the various suppliers, clients or other stakeholders of the company. It's equally about how the people at these stakeholders get treated themselves.

Working (directly or indirectly) with suppliers, clients or other stakeholders who do not treat their people fairly may have an adverse reputational impact on the company.

Social impact is also about the people further down the line: the consumers and general public who may be affected by the organisation directly or indirectly. To take some rather obvious examples, these may be people affected by companies manufacturing weapons or unhealthy snacks. Although these companies may treat their employees fairly and push their various stakeholders to treat their employees similarly, their activities have an adverse effect on those harmed by the weapons or by simply eating the unhealthy snacks.

We can all easily relate to such blatant examples. But the scope of the 'S for social' is much wider. Consider, for example, the behaviour of a bank towards a customer struggling to repay a loan. In practice, depending on circumstances, a fair amount of judgement might be required to assess what can be deemed to be proper social behaviour.

The S in ESG further covers human rights in general, as well as corporate citizenship and philanthropy. You might understandably expect that we are talking only about the social impact on the communities where a company is active — after all, one might say, no company can be expected to carry the burden of the entire world on its shoulders. But in fact it's difficult to draw boundary lines so conveniently. There are no boundaries on major global or regional events, such as war or major earthquakes that displace hundreds of thousands of refugees and have unforeseen knock-on effects on societies and businesses. There are no boundaries on social values, such as tolerance and equality. At any point in their activities, companies may affect or be impacted by events way beyond their community.

Diversity, equity and inclusion

Diversity, equity and inclusion (DE&I) are integral components of social responsibility. DE&I encompasses the principles of embracing diversity in all its forms, ensuring equity in opportunities and treatment, and fostering an inclusive work environment where every individual feels valued and empowered.

A crucial aspect is ensuring equal pay. It serves as a tangible manifestation of DE&I principles, reinforcing the commitment to fairness and eliminating discriminatory practices based on gender, identity, ethnicity, age or other factors. By adhering to the principle of equal pay, organisations send a strong message that they value and respect the contributions of every employee.

Adopting equal pay practices also positions organisations as employers of choice. In an increasingly competitive job market, prospective employees seek organisations that prioritise fairness, equality and inclusion. By emphasising equal pay, organisations attract top talent by showcasing their commitment to providing a work environment where all employees are treated fairly. Being recognised as an employer of choice brings numerous benefits to organisations, including attracting diverse talent, reducing turnover, and enhancing employee engagement and loyalty.

Social performance and impact assessment

All of the above demonstrates that it's not really all that difficult to LIST what is or may be included in the S of ESG: what the issues are and who may be impacted. It may not even be all that complicated for companies to subjectively assess their [direct] social performance according to this list. What's a lot more challenging is to actually – and accurately – measure and report social performance and impact. This difficulty is compounded when attempting to assess the wider social impact down the value chain, and in particular impacts on human rights. **The solution must lie in establishing reliable, standardised data collection, analysis and reporting rather than subjective assessments.**

A PwC study covering ESG-related activities (Figure 15) found that companies identified as ESG champions are typically bigger in size and by consequence have more means to put measures in place to monitor human rights risk areas, for example. 81% of ESG champions already have wide-ranging coverage of all primary human rights risk areas throughout their value chains. Non-champions (94% of the surveyed companies) have a much tougher time to actually monitor the risks arising from the human rights angle.

Figure 15 – Measures implemented to adhere to social and governance guidelines within the supplier collaboration.[37]

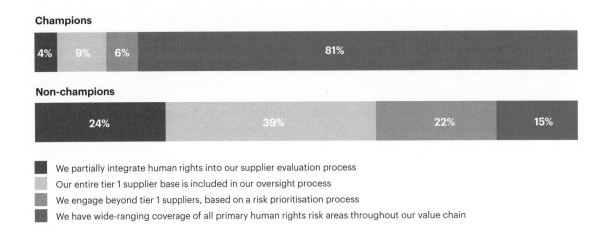

Champions

| 4% | 9% | 6% | 81% |

Non-champions

| 24% | 39% | 22% | 15% |

- ▆ We partially integrate human rights into our supplier evaluation process
- ▆ Our entire tier 1 supplier base is included in our oversight process
- ▆ We engage beyond tier 1 suppliers, based on a risk prioritisation process
- ▆ We have wide-ranging coverage of all primary human rights risk areas throughout our value chain

Scrutiny and reputation

The SDGs highlight the world's growing scrutiny of the social impact of corporate activities. Not only are citizens and regulators scrutinising companies more closely all the time: they are also condemning the 'bad' players, who may suffer any degree of backlash, from adverse publicity, to damaged reputation, boycotting, fines or worse. Companies are expected to hold and meet high standards in all of the areas falling within social performance. Companies leading or even complying in these areas and reporting on them will be positively perceived; failure to do so can result in negative reactions from staff or customers and highly brand-damaging media reports.

Staff complaints and stories of irresponsible company actions can spiral way out of the company's control, and massively impact their reputation, social capital and share value.

Allegations and scandals can spread fast and far, severely damaging a company's reputation.

For example, a major online retailer has faced numerous allegations concerning workforce practices, including: firing people on medical leave; failure to pay workers a living wage; forcing people to work in high temperatures, leading to dehydration and collapse; using scanners to check worker location to check if they are 'idle'; toxic manage-

ment practices leading to mental health issues among workers, and much more. As a result, many consumers have permanently boycotted the brand.

In 2022, a multinational manufacturer and its supplier faced criticism concerning treatment of workers at the supplier's plant in China. Videos released by workers went viral, triggering outrage across the globe. The media reported that in order to keep the plant in operation during a Covid-19 lockdown, factory workers had been forced to live on-site in a closed bubble, living in isolation in dormitories where they faced food shortages and lack of proper access to healthcare.

What a company doesn't do can lead to as much scrutiny as what it has done. In various States across the US, legislation has recently been introduced that has been deemed misogynist, bigoted and anti-LGBTQ+. Scandals have arisen when company staff criticised their management for failure to speak up against the legislation. Some companies quickly tried to retrieve their good will among employees and customers by introducing [costly] benefits (such as financial support for treatments no longer available in the employee's State or no longer covered by medical insurance, time off and financial support for healthcare travel, and so on) and promising to support advocacy groups to combat the legislation. Companies have been under such pressure that several have even taken the radical step of moving their operations to a different State.

Political pressure comes from 'anti' as well as 'pro' sides of the ESG debate, and can damage organisations committed to positive change as well as those whose actions are deemed inadequate. In 2023, for example, the media reported on a group of some of the world's leading insurers and reinsurers, representing a significant percentage of world premium volume globally. It was reported that several major insurance companies – a third of the group's members – had quit, severely curbing the group's collective power and threatening its future. The companies that had quit claimed that the group, and its members, were under attack from Republican politicians in the US who were targeting collective climate action groups perceived to be unfairly hitting the oil and gas industry, with the implication that these attacks were interfering with insurers' efforts to price climate risk, which would harm policyholders, investors and local economies.

This is just one example illustrating how companies are under many pressures, often conflicting, in their efforts to build a sustainable future.

When S and E conflict

Before moving on to measuring and reporting the S, let's briefly look at the interaction with the E.

When endeavouring to comply with ESG requirements, progress in one area does not automatically result in benefits in another. In fact, greening our society comes at a formidable cost, and this cost may result in **options no longer being available or affordable for several groups in our society**. Countless areas of daily life may be affected, from the industrial landscape to housing, transport and much more.

For example, certain products are today produced in a way which harms the environment. Solving this according to the E agenda may lead to significant changes in the industrial landscape as polluting factories are shut down, which may benefit the planet greatly. But these same polluting industries may also create well-paid jobs, pay their taxes and make products which benefit

our society. Putting these activities to an end also adversely affects workers and local communities, at least in the short term.

In the property market, significant investment is required to insulate existing buildings and make them energy efficient. Not everybody is able to afford these investments within the deadlines put forward by the legislator, potentially transforming what used to be a market of buyers into a market where most people will only be able to afford a rental property.

For personal transport, electric cars – or hydrogen cars when they come to market – are expected to remain more expensive than combustion engine cars for quite some time. This may result in cars becoming a luxury product, with ownership available only to the happy few, while the masses only get access to cars in a cheaper car sharing system. Even then, charging facilities may not be widely available as the strain on the networks may result in power shortages, potentially prioritising those who are willing to pay more.

Yet another example can be found in the travel industry. In recent decades, the world has been reduced to a global village, opening the possibility to its populations to travel across the globe with ever-reducing barriers. Reducing the emissions resulting from air travel will undoubtedly lead to a market with fewer, more expensive flights, making air travel unaffordable for many.

Everyday life for many people may also be affected by environmental progress. Certain jobs may become obsolete — finding new employment opportunities may require reskilling that is not necessarily available to everyone in our society. Or cheaper food and other products, previously sourced globally, may no longer be available at an affordable price, resulting in more limited availability of those products to those with less disposable income.

As these trends affect employees, they will impact employers too: an increased cost of living will eventually lead to a higher cost of wages and benefits. Already today, companies are seeing repercussions on business travel, remote work, company car policies, benefits packages, etc.

And no, it's not a surprise

Unfortunately, this could all have been foreseen quite some time ago. We have collectively been living on borrowed time, benefiting from the quick fixes of cheap energy, cheap products and easy travel, instead of investing in a more sustainable future. As a result, we will now need to go through one or two more difficult decades to solve these issues, which will undoubtedly be a burden for an entire generation.

Measuring social performance and impact

Out of the three letters in ESG, the S is generally considered to be the hardest to analyse and measure. Data is more difficult to come by and there is a lack of standardisation around social metrics. This was a clear takeaway from a 2021 Global ESG survey performed by BNP Paribas, where **51% of respondents felt the S to be the most difficult to analyse and embed in investment strategies**.[38]

It's often said that the social side of ESG requires standardisation and quantification in order to allow for proper reporting.

Step 1: Standardisation

Because of the absence of standardisation and formal classification, every company (or NGO) tends to define and measure their social impact or performance differently. For investors – and other stakeholders – that results in unreliable, incomparable and low-value output that cannot be properly interpreted. Some say that you could use the UN's SDGs as a framework, but these were never designed to be used in this way. It would be very hard to attribute any of the SDGs to any discrete social programme or intervention.[39] On the contrary, the SDGs were designed to address pressing global topics in the form of important political goals, which will not be universally relevant to all companies and communities.

Given its importance within the ESG field, we urgently need a standard for social outcomes or performance to allow companies to measure the quantum of social change that was realised as a result of a programme, strategy or intervention.

In the interim, i.e. while we wait for standardisation and classification, companies can of course make efforts to set their own measurable (SMART) objectives. These objectives can then be used to set (senior) management's KPIs and to assess them based on the achievement of said objectives.

Step 2: Quantification

Once social impacts can be standardised and classified, then of course they need to be quantified. This implies that the standards applied should determine what constitutes a 'unit of impact' for the areas concerned.

The use of standardised and quantified social impact analysis would also allow companies to produce more comparable data. This would in turn then generate more reliable benchmarks from other companies to rely on. Furthermore, rating agencies will also be better equipped to assess whether companies are making the right level of progress to make them a valuable investment for the future.

Social performance and impact reporting

Reporting in general, but in particular when it comes to ESG, is all about the disclosure of material risks: making sure information is made available about things that could negatively affect corporate performance and which therefore merits disclosure. For the risk to be material, there is typically a substantial likelihood that a reasonable stakeholder would find the risk sufficiently important to base a decision on.

But this materiality can also be about something positive, i.e. a company initiative that positively impacts its performance. Initiatives to drive an inclusive and caring culture through the organisation, for example, may vastly improve a company's productivity and even brand reputation, positively impacting its financial results.

Tony's Chocolonely

Tony's Chocolonely is an example of a brand committed not just to improving the social performance of their own operations, but of raising awareness of inequality in an entire industry sector.[40]

Tony's actively campaigns against the practice of mass balance trading, whereby major chocolate companies buy cocoa without duly considering or taking responsibility for the circumstances in which the farmers that produce the cocoa work and without guaranteeing humane labour conditions or a living wage for cocoa workers. The company also claims to rigorously seek out and eliminate labour malpractice in its own supply chain.

Tony's Chocolonely is an increasingly popular brand in the Netherlands, with around 20% market share of chocolate bars, and 8% market share of the whole chocolate category.[41]

Figure 16 – The design of the Tony's Chocolonely chocolate bar represents inequality in the share of benefits from the chocolate supply chain.[42]

Respecting human rights in a corporate and deals environment

By prioritising human rights, companies can demonstrate their social responsibility, leading to **increased trust and loyalty**. This can then translate into a competitive advantage and long-term profitability. Failure of a company to comply with human rights legislation – or the violation of supply chain integrity in relation to human rights – can result in legal liabilities, lawsuits and fines, and can lead to significant damage to a company's reputation.

Respecting human rights in the workplace, across the value chain, can also have a **positive impact on employee's engagement**. When employees are granted an inclusive workplace, fair wages and safe working conditions, they will feel valued and motivated, which in turn will boost employee satisfaction, productivity and retention. A commitment to human rights also attracts top talent, as today employees often prioritise working for companies that align with their own core values.

Upholding human rights could also create investment opportunities in and by companies engaging in responsible business practices. For example, a clothing manufacturer will not get a loan from a bank if child labour or modern slavery are identified in the supply chain.

Modern slavery – including human trafficking, slavery, forced and child labour – is a growing global criminal industry that businesses could become associated with unknowingly. Implementing human rights due diligence measures can thereby help identify and address potential financial and reputational risks before they escalate.

By integrating respect for human rights into their core values and operations, ensuring compliance with the legislative framework and mitigating violations of supply chain integrity, companies can build a positive reputation and brand image, enhance productivity, attract and retain talent, improve competitiveness and ensure long-term sustainability.

05.
G for Governance

Key takeaways

1. Governance underpins all corporate E and S initiatives and achievements.

2. 'G for Governance' means governance *founded on* environmental and social principles, not just governance of E + S matters.

3. Effective corporate governance is essential to ensuring that ESG ambitions translate into concrete action and systemic change.

4. In companies, the board has ultimate responsibility for ESG, as part of responsible corporate management.

5. The board is responsible for allocating formal ownership (i.e. accountability and decision-making power) of different aspects of ESG where appropriate. This ownership does not absolve the board of ownership and responsibility.

6. A transition from shareholder value to stakeholder value is required.

7. Thinking 'sustainable' requires shifting from short term to long term reporting.

What's behind the 'G'?

First, what is 'governance'?

There are arguably as many different definitions or codes of governance as there are governance styles! The European Corporate Governance Institute (ECGI) publishes the full texts of several hundred national, regional and sector-specific versions.[43] The European Corporate Governance Codes Network (ECGCN) has members from 25 countries.[44]

In the strictest sense, 'governance' of companies means all of the practices, processes and policies used to steer the business. This includes corporate-level decision making, policy making and the distribution of rights and responsibilities among the various participants in companies. It traditionally encompasses all policies and measures taken to ensure proper operations at all levels and in all activities. It covers business ethics, integrity, risk management, board diversity and equity, and much more.

Governance in an ESG context

Much like the S in ESG, it's sometimes said that insufficient attention is being paid to the G.[45] And just like for the S, that may be because a lot of time and effort has already been spent on improving things in the past. As the ECGI list illustrates, many initiatives have already been taken over the years to define and improve corporate governance, to introduce segregation of duties and rules on potential conflicts of interest, to establish committees on audits and remuneration, and so on. Technically, the governance of a great many companies has vastly improved in recent years and investors have applauded these changes.

The G is the cornerstone of ESG

In reality, despite there being less obvious focus on it, the G underpins much of the E and the S in ESG. Governance spearheads corporate sustainability initiatives, and is fundamental to the realisation of environmental and social objectives. Behind each successful ESG initiative lies successful governance. And behind each breach of a company's environmental or social commitments lies ineffective corporate governance. Governance is of course also at the heart of a company's ESG disclosures, determining their integrity and whether ESG indicators are efficiently and ethically pursued and reported.

So, while social but especially environmental challenges have dominated the public debate in recent years, **effective corporate governance is essential to ensuring that ESG ambitions translate into concrete action and systemic change.**[46]

However, while it's true that not much can improve under E and S without the right governance, taking care of the E+S is _not_ what the G for governance is all about.

So, practically speaking, what exactly falls within the scope of G for governance in ESG?

ESG means E+S+G, not (E+S)*G

The term ESG originated in a 2004 joint report by financial institutions to the United Nations[47] proposing guidelines and recommendations on how to better integrate environmental, social and corporate governance issues in asset financial management. That report referred to environmental _and_ social _and_ governance (E+S+G) issues:

> "In an increasingly complex and interconnected world, the importance of actively managing risks and opportunities related to emerging environmental and social trends, _in combination with_* rising public expectations for better accountability and corporate governance, presents a new set of challenges with far-reaching financial consequences for corporations. This is true both at the level of companies and at the level of investment portfolios."

Somehow, since then, the original meaning became distorted so that the G was often understood more narrowly to mean 'environmental and social governance' – i.e., (E+S)*G.

In other words, when addressing the G in ESG, in many sources there's an underlying assumption

* (note: our emphasis)

that the G refers *only* to the governance of environmental- and social-related matters. Or only to governance of 'sustainability'-related functions and operations, where the word 'sustainability' is being used meaning 'environmentalism and social reform'.

In the (E+S)*G mindset, the G in ESG is about all the practices, processes and policies that help govern the E+S initiatives, and the allocation of roles and responsibilities and related chain of command. The G in ESG is solely about setting up this chain of command, as well as compliance regarding, for example, diversity, gender equality and equal pay at board level.

This is a narrow approach that is being superseded by a broader perspective. In reality, there's a wide overlap between 'sustainability governance' and 'governance' in its broadest sense. And indeed, with the increasing focus on ESG, the meaning of the term 'sustainability' itself is expanding: it's in the process of blending into a hybrid word meaning both economic sustainability AND environmental and social sustainability.

The impact of limiting the scope of G

Why this [mathematical-level] nitpicking, you may ask? Because **misreading the term ESG, or limiting the reach of G to environmental and social matters, has wide-reaching effects**. It disconnects E+S matters from the core business strategy and direction, introducing inherent risks of lack of oversight, governance or accountability. And it puts companies at risk of missing opportunities for synergies and transformations that could move the business forward responsibly.

Towards a more comprehensive governance model

Governance founded on E+S principles

Today, some companies are being more forward-thinking about ESG, with a mindset that the **overall corporate governance policy needs to be founded on environmental and social principles**. The E+S are therefore not separate verticals or 'limbs' of the organisation; they are in its very bloodstream.

What does it mean in practice?

In an E+S+G mindset, of governance founded explicitly on E+S principles, company leaders would put E+S considerations at the heart of corporate decision making. With E+S embedded in the corporate strategy and culture, the focus would be not merely, for example, on strict compliance with E+S legislation, but on being several steps ahead of legislation, having higher ambitions, inspiring employees, fostering innovation and communicating this mindset to their stakeholders.

In this mindset, the components of ESG governance — including in an ESG context — are comprehensive, not limited to environmental and social matters per se.

Governance founded on E+S principles is not [entirely] new!

When you consider what's behind E and S – essentially, taking care of people and of the planet where we live – these fundamentals are already *implicitly* built into many of the 'traditional' components of governance. Ethics. Purpose and values. Leadership and responsibility. Risk management, mitigation and compliance. Transparency, integrity and fair practices...

A key to achieving governance *explicitly* founded on E+S principles is to embed ESG into the core of your business, by building it into the top-level corporate strategy. This is explained further in Chapter 8.

How to transform your governance model to a sustainability-driven model within an ESG transformation is addressed in Chapter 10.

An example of this is the Belgian Code on Corporate Governance.[48] It translates corporate governance activities into 10 specific principles. These cover governance structure, remits, composition, activities and behaviour and responsibilities.

There is no specific EU code of governance: rather, the responsibilities under governance fall under a wide range of EU regulations and directives.[49] For example, binding EU due diligence rules would require companies to identify, address and modify aspects of their value chain (all operations, direct or indirect business relationships, suppliers and investment chains) that could be detrimental to:

- the environment (including the contribution to climate change or deforestation)
- human rights (including social, trade and labour rights)
- good governance (such as corruption or bribery).

Sustainability accountability is a starting point

Some large companies already have the bones of a governance model based on environmental and social principles. Typically, it's the responsibility of their Sustainability group, however that is structured, with a comprehensive, value-chain-level structure of accountability.

Indeed, an organisation's sustainability setup may be a very good starting point for building a corporate governance model based on E+S principles. Especially if 'sustainability' is considered in the broadest sense of ensuring the long-term success and viability of the company. If the term 'sustaina-

bility' is interpreted in its narrower sense of environmental responsibility, then there's room to reconsider what sustainability really means in the context of the company's long-term business ambition.

Compliance and reporting

A governance model explicitly based on E+S principles is by nature aspirational, based on ethical values and sustainability ambitions, rather than only about regulatory compliance. Nonetheless, a prime responsibility of governance is to ensure compliance with all relevant legal requirements and standards as well as adherence to relevant selected guidelines and good practices. This is secured by means of standards, rules, policies and procedures, where training is provided so that everyone understands their roles and responsibilities. It is enforced by means of controls and sanctions for deviating conduct. All this is underpinned by accurate and transparent reporting.

Compliance failures may result in penalties for the company ranging from fines, to sanctions, to loss of licence to operate, and to reputational damage or even liability charges against individual officers or directors.

Typically, compliance models are either centralised, decentralised or a mix (Figure 17).

Figure 17 – Typical compliance models.

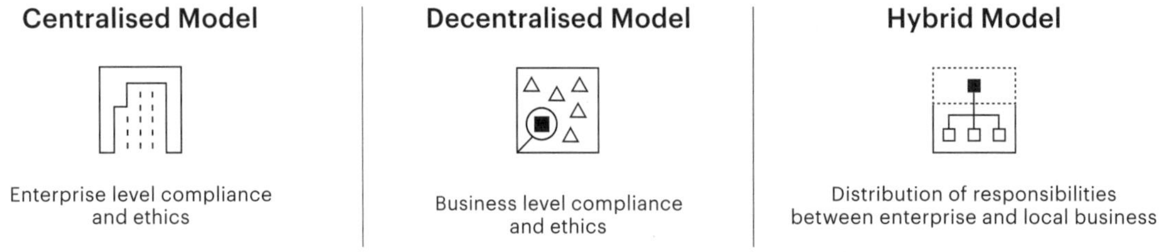

Centralised Model	Decentralised Model	Hybrid Model
Enterprise level compliance and ethics	Business level compliance and ethics	Distribution of responsibilities between enterprise and local business

In a **centralised compliance model**, a central, enter-prise-level (i.e. head office) compliance function is responsible and accountable for compliance and ethics across the organisation, and for both strategy and day-to-day management of compliance for all regulatory verticals. The advantage of a centralised model is that ownership and accountability sit at the top of the organisation. The disadvantage is that, for a large organisation, there's just too much to be responsible and accountable for, so that head office doesn't always know what happens down the line.

In a **decentralised model**, ownership and account-ability for compliance and ethics are determined at regional level, or spread across the different oper-ational functions, with – ideally – enterprise-level oversight and coordination. The advantage is, per-haps, greater transparency across the value chain. The disadvantage is, in practice, lack of ownership at the highest level of the organisation and, there-fore, often no consistent framework, no progress reports to a central compliance team, and no real oversight or coordination.

A **hybrid model** offers the best of both worlds, through distribution of responsibilities between head office and local businesses. The [local] business compliance function is responsible and accountable for day-to-day execution. The enter-prise compliance function provides a strategy and oversight.

Chapter 10 provides practical guidance on building an effective compliance programme (*Chapter 10, Sustainable governance transformation*).

The regulatory universe

A comprehensive, hybrid compliance programme covers all important regulations applicable to the organisation. As Figure 18 shows, many of the topics fall within the E and S of ESG (e.g. envi-ronmental laws, labour and employment), while others are typical governance issues (e.g. finan-cial reporting, competition law).

Figure 18 – The regulatory universe comprises environmental, social and governance areas.[50]

Changing the mindset

Within the ESG governance context, two important challenges persist, both related to sustainable business strategies. The first has to do with the shift from shareholder value to stakeholder value. And the second one relates to the short-termism linked to quarterly and annual reporting.

The shift from shareholder to stakeholder value

Most, if not all, changes to corporate governance in recent years have been introduced to ensure appropriate behaviour of a company's management to the benefit of its shareholders. And these shareholders are in turn solely focused on generating a financial return, especially if these are investment funds that themselves are under pressure to chew out significant financial returns. And so the so-called improvements to corporate governance provided tools for shareholders to challenge a company's management if and insofar as they had not acted in their [the shareholders'] best [financial] interest. Rating agencies also largely judge companies' corporate governance on this basis.

If companies want to bring their corporate governance rules into line with ESG requirements, and to shift to a more ESG-based governance model, the current challenge is to ensure respectful treatment of all stakeholders.

Many aspects of what one might call 'respectful' corporate governance already fall under national and regional legislation, and under the 'S for social' examples mentioned in Chapter 4, such as securing workforce diversity and equal pay. Standard governance examples might include diversity and gender equality on boards, compliance, and independent oversight and control of board effectiveness.

An **ESG-based governance model that encompasses the whole value chain needs to shift focus from shareholders to stakeholders**. ESG-based governance also includes policy-making, risk management and setting codes of conduct as regards the treatment of, and the impact of operations on, a much wider group of stakeholders: farmers, people living near factories, children and families of employees, contractors, and so on.

The shift from short term to longer term reporting

The second governance challenge in the ESG context is that of time. Corporate governance should strive for sustainability, which de facto refers to a long period of time. We live in a world where short-termism has nested itself at the very core of our society, resulting in increased pressure on all actors to perform without any reasonable delay. This push for immediacy regularly leads to plights of all sorts, both in corporate life (e.g. fraudulent representation of financial performance) and in personal life (e.g. the vast increase in the number of burnouts).

We need to allow companies to take things down a notch or two and once more accept that some things take time to complete, starting with the time to reflect and determine a strategy, all the way to the execution of that same strategy.

During his tenure as CEO of Unilever, Paul Polman abolished quarterly reporting to achieve exactly this and allow for a more long term – more sustainable – strategy to be executed.[51] Not only did Unilever become a more sustainable company, it also became more profitable. The Unilever case demonstrates that sustainability and profitability can be combined.

This chapter has explored the meaning of governance and the meaning of governance in an ESG context. We hope it has inspired you to ask whether your business wants or needs to embrace sustainability in a more fundamental way. In *Chapter 10, Sustainable governance transformation*, we explore what this can entail.

06.
From ESG to SDG

Key takeaways

1. In 2015, the UN developed 17 Sustainable Development Goals (SDGs).

2. SDGs can be a good framework to evaluate where a company is having a positive or negative impact on our world.

3. As a whole (citizens, countries and companies), we are not making fast enough progress towards meeting the SDGs.

4. While many companies report on SDG actions, as few as 1% of them actually measure and report the impact on the selected SDGs.

5. The SDGs can provide a framework for business transformation.

6. Increasing legislation on mandatory sustainability reporting makes greenwashing and greenhushing practices more difficult to sustain.

As the preceding chapters illustrate, environmental, social and governance are not three distinct entities within the concept of ESG. Together they touch on virtually every aspect of human activity; they are therefore, inevitably, broadly interconnected, overlapping and even conflicting.

Over the past decades, as the world became increasingly aware of the growing challenges to the Earth's very survival in the long term, governments and organisations started to come together to address the many sustainability issues that were being identified.

Figure 19 shows key milestone events, leading up to today, where ESG has become a burning platform.

One of the key defining moments was the creation of the Sustainable Development Goals or SDGs.

In order to break the challenges down into a workable framework for action, it was seen as necessary to pinpoint different areas of focus. This is how the sustainable development goals arose.

Figure 19 – ESG milestone events.[52]

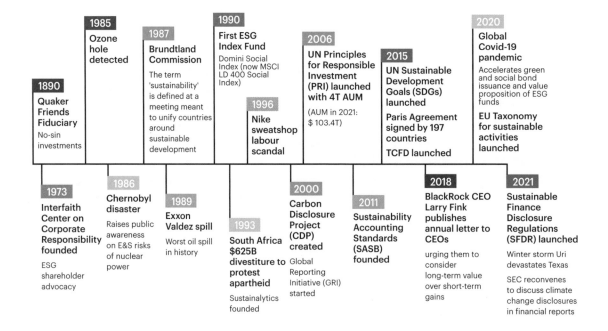

The 17 sustainable development goals and their history

In September 2015, the United Nations General Assembly adopted the 2030 Agenda for Sustainable Development. The core of the agenda was built around 17 sustainable development goals (SDGs). Each of these SDGs has a set of targets, totalling 169 targets across all of the areas in scope.

The overall objective was to build a shared blueprint for peace and prosperity for people and the planet, now and into the future.

Becoming truly prosperous as a country and planet entails making progress on all 17 elements at the heart of the 2030 Agenda.

Figure 20 – The 17 Sustainable Development Goals.[53]

Are the SDGs working?

In a nutshell, no. Or not enough. Each year a progress report is published that tracks the global and regional progress towards the 17 goals. With each one, the difficulty of meeting the targets becomes more apparent. Where countries might improve in one area, there may be a cost somewhere else. Unforeseen events, Covid-19 being the most obvious, can have devastating consequences.[54]

For the first time in decades, we have seen a rise in deaths from tuberculosis and malaria. A quarter of the global population is now living in countries affected by conflict, creating a record flow of refugee migration.

On climate goals, we need to hit peak GHG emissions by 2025 but national commitments will not meet this requirement and even point to a 14% increase by 2030.

The 17 SDGs are easy to criticise as utopic, unrealistic, unachievable. Companies are accused of greenwashing under the banner of the SDGs. Progress has been patchy at best.

But it would be foolhardy to dismiss the SDGs. Every strategy needs targets, and these are the targets the world has agreed on. Nothing will improve by removing or arguing about the vision. Nothing will change without hope and action.

In short, **the SDGs represent a lifeline for our planet. We must do our best to grab it.**

Figure 21 – SDG status report

1 NO POVERTY — END POVERTY IN ALL ITS FORMS EVERYWHERE

MORE THAN
4 YEARS OF PROGRESS
= AGAINST POVERTY =
HAS BEEN ERASED
BY COVID-19

WORKING POVERTY
RATE ROSE FOR THE FIRST
TIME IN **TWO DECADES**

6.7% 7.2%

2019 2020

PUSHING AN ADDITIONAL
8 MILLION WORKERS
INTO POVERTY

RISING INFLATION AND IMPACTS OF WAR
IN UKRAINE FURTHER DERAIL PROGRESS

NUMBER OF PEOPLE LIVING IN EXTREME POVERTY IN 2022

581 MILLION
PRE-PANDEMIC PROJECTION

657-676 MILLION
CURRENT PROJECTION

UNEMPLOYMENT CASH BENEFITS
DURING THE **PANDEMIC** (2020)

HIGH-INCOME COUNTRIES — 52.2%
LOW-INCOME COUNTRIES — 0.8%

DISASTER-RELATED DEATHS ROSE SIXFOLD IN 2020
LARGELY AS A RESULT OF THE PANDEMIC

2 ZERO HUNGER — END HUNGER, ACHIEVE FOOD SECURITY AND IMPROVED NUTRITION AND PROMOTE SUSTAINABLE AGRICULTURE

CONFLICT, COVID-19, CLIMATE CHANGE
AND GROWING INEQUALITIES
ARE CONVERGING TO UNDERMINE
FOOD SECURITY WORLDWIDE

ABOUT 1 IN 10 PEOPLE
WORLDWIDE ARE
SUFFERING FROM HUNGER

NEARLY 1 IN 3 PEOPLE
LACK REGULAR ACCESS
TO ADEQUATE FOOD (2020)

SOARING FOOD PRICES
AFFECTED

47%
OF COUNTRIES IN 2020
(UP FROM 16% IN 2019)

149.2 MILLION
CHILDREN
UNDER AGE 5
SUFFER FROM **STUNTING**
(2020)

TO REDUCE STUNTING IN
CHILDREN BY 50% BY 2030,
ANNUAL RATE OF DECLINE
MUST **DOUBLE**
(FROM 2.1 TO 3.9% PER YEAR)

UKRAINE CRISIS TRIGGERED FOOD SHORTAGES FOR THE WORLD'S POOREST PEOPLE

UKRAINE AND THE RUSSIAN
FEDERATION SUPPLY
GLOBAL EXPORTS:

 30% OF WHEAT
 20% OF MAIZE
 80% OF SUNFLOWER SEED PRODUCTS

3 GOOD HEALTH AND WELL-BEING — ENSURE HEALTHY LIVES AND PROMOTE WELL-BEING FOR ALL AT ALL AGES

COVID-19
IS THREATENING DECADES OF PROGRESS IN GLOBAL HEALTH

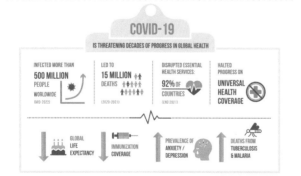

INFECTED MORE THAN
500 MILLION PEOPLE
WORLDWIDE
(MID-2022)

LED TO
15 MILLION DEATHS
(2020-2021)

DISRUPTED ESSENTIAL
HEALTH SERVICES:
92% OF COUNTRIES
(END 2021)

HALTED PROGRESS ON
UNIVERSAL HEALTH COVERAGE

GLOBAL LIFE EXPECTANCY ↓
IMMUNIZATION COVERAGE ↓
PREVALENCE OF ANXIETY / DEPRESSION ↑
DEATHS FROM TUBERCULOSIS & MALARIA ↑

22.7 MILLION CHILDREN
MISSED BASIC
VACCINES IN 2020
3.7 MILLION
MORE THAN IN 2019

PANDEMIC CLAIMED THE LIVES OF
115,500 FRONT-LINE HEALTH-CARE WORKERS

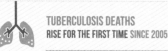
TUBERCULOSIS DEATHS
RISE FOR THE FIRST TIME SINCE 2005

1.2 MILLION — 2019
1.3 MILLION — 2020

4 QUALITY EDUCATION — ENSURE INCLUSIVE AND EQUITABLE QUALITY EDUCATION AND PROMOTE LIFELONG LEARNING OPPORTUNITIES FOR ALL

COVID-19 PANDEMIC
— HAS DEEPENED A —
GLOBAL LEARNING CRISIS

147 MILLION CHILDREN
MISSED OVER HALF
OF IN-PERSON
INSTRUCTION
IN 2020-2021

24 MILLION LEARNERS
(PRE-PRIMARY TO UNIVERSITY LEVEL)
MAY NEVER RETURN TO SCHOOL

EDUCATION IS A LIFELINE
FOR CHILDREN IN CRISES

ENTRENCHED INEQUITIES IN EDUCATION HAVE
ONLY **WORSENED** DURING THE PANDEMIC

REMOTE LEARNING
IS OFFERED TO
3 MILLION
UKRAINIAN CHILDREN
IN THE CHAOS OF WAR
(APRIL 2022)

MANY COUNTRIES ARE **IMPROVING** SCHOOL INFRASTRUCTURE AS CLASSROOMS REOPEN

GLOBALLY, PRIMARY SCHOOLS (2019-2020)
25% LACK — ELECTRICITY, DRINKING WATER, BASIC SANITATION
50% LACK — COMPUTERS, INTERNET ACCESS

SDG 5

 5 GENDER EQUALITY

ACHIEVE GENDER EQUALITY AND EMPOWER ALL WOMEN AND GIRLS

IT WOULD TAKE ANOTHER
40 YEARS
FOR WOMEN AND MEN TO BE REPRESENTED EQUALLY IN NATIONAL POLITICAL LEADERSHIP AT THE CURRENT PACE

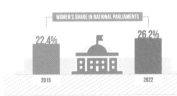

WOMEN'S SHARE IN NATIONAL PARLIAMENTS

22.4% 2015 — **26.2%** 2022

 GENDER-RESPONSIVE BUDGETING NEEDS TO BE STRENGTHENED

PROPORTION OF COUNTRIES WITH SYSTEMS TO TRACK GENDER-BUDGET ALLOCATIONS (2018-2021)

- **26%** COMPREHENSIVE SYSTEMS
- **59%** SOME FEATURES OF A SYSTEM
- **15%** LACKING MINIMUM ELEMENTS OF SUCH A SYSTEM

WOMEN ACCOUNTED FOR
39% OF TOTAL EMPLOYMENT IN 2019, BUT **45%** OF GLOBAL EMPLOYMENT LOSSES IN 2020

MORE THAN 1 IN 4 WOMEN (15+ YEARS)

HAVE BEEN SUBJECTED TO INTIMATE PARTNER VIOLENCE (641 MILLION) AT LEAST ONCE IN THEIR LIFETIME

ONLY **57%** OF WOMEN (15-49 YEARS) ARE MAKING THEIR OWN INFORMED DECISIONS ON SEX AND REPRODUCTIVE HEALTH CARE
(64 COUNTRIES, 2007-2021)

SDG 6

 6 CLEAN WATER AND SANITATION

ENSURE AVAILABILITY AND SUSTAINABLE MANAGEMENT OF WATER AND SANITATION FOR ALL

THE WORLD'S WATER-RELATED
ECOSYSTEMS
ARE BEING DEGRADED AT AN ALARMING RATE

OVER THE PAST 300 YEARS,
OVER 85%
OF THE PLANET'S WETLANDS HAVE BEEN LOST

MEETING DRINKING WATER, SANITATION AND HYGIENE TARGETS BY 2030 REQUIRES A **4X** INCREASE IN THE PACE OF PROGRESS

AT CURRENT RATES, IN 2030

1.6 BILLION PEOPLE WILL LACK SAFELY MANAGED DRINKING WATER

2.8 BILLION PEOPLE WILL LACK SAFELY MANAGED SANITATION

1.9 BILLION PEOPLE WILL LACK BASIC HAND HYGIENE FACILITIES

FOR AT LEAST 3 BILLION PEOPLE, THE QUALITY OF THE WATER THEY DEPEND ON IS UNKNOWN DUE TO A LACK OF MONITORING

733+ MILLION PEOPLE

 LIVE IN COUNTRIES WITH HIGH AND CRITICAL LEVELS OF WATER STRESS (2019)

 ONLY ONE QUARTER OF REPORTING COUNTRIES HAVE >90% OF THEIR TRANSBOUNDARY WATERS COVERED BY OPERATIONAL ARRANGEMENTS (2020)

SDG 7

 7 AFFORDABLE AND CLEAN ENERGY

ENSURE ACCESS TO AFFORDABLE, RELIABLE, SUSTAINABLE AND MODERN ENERGY FOR ALL

IMPRESSIVE PROGRESS IN ELECTRIFICATION
HAS SLOWED
DUE TO THE CHALLENGE OF REACHING THOSE HARDEST TO REACH

NUMBER OF PEOPLE WITHOUT ELECTRICITY

- **1.2 BILLION** 2010
- **733 MILLION** 2020
- **679 MILLION** 2030 (BASED ON CURRENT TREND)

INTERNATIONAL FINANCIAL FLOWS TO DEVELOPING COUNTRIES FOR RENEWABLES DECLINED FOR A SECOND YEAR IN A ROW

- **$24.7 BILLION** 2017
- **$14.3 BILLION** 2018
- **$10.9 BILLION** 2019

PROGRESS IN ENERGY EFFICIENCY NEEDS TO SPEED UP TO ACHIEVE GLOBAL CLIMATE GOALS

ANNUAL ENERGY-INTENSITY IMPROVEMENT RATE

- **1.9%** ACTUAL (2010-2019)
- **3.2%** NEEDED (TO 2030)

2.4 BILLION PEOPLE STILL USE INEFFICIENT AND POLLUTING COOKING SYSTEMS (2020)

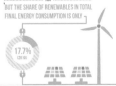

TOTAL RENEWABLE ENERGY CONSUMPTION INCREASED BY A QUARTER BETWEEN 2010 AND 2019, BUT THE SHARE OF RENEWABLES IN TOTAL FINAL ENERGY CONSUMPTION IS ONLY **17.7%** (2019)

SDG 8

8 DECENT WORK AND ECONOMIC GROWTH

PROMOTE SUSTAINED, INCLUSIVE AND SUSTAINABLE ECONOMIC GROWTH, FULL AND PRODUCTIVE EMPLOYMENT AND DECENT WORK FOR ALL

GLOBAL ECONOMIC RECOVERY
IS HAMPERED BY:

 NEW WAVES OF COVID-19
 RISING INFLATION
 SUPPLY-CHAIN DISRUPTIONS
 POLICY UNCERTAINTIES
 LABOUR MARKET CHALLENGES

GLOBAL ECONOMIC RECOVERY IS FURTHER SET BACK BY THE UKRAINE CRISIS

ANNUAL GROWTH RATE OF GLOBAL REAL GDP PER CAPITA (%) (2019-2023)

- 2.1 (2018)
- -4.4 COVID-19 (2020)
- 4.4 RECOVERY (2021)
- 3.0 / 2.4 UKRAINE CRISIS
- 2.5 (2023, PROJECTED)

GLOBAL UNEMPLOYMENT
TO REMAIN ABOVE PRE-PANDEMIC LEVEL UNTIL AT LEAST **2023**

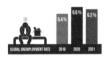

GLOBAL UNEMPLOYMENT RATE

- 5.4% 2019
- 6.6% 2020
- 6.2% 2021

1 IN 10 CHILDREN ARE ENGAGED IN CHILD LABOUR WORLDWIDE

160 MILLION TOTAL CHILDREN (2020)

WORKER PRODUCTIVITY HAS REBOUNDED, BUT NOT IN LDCs

GROWTH IN OUTPUT PER WORKER

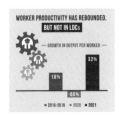

- 1.6% 2016-2019
- -0.6% 2020
- 3.2% 2021

9 INDUSTRY, INNOVATION AND INFRASTRUCTURE
BUILD RESILIENT INFRASTRUCTURE, PROMOTE INCLUSIVE AND SUSTAINABLE INDUSTRIALIZATION AND FOSTER INNOVATION

GLOBAL MANUFACTURING
HAS REBOUNDED FROM THE PANDEMIC
BUT LDCs ARE LEFT BEHIND

MANUFACTURING GROWTH

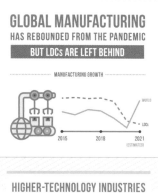

WORLD
LDCs
2015   2018   2021 (ESTIMATED)

HIGHER-TECHNOLOGY INDUSTRIES
ARE FAR MORE RESILIENT IN CRISES
THAN THEIR LOWER-TECH COUNTERPARTS

MANUFACTURING PRODUCTION INDEX

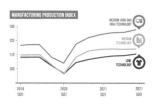

MEDIUM-HIGH AND HIGH TECHNOLOGY
MEDIUM TECHNOLOGY
LOW TECHNOLOGY

130
120
110
100

2019 (Q3)   2020 (Q2)   2021 (Q3)   2021 (Q4)

SMALL-SCALE INDUSTRIES
LACK ACCESS TO FINANCIAL SUPPORT FOR RECOVERY

ONLY 1 IN 3 SMALL MANUFACTURERS
ARE BENEFITING FROM A LOAN OR LINE OF CREDIT
(2020-2021)

PASSENGER AIRLINE INDUSTRY
=== IS STILL STRUGGLING TO ===
RECOUP CATASTROPHIC LOSSES

4.5 BILLION
2.3 BILLION
2019   2021

2.3 BILLION PASSENGERS IN 2021,
COMPARED WITH 4.5 BILLION IN 2019

1 IN 3 MANUFACTURING JOBS
ARE **NEGATIVELY IMPACTED** BY THE CRISIS

---

10 REDUCED INEQUALITIES
REDUCE INEQUALITY WITHIN AND AMONG COUNTRIES

PANDEMIC
HAS CAUSED THE FIRST RISE IN
BETWEEN-COUNTRY INCOME INEQUALITY IN A GENERATION

CHANGE IN BETWEEN-COUNTRY INCOME INEQUALITY
(2013-2021)

2013-2017   2017-2021
1.2% COVID-19 PROJECTION
-2.0% WITHOUT COVID-19 PROJECTION
-3.8%

5,895 MIGRANTS

LOST THEIR LIVES IN 2021

THE **DEADLIEST** YEAR SINCE 2017 FOR MIGRANTS

1 IN 5

PEOPLE HAVE EXPERIENCED
DISCRIMINATION
ON AT LEAST ONE OF THE GROUNDS PROHIBITED UNDER INTERNATIONAL HUMAN RIGHTS LAW

GLOBAL REFUGEE FIGURE
HITS RECORD HIGH

WAR IN UKRAINE PUSHES
THE WORLD TOTAL **EVEN HIGHER**

NUMBER OF REFUGEES OUTSIDE THEIR COUNTRY OF ORIGIN
INCREASED BY 44% BETWEEN 2015 AND 2021

216 PER 100,000 PEOPLE (2015)
311 PER 100,000 PEOPLE (MID-2021)

---

11 SUSTAINABLE CITIES AND COMMUNITIES
MAKE CITIES AND HUMAN SETTLEMENTS INCLUSIVE, SAFE, RESILIENT AND SUSTAINABLE

NUMBER OF COUNTRIES
WITH LOCAL DISASTER RISK REDUCTION STRATEGIES
NEARLY DOUBLED
BETWEEN 2015 **AND** 2021
(51 TO 98 COUNTRIES)

=== LEAVING NO ONE BEHIND ===
WILL REQUIRE AN **INTENSIFIED FOCUS** ON
1 BILLION SLUM DWELLERS

AS CITIES GROW, MUNICIPAL SOLID WASTE
PROBLEMS MOUNT

GLOBALLY,
MUNICIPAL SOLID WASTE

82% COLLECTED
55% MANAGED IN CONTROLLED FACILITIES (2022)

IN SUB-SAHARAN AFRICA,
LESS THAN 1/3 OF CITY DWELLERS HAVE CONVENIENT
ACCESS TO **PUBLIC TRANSPORTATION**

99%
=== OF THE ===
WORLD'S URBAN POPULATION BREATHE
POLLUTED AIR
ACCORDING TO NEW WORLD HEALTH ORGANIZATION AIR QUALITY GUIDELINES OF PM2.5 >5 UG/M³

---

12 RESPONSIBLE CONSUMPTION AND PRODUCTION
ENSURE SUSTAINABLE CONSUMPTION AND PRODUCTION PATTERNS

UNSUSTAINABLE PATTERNS
OF CONSUMPTION AND PRODUCTION ARE ROOT CAUSE OF

=== TRIPLE PLANETARY CRISES ===

CLIMATE CHANGE   BIODIVERSITY LOSS   POLLUTION

OUR RELIANCE ON
NATURAL RESOURCES
IS INCREASING

RISING OVER
65% GLOBALLY
FROM
2000 TO 2019

TOO MUCH FOOD IS BEING LOST OR WASTED
=== IN EVERY COUNTRY EVERY DAY ===

HARVESTING   TRANSPORT   STORAGE   PROCESSING

13.3% OF THE WORLD'S FOOD IS LOST AFTER HARVESTING
AND BEFORE REACHING RETAIL MARKETS

HOUSE   GROCERY STORE   HOUSEHOLD   RESTAURANT

17% OF TOTAL FOOD IS WASTED AT THE
CONSUMER LEVEL

VAST MAJORITY OF THE
WORLD'S ELECTRONIC WASTE IS
NOT BEING SAFELY MANAGED

E-WASTE COLLECTION RATES (2019)

1.2% LATIN AMERICA AND THE CARIBBEAN
1.6% SUB-SAHARAN AFRICA
46.9% EUROPE AND NORTHERN AMERICA
22.8% GLOBAL AVERAGE

13 CLIMATE ACTION — TAKE URGENT ACTION TO COMBAT CLIMATE CHANGE AND ITS IMPACTS

CLIMATE CHANGE
IS HUMANITY'S "CODE RED" WARNING

OUR WINDOW TO AVOID CLIMATE CATASTROPHE IS CLOSING RAPIDLY

DIFFERENT TEMPERATURE SCENARIOS FOR CORAL REEFS

70%-90% GONE	DIE OFF COMPLETELY
1.5 °C SCENARIO	2 °C SCENARIO

CORAL REEFS

SEA LEVEL WILL RISE 30-60 CM BY 2100

SEA LEVEL RISE

DROUGHT ESTIMATED TO DISPLACE 700 MILLION PEOPLE BY 2030

DROUGHTS

MEDIUM- TO LARGE-SCALE DISASTERS WILL INCREASE 40% FROM 2015 TO 2030

DISASTERS

ENERGY-RELATED CO₂ EMISSIONS INCREASED

6% IN 2021

REACHING HIGHEST LEVEL EVER

CLIMATE FINANCE FALLS SHORT OF $100 BILLION YEARLY COMMITMENT

DEVELOPED COUNTRIES PROVIDED $79.6 BILLION IN CLIMATE FINANCE IN 2019

RISING GLOBAL TEMPERATURES CONTINUE UNABATED, LEADING TO **MORE EXTREME WEATHER**

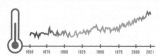

1650 1875 1900 1925 1950 1975 2000 2021

---

14 LIFE BELOW WATER — CONSERVE AND SUSTAINABLY USE THE OCEANS, SEA AND MARINE RESOURCES FOR SUSTAINABLE DEVELOPMENT

OUR OCEAN
THE PLANET'S LARGEST ECOSYSTEM
IS ENDANGERED

PLASTIC/MARINE POLLUTION

OVER-FISHING

OCEAN WARMING

ACIDIFICATION

EUTROPHICATION

INCREASING ACIDIFICATION
IS THREATENING MARINE LIFE AND LIMITING THE OCEAN'S CAPACITY TO MODERATE CLIMATE CHANGE

THE OCEAN ABSORBS AROUND 1/4 OF GLOBAL ANNUAL CO₂ EMISSIONS

PLASTIC POLLUTION
IS CHOKING THE OCEAN

17+ MILLION METRIC TONS OF PLASTIC ENTERED THE OCEAN IN 2021

PROJECTED TO DOUBLE OR TRIPLE BY 2040

90% OF THE
WORLD'S FISHERS ARE EMPLOYED IN SMALL-SCALE FISHERIES

WHO NEED ACCELERATED SUPPORT DUE TO THE **PANDEMIC**

---

15 LIFE ON LAND — PROTECT, RESTORE AND PROMOTE SUSTAINABLE USE OF TERRESTRIAL ECOSYSTEMS, SUSTAINABLY MANAGE FORESTS, COMBAT DESERTIFICATION, AND HALT AND REVERSE LAND DEGRADATION AND HALT BIODIVERSITY LOSS

10 MILLION

HECTARES OF FOREST ARE DESTROYED EVERY YEAR

ALMOST **90% OF GLOBAL DEFORESTATION**
IS DUE TO **AGRICULTURAL EXPANSION**

49.6%
CROPLAND EXPANSION

38.5%
LIVESTOCK GRAZING

133 PARTIES HAVE RATIFIED **THE NAGOYA PROTOCOL,** WHICH ADDRESSES ACCESS TO **GENETIC RESOURCES** AND THEIR FAIR AND EQUITABLE USE

BIODIVERSITY
IS LARGELY NEGLECTED
IN COVID-19 RECOVERY SPENDING

AROUND **40,000 SPECIES** ARE DOCUMENTED TO BE AT RISK OF EXTINCTION OVER THE COMING DECADES

NEARLY HALF OF FRESHWATER, TERRESTRIAL AND MOUNTAIN KEY BIODIVERSITY AREAS **ARE PROTECTED**

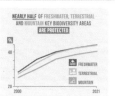

FRESHWATER
TERRESTRIAL
MOUNTAIN

2000   2021

---

16 PEACE, JUSTICE AND STRONG INSTITUTIONS — PROMOTE PEACEFUL AND INCLUSIVE SOCIETIES FOR SUSTAINABLE DEVELOPMENT, PROVIDE ACCESS TO JUSTICE FOR ALL AND BUILD EFFECTIVE, ACCOUNTABLE AND INCLUSIVE INSTITUTIONS AT ALL LEVELS

PLEAS FOR
GLOBAL PEACE
GROW LOUDER

WORLD IS WITNESSING LARGEST NUMBER OF VIOLENT CONFLICTS **SINCE 1946**

AND

A QUARTER OF THE GLOBAL POPULATION LIVES IN CONFLICT-AFFECTED COUNTRIES (END 2020)

A RECORD **100 MILLION PEOPLE**

HAD BEEN **FORCIBLY DISPLACED** WORLDWIDE (MAY 2022)

1/3 OF THE WORLD'S POPULATION
MOSTLY WOMEN
FEAR WALKING ALONE IN THEIR NEIGHBOURHOODS AT NIGHT

GLOBAL HOMICIDE RATE DECLINED

5.2% BETWEEN 2015 AND 2020

FALLS SHORT OF THE "SIGNIFICANT REDUCTION" BY 2030 TARGETED IN THE SDGs

CORRUPTION IS FOUND IN EVERY REGION

ALMOST **1 IN 6** BUSINESSES HAVE RECEIVED BRIBE REQUESTS FROM **PUBLIC OFFICIALS**

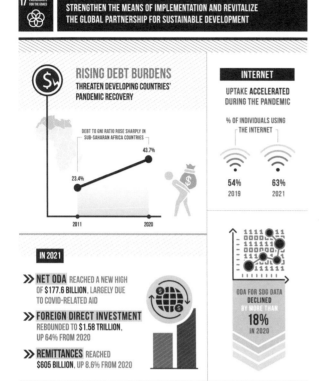

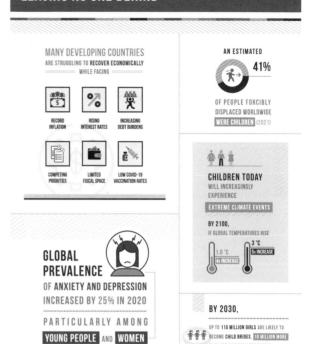

Most companies are working with the SDGs ...

Despite their flaws, legislative authorities and companies are continuing to use the SDGs to inspire and inform their strategic targets and planning.

Ongoing data and statistics are needed to further understand and develop our roadmap to address the SDGs. Meanwhile, the business world recognises that no matter the difficulties of reaching the SDG targets, if they don't even try, at the very least they will severely damage their brand and reputation.

Indeed, according to a PwC analysis of over 1,000 companies in 31 countries,[55] nearly three-quarters mentioned SDGs in their reporting, of which 59% referenced them as part of their sustainability report while 51% mentioned them in their annual report. However, only 14% mentioned specific SDG targets (Figure 22).

Figure 22 – Results of an analysis of companies' engagement with ESG.[56]

72%	21%	25%	65%	14%	1%
of companies mentioned the SDGs in their reporting	of companies include reference to the SDGs in their CEO or Chair statement	of companies included the SDGs in their published business strategy	of companies referred to specific SDGs	of companies included specific SDG targets	of companies measured their performance against SDG targets

Figure 23 – Analysis of companies' engagement with specific SDGs (*=SDG target number).[57]

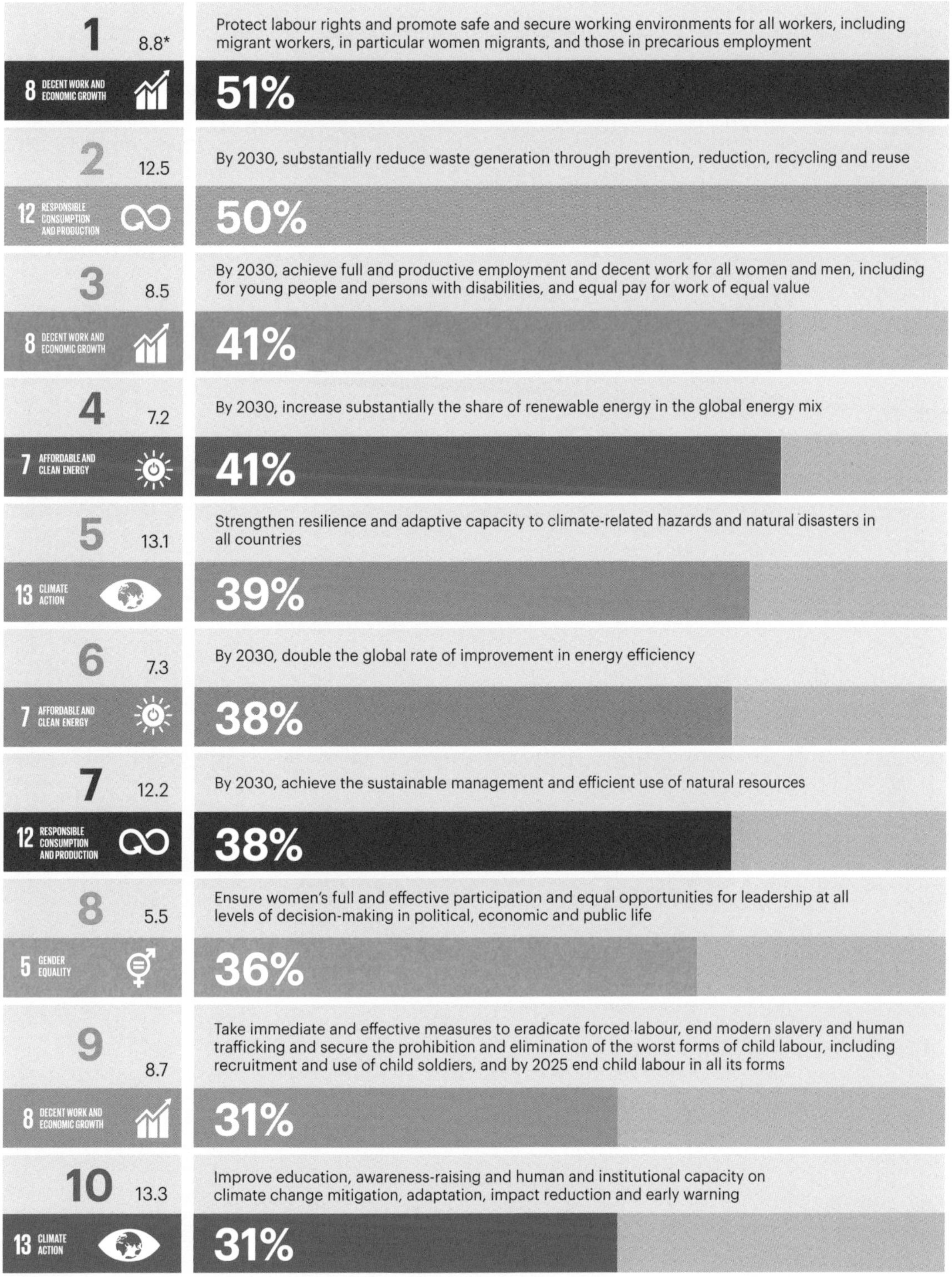

1 8.8*	Protect labour rights and promote safe and secure working environments for all workers, including migrant workers, in particular women migrants, and those in precarious employment	
8 DECENT WORK AND ECONOMIC GROWTH	**51%**	
2 12.5	By 2030, substantially reduce waste generation through prevention, reduction, recycling and reuse	
12 RESPONSIBLE CONSUMPTION AND PRODUCTION	**50%**	
3 8.5	By 2030, achieve full and productive employment and decent work for all women and men, including for young people and persons with disabilities, and equal pay for work of equal value	
8 DECENT WORK AND ECONOMIC GROWTH	**41%**	
4 7.2	By 2030, increase substantially the share of renewable energy in the global energy mix	
7 AFFORDABLE AND CLEAN ENERGY	**41%**	
5 13.1	Strengthen resilience and adaptive capacity to climate-related hazards and natural disasters in all countries	
13 CLIMATE ACTION	**39%**	
6 7.3	By 2030, double the global rate of improvement in energy efficiency	
7 AFFORDABLE AND CLEAN ENERGY	**38%**	
7 12.2	By 2030, achieve the sustainable management and efficient use of natural resources	
12 RESPONSIBLE CONSUMPTION AND PRODUCTION	**38%**	
8 5.5	Ensure women's full and effective participation and equal opportunities for leadership at all levels of decision-making in political, economic and public life	
5 GENDER EQUALITY	**36%**	
9 8.7	Take immediate and effective measures to eradicate forced labour, end modern slavery and human trafficking and secure the prohibition and elimination of the worst forms of child labour, including recruitment and use of child soldiers, and by 2025 end child labour in all its forms	
8 DECENT WORK AND ECONOMIC GROWTH	**31%**	
10 13.3	Improve education, awareness-raising and human and institutional capacity on climate change mitigation, adaptation, impact reduction and early warning	
13 CLIMATE ACTION	**31%**	

...But it's not easy or comprehensive

While awareness has really been rising, it remains a challenge to include specific SDG targets in company reporting and actually measure performance versus those targets. Most reporting covers elements of labour rights and working environments, responsible consumption and production, and of course energy. Only a minority of companies reports on all SDGs; this makes sense, as not all are material for each company, but it's important to make progress on those that can shift the needle.

UNDP framework for integrating SDGs

The United Nations Development Programme (UNDP) has developed SDG impact standards for enterprises to help companies integrate the SDGs in their strategy. It can serve as a helpful framework based on four standards (Strategy, Management Approach, Transparency and Governance) to define the way to address the transformation ahead, based on 12 action points (Figure 24).[58]

Figure 24 – UNDP 12 action points for addressing transformation.[59]

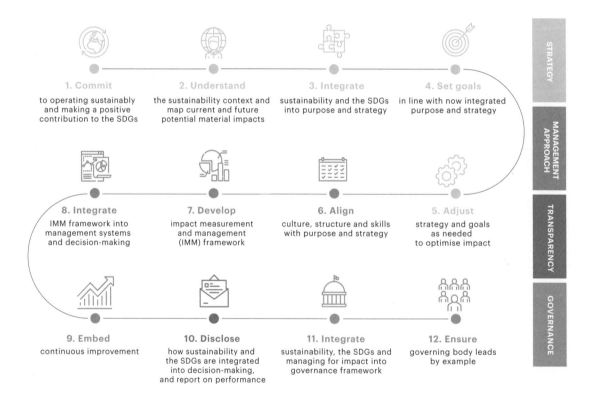

1. **Commit** to operating sustainably and making a positive contribution to the SDGs

2. **Understand** the sustainability context and map current and future potential material impacts

3. **Integrate** sustainability and the SDGs into purpose and strategy

4. **Set goals** in line with now integrated purpose and strategy

8. **Integrate** IMM framework into management systems and decision-making

7. **Develop** impact measurement and management (IMM) framework

6. **Align** culture, structure and skills with purpose and strategy

5. **Adjust** strategy and goals as needed to optimise impact

9. **Embed** continuous improvement

10. **Disclose** how sustainability and the SDGs are integrated into decision-making, and report on performance

11. **Integrate** sustainability, the SDGs and managing for impact into governance framework

12. **Ensure** governing body leads by example

STRATEGY

MANAGEMENT APPROACH

TRANSPARENCY

GOVERNANCE

The impacts of greenwashing or greenhushing

Greenwashing is a familiar term denoting false assertions about environmental credentials, such as claims about eco-friendly products, green investment funds, etc. Research by the European Commission in 2021 revealed that national consumer authorities suspected that **42% of online green claims from various business sectors were exaggerated, false or deceptive.**[60]

Once the accusation of greenwashing is thrown at a company, their brand reputation is tarnished. It can be difficult to recover from the slur, whether deserved or not.

Greenwashing can range from the relatively minor claims, such as describing a product as 100% organic when it's not, or outright dangerous, such as falsely claiming to be reducing your carbon footprint. At COP 26, the UN launched an initiative to bring greenwashing into the light, coming up at COP 27 with a 'zero tolerance for greenwashing' report, bringing 10 practical recommendations to the table.[61] Launching the report, UN Secretary-General António Guterres described *"bogus 'net-zero' pledges to cover up massive fossil fuel expansion"* as a *"reprehensible ... toxic cover-up [that] could push our world over the climate cliff."*

To avoid the perils of greenwashing accusations, more and more enterprises are choosing greenhushing: the practice of concealing their climate or sustainability plans from public scrutiny. A study from South Pole indicated that out of 1200 big firms surveyed, a quarter have set themselves stringent emission reduction targets but do not intend to publicise them.[62]

South Pole argued that *"Doing so makes corporate climate targets harder to scrutinise and limits knowledge-sharing on decarbonisation, potentially leading to less ambitious targets being set, and missed opportunities for industries to collaborate."*

The EU Corporate Sustainability Reporting Directive (CSRD) makes it increasingly difficult for companies to sustain greenhushing practices, ensuring greater transparency through mandatory sustainability reporting. (See *Chapter 9 – Reporting*.)

SDGs: a foundation for transformation

The 17 UN SDGs serve as a guide for companies and establish parameters for meeting ESG targets. But they are not intended just for inspiration or information. The SDGs are grounded in international law and closely linked to the Paris Climate Agreement, which is legally binding for its Parties; 193 States plus the European Union.

Governments and other legislative authorities use the SDGs when setting targets, legislation and recommendations for organisations and citizens in their jurisdiction.

Many companies also use the SDGs to inform and determine their ESG/sustainability journey, to help them build a strategy and roadmap for integrating sustainability and transforming their business.

07.
From SDG to circular economy

Key takeaways

1. We cannot continue depleting natural resources.

2. Circular economy is an ecosystem oriented at finding ways to close the loop, so that we can keep on using the same resources, by reusing, repairing, refurbishing and recycling existing materials and products.

3. Due to resource depreciation and definitive waste, no 'circular' model is genuinely hermetic. What is called a 'circular economy' could more accurately be described as a 'spiral economy'.

4. A growing number of companies declare a wish to build a circular business, but intentions don't always match with reality.

5. Critical success factors for a circular economy model are: integrated; market relevant; holistic and systematic; access to supportive micro- and macro-economic instruments; collaborative; and the right technology.

Outlining ESG issues and the SDG framework in a logical sequence makes all these challenges seem if not easily manageable, at least coherent. In reality, it's all part of a complex maelstrom of change that seems to be happening at an accelerating pace.

And all this to a backdrop of major demographic shifts – population explosion and urbanisation, and the growth of the middle-class – fuelling demand for products and services. Not to mention changing consumer demands and expectations, trade wars, political turmoil and ever more-frequent catastrophic weather events across the world...

It's not easy to pinpoint long term consequences of all of this. However, there is one more theme, **closely entangled with ESG**, that is rising to the fore for business leaders: **scarcity**.

SDG 6 – Clean water and sanitation – addresses the issue of populations and communities affected by water scarcity. In a business context, however, scarcity is a wider issue of meeting the world's needs for all natural resources (and as such, it touches on several of the SDGs).

Resource scarcity

Scarcity has been defined as the gap between limited resources and [potentially] limitless wants.

Resource scarcity results in price volatility, structural supply chain disruptions, uncertainty and other unforeseen consequences. This can ultimately lead to the extinction of unfit companies and inadequate value chain models.

What is considered 'scarce' is changing. Some commodities, metals and elements once considered almost infinite in supply are now fast running out. In this century, perhaps just decades from now, it's conceivable that reserves of oil, gas, coal, uranium, lead, antimony, gold, copper, silver, zinc, indium and many rare earths will have run out or become so expensive to extract that production will stop.

Figure 25 provides an interesting illustration of how fast minerals and other natural resources could be depleted in the lifetime of a person born in 2010.

Figure 25 – Reserves of selected commodities and metals.[63]

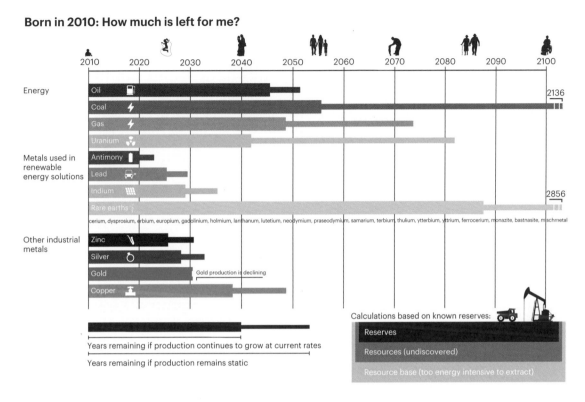

Born in 2010: How much is left for me?

Where to find the leftovers?

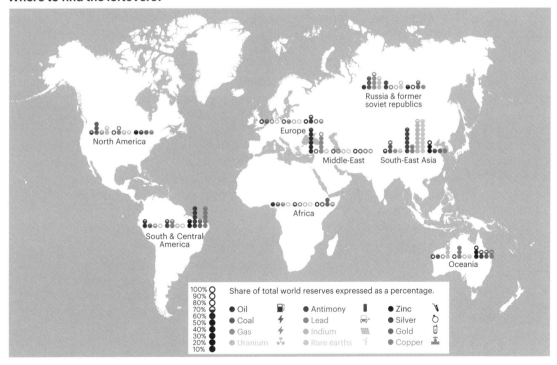

But there's more to find, right?

The information in Figure 25 is quite easy to challenge. The graphic is old, from 2014. Some more recent sources show larger reserves of, say, gold, than suggested here. Whereas extraction of many of these resources, particularly rare earths, has only accelerated since this was first published, depleting reserves faster than then expected.

Some say that resource scarcity is less of a problem than environmental 'doomsayers' claim. Put simply, the argument states that calculations of reserves are based on known reserves, and that there is plenty of scope to find new reserves. To quote just one source, *"Resource availability is not determined by the finite amount of the resource, but by our ability to obtain it. Historically, technology needs to advance to extract a greater amount of resources, and we don't have any reason to assume this won't keep happening."*[64]

Perhaps. But quibbling about **whether a resource will run out a couple of decades sooner or later is missing the point**. It's a short-sighted approach. Plundering the earth's reserves to the very last is merely another way – or excuse – to keep on damaging the biosphere and letting future generations take the consequences. From a business perspective, it's most definitely not a sustainable strategy.

Circular economy: a first step towards solving scarcity

Companies and industry sectors, but also governments and regulators, are increasingly and acutely being challenged to transform and adapt to a world of scarcity. Many have come to realise that in order to understand and take greater control of their total value chain, they need to start thinking in terms of a circular economy.

What is the circular economy?

"Circular economy is a production and consumption model that involves reusing, repairing, refurbishing and recycling existing materials and products to keep materials within the economy. It implies that waste becomes a resource, consequently minimising the actual amount of waste. The circular model is generally the antithesis of a traditional, linear economic model, which is based on a 'take-make-consume-throw away' pattern."[65]

There are many definitions of circular economy, and many, like that above, are variations of what's become well known as the **3 Rs – reduce, reuse, recycle**. It's an economic system that minimises the use of energy and resources, reduces waste, and maximises the value of resources and products by extending their life span.

The circular economy framework enables the reduction of the GHG emissions and environmental degradation associated with traditional linear production systems. It's about keeping products, components and materials circulating in the economy by designing for durability, recycling, reuse and remanufacturing, eliminating waste and pollution across the whole value chain, promoting sustainable consumption patterns and, where possible, regenerating nature.

The intention is to reduce the negative impact on the environment while sustaining or building value and trust with customers, investors, employees, governments and society at large.

Circular economy is an answer to scarcity... and a driver for growth

The circular economy is traditionally overwhelmingly connected with climate change abatement or net-zero strategies and initiatives. Certainly, circular business models will often contribute positively to the reduction of GHG emissions. But the circular agenda should not be determined by net-zero or GHG abatement strategies alone. The agenda is predominantly connected with survival, growth and gaining competitive advantage in a world of constrained resources.

In order to use the circular economy concept as a foundation for business strategy, it's helpful to break this rather fluid concept into more concrete principles. A useful model is the butterfly diagram, proposed by the Ellen MacArthur foundation (Figure 26).

"The circular economy system diagram, known as the butterfly diagram, illustrates the continuous flow of materials in a circular economy. There are two main cycles – the technical cycle and the biological cycle. In the technical cycle, products and materials are kept in circulation through processes such as reuse, repair, remanufacture and recycling. In the biological cycle, the nutrients from biodegradable materials are returned to the Earth to regenerate nature."[66]

Figure 26 – The butterfly diagram: visualising the circular economy.[67]

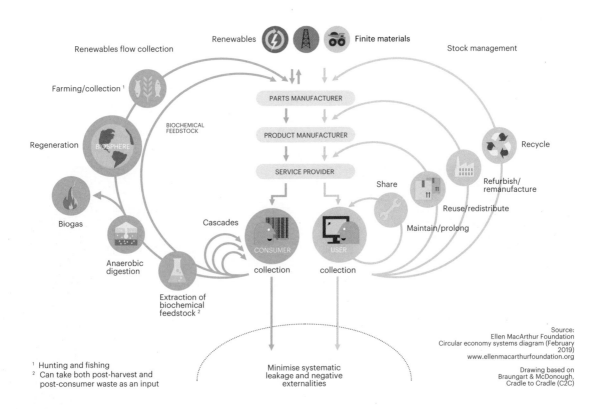

¹ Hunting and fishing
² Can take both post-harvest and
  post-consumer waste as an input

Source:
Ellen MacArthur Foundation
Circular economy systems diagram (February 2019)
www.ellenmacarthurfoundation.org

Drawing based on
Braungart & McDonough,
Cradle to Cradle (C2C)

More spiral than circular

A pure circular model would imply infinite incorporation of resources into the production and consumption chain, which is impossible. Inevitably, the life span of resources, products and components is limited: they cannot be reused *ad infinitum*. Most depreciate with each reuse.

This depreciation, together with the 'definitive' waste generated by the system, means that no 'circular' model is a genuinely hermetic system that operates in a completely circular way. Such models are never 100% self-sufficient, and still exchange both material and energy with the environment. In the butterfly diagram above, this is what is being referred to under the label 'Minimise systematic leakage and negative externalities'.

To account for these 'leakages' and 'externalities', the term 'circular economy' is in some contexts being overtaken by a newer term, 'spiral economy'.[68]

The book *The Spiral-Circular Economy*[69] states that:

> "It is not true that everything can be recycled because there are thermodynamic and economic limits, since the processes take place in a 'spiral loop' system that involves a certain dissipation of the materials through their use."

Thinking in terms of a spiral economy helps to make the requirements and limitations of the circular economy more tangible. It also helps to open the mind to additional opportunities beyond one's own 'internal' circular economy model. Roland Harwood has described the spiral economy as a world *"where the by-products of one organisation or industry not only form a component of another one, but rather become a platform which spawns endlessly unfolding opportunities at varying scales much like the famous Fibonacci sequence."*[70]

Keeping the idea of the spiral economy in mind helps steer one away from the idea that the circular economy is 'the' solution. However, in this book, we will continue to refer to the more universally understandable term 'circular economy', albeit in the broadest sense including its spiral aspects. It remains a useful term to refer to more sustainable operations and practices in a business and regulatory context.

Interest in circular economy models is rising...

More and more organisations are incorporating a circular economy model into their business and operations strategy. For example, the aforementioned PwC study covering ESG-related activities found that 65% of respondents intended to implement a circular business model within the next two years, exceeding intentions for any other ESG measure (Figure 27).[71]

Figure 27 – Circular business model implementation compared to other ESG intentions

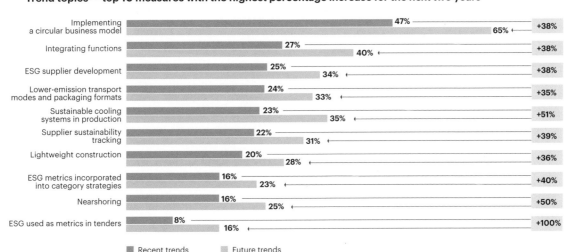

Trend topics — top 10 measures with the highest percentage increase for the next two years

Measure	Recent trends	Future trends	Increase
Implementing a circular business model	47%	65%	+38%
Integrating functions	27%	40%	+38%
ESG supplier development	25%	34%	+38%
Lower-emission transport modes and packaging formats	24%	33%	+35%
Sustainable cooling systems in production	23%	35%	+51%
Supplier sustainability tracking	22%	31%	+39%
Lightweight construction	20%	28%	+36%
ESG metrics incorporated into category strategies	16%	23%	+40%
Nearshoring	16%	25%	+50%
ESG used as metrics in tenders	8%	16%	+100%

■ Recent trends   ■ Future trends

...But not yet well established

The PwC survey revealed, however, that intentions and reality don't always match up. In many cases, organisations state that they already do a lot — and when looking at the different initiatives and systems put in place across regions and industry sectors one cannot deny that a lot has been and is happening, depending on the industry sector and the country.

Most of the top 10 measures implemented by the survey respondents are those that have a direct impact on costs, such as resource efficiency and waste management (Figure 28).

Figure 28 – Top 10 ESG/circular initiatives.

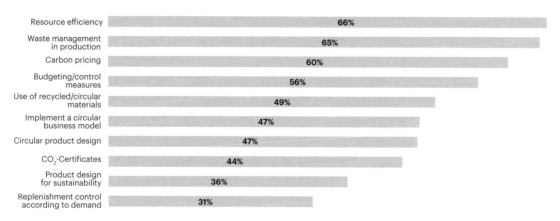

Today's top 10 measures

Measure	%
Resource efficiency	66%
Waste management in production	65%
Carbon pricing	60%
Budgeting/control measures	56%
Use of recycled/circular materials	49%
Implement a circular business model	47%
Circular product design	47%
CO_2-Certificates	44%
Product design for sustainability	36%
Replenishment control according to demand	31%

However, when looking a bit closer into individual organisations and initiatives, a wide range of issues can be seen.

- Targets and instruments are fragmented, opportunistic and disconnected, with deployment of ESG/circular activities being ad hoc rather than systemic.
- There is no strategy-led ability to translate market expectations, or to develop and implement ESG/circular strategies to realise economies of scale, cost optimisation, compliance, etc.
- There are no clearly defined business targets and strategies developed to respond to ESG/circular expectations from regulators, customers, investors and suppliers.
- There are numerous blind spots, whether related to focus, instruments, opportunities or stakeholders.
- There is a lack of enabling instruments to orient, steer, strategise, manage and measure the realisation of the overall circular objective.
- There is no/insufficient transparency and traceability of product ESG parameters and performance to duly inform customers and other stakeholders.
- The performance of management systems with suppliers is inadequate (e.g. with regard to supply chain legislation, due diligence obligation, digital product passports, CSRD deforestation legislation, grievance mechanisms, etc.).

- There is a lack of vision in transforming relationships with suppliers and customers into partnerships that would create profitable revenue models that both decarbonise and secure access (greenfield or not) to resources in a cost-effective manner.

[A few] ESG champions are ahead of the game

The PwC report shows that there is quite a clear demarcation between ESG champions and the rest. Their research shows that there is a subset of ESG champions emerging: these enjoy top management support and have a clear ESG strategy and vision. Perhaps what is most worth noticing is that they have a balanced rather than piecemeal focus on all ESG aspects (Figure 29).

These companies have rethought the value chain end to end in view of making their business more resilient. They have, typically, reengineered their supplier network, own footprint and product design, and adjusted their own business models towards circularity.

The ESG champions tend to be companies with revenues over €3 billion. North America and Asia are ahead of Europe and the industrial manufacturing and retail/consumer goods industry is leading, whereas the process and service industries are lagging behind.

Figure 29 – ESG champions are ahead of the game in developing and implementing ESG/circular strategies

Implementation rate of circular business strategies to achieve ESG goals

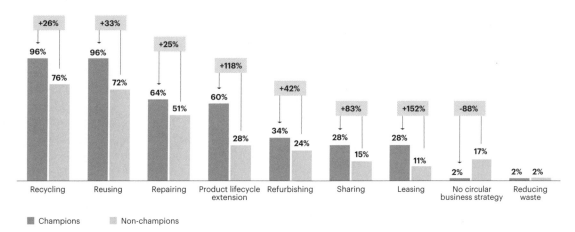

■ Champions ■ Non-champions

6 circular economy critical success factors

What are the keys to a successful circular economy model? First, it must be strategy-driven and fully integrated into the overall business strategy. Secondly, there must be a demand for the product or service proposed. Thirdly, because by its very nature a circular economy model is comprehensive, it almost goes without saying that it should be holistic. It must also be feasible, collaborative and have the right technology in place.

1. Integrated into the business strategy

Any circular business model needs to be an integral part of the organisation's overall business strategy. Without this, ventures into circular strategies are doomed to remain in the drawer or remain accessory to the core business. Joined-up thinking is required to fully integrate circular initiatives into the business, ideally to replace the existing business strategy, or at least to be fully connected with and integrated into existing processes.

Natura&Co
Natura&Co is an example of such joined-up thinking. Natura&Co is a Brazilian multinational producer of cosmetics, hygiene and beauty products (better known under their commercial brands Avon, The Body Shop, Aesop and Natura). Sustain-

able commitments are a core part of Natura&Co's brand and business strategy.[72] The company has been CO_2 neutral since 2007, all cosmetics are certified without animal testing and their brands are known for their commitment to forest conservation. They are circular in the design of their packaging, which is made entirely from recycled plastics, and refills with green plastics from sugar cane instead of petrochemicals.

In parallel, they also practise fair trade with local communities. Natura is one of the largest B-CORP[73] certified companies, demonstrating strong ethics and social and environmental responsibility.

It all adds up to a single, integrated vision and strategy that drives every aspect of the business.

2. Market relevant

A circular economy model needs to deliver products and services for which a (profitable) market is available. Where the market conditions are not present, focus should be on the creation of such a market — if there is a solid business case. Measuring the market relevance should consider all relevant impact dimensions to avoid blind spots in the decision process.

For example, several large brands are currently introducing circular model schemes to reuse and recycle products returned by customers.

H&M

H&M is a Swedish multinational and one of the world's largest clothing brands. Its sustainability initiatives include a scheme to collect returned items from stores, sorting it into items for rewear (to be sold as second-hand clothing), reuse (to be turned into other textile products such as cleaning cloths) or recycling (e.g. to be turned into fibres for insulation).[74]

This is a circular initiative rather than a comprehensive business model, but it does serve as an example of a company testing the waters of circularity.

It could be argued that, for a brand such as H&M, a circular business model is not just relevant but even essential to survival in current market conditions, where there's growing intolerance of what is perceived as 'fast fashion' and 'throwaway' clothes. H&M's scheme is part of a wider resurgence of demand for second-hand clothes, as evidenced by the popularity of online platforms such as thredUP or Vinted.[75]

3. Holistic and systematic

Circular economy strategies require a comprehensive, holistic and systematic approach. However, in many cases companies and organisations start a range of different, sometimes unrelated, initiatives without consideration of all the different dimensions.

A more successful approach is to take a holistic look at the design and manufacturing of the products and services throughout the intended life cycle. When viewed as a whole system, any part of the resources, products, processes and value propositions chain can create opportunities for innovation, growth and potential new profit pools, and improved customer intimacy and satisfaction.

Aside from those 'static' assessments, the approach needs to take into account the capabilities and instruments that will enable and facilitate the creation of the intended loops or results.

IKEA

The global home furnishings brand, IKEA, could be said to have operated under a 'circular-ish' business model almost since its inception: the organisation is structured with ownership control across their value chain, from product design to procurement, manufacturing, distribution, sales and service.

Sustainable processes are built into the IKEA mindset;[76] a mindset originally aimed at cutting costs and increasing sales but that fully aligns with today's concern for saving the environment. Whatever the reason, IKEA has long been a leader in sustainable practices. Its products have always been designed in accordance with principles of resource efficiency and minimal waste, and any waste is reused in other products as far as possible. For many decades, all IKEA stores have included areas where used/returned products are sold at reduced prices. Spare parts to reassemble or repair IKEA products are available to customers, on request, usually free of charge.

Today, IKEA is on the way to turning its entire business model into a circular model by 2030.[77] As with H&M, this strategic business transformation is market relevant, by meeting a growing demand for [even] cheaper and/or used home furnishings, as well as in line with consumer demand for greater sustainability.

4. Supportive micro- and macro-economic instruments

Shifting towards a more circular economy can contribute to reducing pressures on ecosystems, enhancing the security of supply of raw materials, and increasing competitiveness, innovation, growth and jobs. However, the shift also entails a number of challenges, not least in terms of financing, skills, consumer acceptance, governance, and so on.

To support the drive towards circularity, a wide range of appropriate and adequate micro- and macro-economic instruments need to be in place to help companies close and or extend product and resource loops.

In 2020, the European Commission adopted a new Circular Economy Action Plan (CEAP).[78] It's a comprehensive plan covering product design, circularity in production processes and value chains, waste, toxicity, raw materials, etc. It serves as a framework for the EU to accelerate the transition towards a regenerative growth model.

Other measures to support circularity – in addition to environmental policies and regulations – include, for example, subsidies, indirect taxes, competition policy, price controls, and fiscal, monetary and exchange rate policies.

5. Collaborative

A successful circular economy at country or market level will in most cases require a collaborative effort between companies and their stakeholders across the value chain, governments, and other relevant stakeholders in their communities. This can take several shapes such as alliances, ecosystems, the cooperation and joint development of regulatory instruments, governance and compliance models, etc.

Walking the circular road will allow or force you to look at creating closed loops that can only be developed through new ways of working across the supply chain. Yes, seeking to engage and collaborate with all stakeholders might be perceived as a hassle and additional burden. However, if well designed and understood by the participating organisations, establishing such collaboration will create the opportunity for sustainable resilience and increased shared value across the value chain. And it will help shift the social licence to operate to the level of value chains, rather than to a single company.

In the traditional way of doing business, most agreements are highly transactional in terms of negotiation and allocation of value derived from the agreement. Collaborative partnerships, however, distribute value on the basis of the overall success and performance of the ecosystem, rather than being only the result of how well you were able to position yourself in that chain.

6. The right technology

Developing and realising a circular business model, including long-term sourcing strategies and product innovation programmes, puts heavy demands on companies in terms of availability of trusted data, alignment of processes and access to information.

Irrespective of its size, it's extremely complex for an individual company to manage and master the requirements, with a huge number and diverse landscape of stakeholders, markets, regulations, etc., often at global level.

To make a circular economy successful, firms must have access to the necessary technology. Industry 4.0 – the fourth industrial revolution or 4IR – refers to the digitalisation of manufacturing. It has brought tools and solutions that enable and speed up the transition towards a circular economy, including:

- digital tools such as data automation, data warehousing, artificial intelligence, blockchain and data analytics to maximise the efficiency of the system
- advanced-manufacturing technology, e.g. equipment and infrastructure, augmented reality, machine automation, robotics, etc.

Leveraging the power of digital technologies for circular ecosystems
These technology advances form the backbone for effective management of connected, innovative and optimised ecosystems. Together, they can deliver end-to-end traceability and transparency of the resources inside the ecosystem, creating trust and reliability, and development of resilient markets.

Just as technology advances are changing what is possible in circular ecosystems and sustainable value chains, so the demands of these are pushing the boundaries of traditional digital solutions. A circular economy-focused technology solution requires going beyond traditional data/technology solutions, which typically might end at the first consumer. A circular economy model would, for example, also need to cover packaging waste, reuse/repair/repurpose logistics and service platforms, product value through the life cycle, and recycling data (recovery of valuable resources, unit recycling costs and footprint, etc.) (Figure 30).

Figure 30 – ESG/circular measures across the value chain

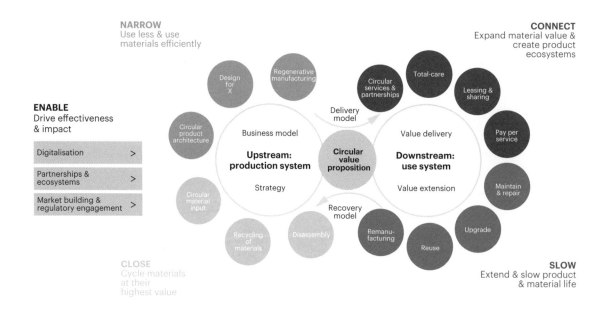

Figure 31 provides examples of ESG/circular measures that can be applied at different stages in the supply chain. In practice, many companies select just one or a small selection of measures, adapting individual parts of their supply chain ad hoc. That's because many companies simply do not have the resources – whether financial or practical – to do otherwise. And indeed, any measures can potentially generate important cost- and materials savings.

Nonetheless, we have already seen that ad hoc deployment of measures in a fragmented way is not the most effective way to build a sustainable business. To build and implement a more sustainable (circular) business model, using our natural capital more efficiently and mitigating the challenges of resource scarcity, will require applying ESG/circular economy principles across the board.

Chapter 8 explores how to create a strategy framework for setting it into action.

Figure 31 – Applying ESG/circular principles at different stages in the supply chain.

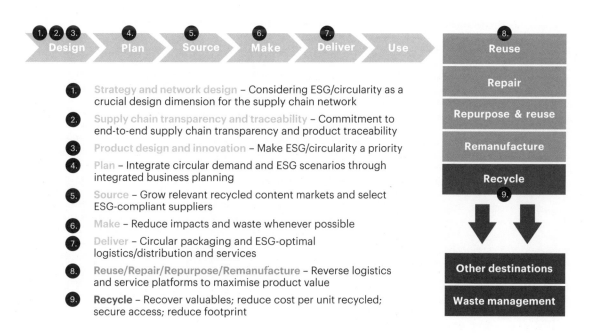

1. **Strategy and network design** – Considering ESG/circularity as a crucial design dimension for the supply chain network
2. **Supply chain transparency and traceability** – Commitment to end-to-end supply chain transparency and product traceability
3. **Product design and innovation** – Make ESG/circularity a priority
4. **Plan** – Integrate circular demand and ESG scenarios through integrated business planning
5. **Source** – Grow relevant recycled content markets and select ESG-compliant suppliers
6. **Make** – Reduce impacts and waste whenever possible
7. **Deliver** – Circular packaging and ESG-optimal logistics/distribution and services
8. **Reuse/Repair/Repurpose/Remanufacture** – Reverse logistics and service platforms to maximise product value
9. **Recycle** – Recover valuables; reduce cost per unit recycled; secure access; reduce footprint

How to operate with positive impact

Roadmap towards a sustainable operating model

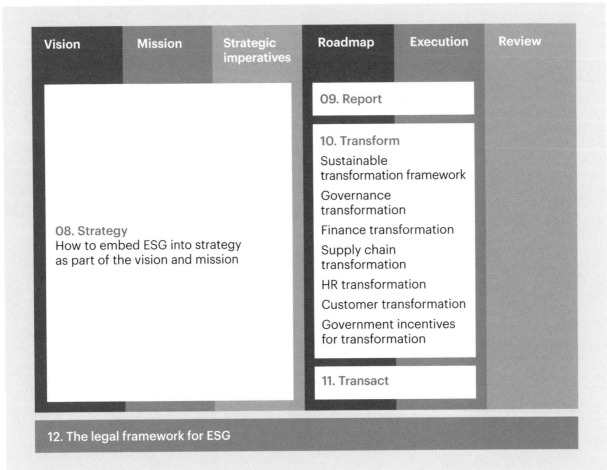

Vision	Mission	Strategic imperatives	Roadmap	Execution	Review

08. Strategy
How to embed ESG into strategy as part of the vision and mission

09. Report

10. Transform
Sustainable transformation framework
Governance transformation
Finance transformation
Supply chain transformation
HR transformation
Customer transformation
Government incentives for transformation

11. Transact

12. The legal framework for ESG

In Part 2, we explore the specific requirements and challenges that companies are facing to become more sustainable, and how you can deal with them. We outline rules and principles and provide practical solutions and examples.

Strategy — Chapter 8 provides an overview of the importance of ESG being part of the top level corporate strategy, and a framework to build a strategy, including measuring your ESG maturity.

Report — Chapter 9 dives into the reporting and compliance landscape. Complying with regulations and law is often the first concern when looking at ESG. This chapter explores the existing frameworks and how these can help to establish a baseline and a transformation plan to improve a range of ESG metrics.

Transform — Chapter 10 presents a practical playbook on ESG business transformation, to accelerate the sustainability journey. Implementing ESG into the business model and operations of a company is not easy. This chapter sheds light onto how to address the execution and integration of an ESG strategy into different segments of your business, and provides some insights on successful examples. It covers transformations in all areas of the business (operations, supply chain, HR, finance, customers) and outlines some of the incentives and grants available that can speed up transformation.

Transact — Chapter 11 addresses how to incorporate ESG into the mergers and acquisitions agenda, listing some of the pitfalls and how to deal with them. As ESG has dominated boardroom discussions, it is inevitable that it also influences the acquisitions agenda.

Legal — Chapter 12 aims to provide a better understanding of the legal landscape that is impacting the ESG agenda and the company as a whole.

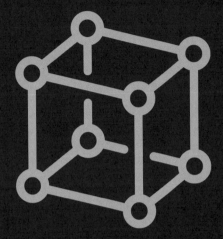

08.
A framework for ESG strategy

Key takeaways

1. ESG needs to be part of the organisation's top-level corporate strategy.

2. A first step is to determine your overriding strategic ambition: conformist, pragmatist, strategist or idealist? Articulating an ESG-focused mission helps to identify your strategic imperatives.

3. Your strategy needs to be complemented with a credible roadmap for implementation, with clear targets and ambitions.

4. What is your ESG maturity level and your reporting maturity?

5. When making pledges, ensure your roadmap to achieve them is credible.

6. How to progress from ESG beginner to ESG champion.

Businesses thrive when built on a well defined strategy to create a unique space in the market. Having a clear purpose, mission and vision leads to better results and higher growth.[79]

When it comes to ESG, the first reflex is often a quest for compliance. However, ESG can and should be far more deeply ingrained and integrated into the corporate strategy. And not only to meet lofty sustainability goals for people and the planet. Embedding ESG in the corporate strategy provides access to cheaper capital, better talent and more customers. And secures the long term viability of the business model.

Fully embracing ESG in the business strategy, however, requires a mindshift, from a narrow focus on shareholder value to a broader perspective of stakeholder value.

ESG is reshaping the boardroom

The business world is moving on from Milton Friedman's narrow doctrine of shareholder capitalism, which has pervaded business for the past 50 years. A broader stakeholder capitalism is taking root in its place, fertilised by ESG principles.

This change has many drivers, from the moral to the pragmatic. But whatever the driver, it's increasingly clear that, in today's world, the boardroom needs to actively nourish the company's social licence to operate, taking into account all stakeholders, not just the shareholders. And that there are major consequences if public opinion, financial institutions or governments no longer support your business.

Sustainability is truly a strategic topic — one for which company boards do bear responsibility. Securing both financial capital AND human, social and natural capital should be part of what keeps board members awake at night.

This requires that board members be educated and knowledgeable about the frameworks and the legal landscape (see *Chapter 12 – The legal framework for ESG*). Too often, ESG is still seen as a matter of reporting, left in the hands of a specific group of experts who need to beg other departments for information so that a nice report can be published on the website. The sustainability agenda should be far more impactful than that and part of the overall company strategy.

A 2015 review concluded that the business case for ESG investing is empirically well founded: analysis of aggregated evidence from more than 2000 empirical studies revealed that more than two-thirds found a positive correlation between ESG investment and corporate financial performance.[80] Moreover, the positive impact of ESG investment on corporate financial performance is stable over time. On top of that, in the intervening years since this review, ESG has garnered considerably more gravitas and attention by companies, shareholders, consumers, governments and the general public.

For companies everywhere, investing in ESG provides far more positive returns than not doing so.

It is now crucial for boardrooms to deliver a clear agenda on how management needs to incorporate ESG matters into the business. The ambition level, targets and incentive structure should mobilise the full management and avoid reporting purgatory.

The importance of bringing ESG to the boardroom has been increasing over the years and it will certainly stay on the agenda in the years to come. Annual surveys of corporate directors by PwC illustrate the growing interest in ESG topics. For example, the proportion of respondents stating that ESG issues are regularly on the board agenda rose from 34% in 2019 to 55% just three years later (Figure 32).

Figure 32 – Corporate Directors' attitudes to ESG.[81]

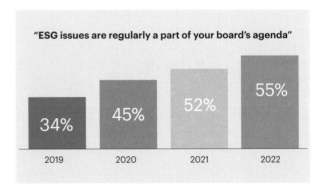

Almost two-thirds of directors (65% in 2022, up from 62% in 2021) say that ESG is part of the board's enterprise risk management (ERM) discussions, meaning it is being built into the central board discussions of company-wide risk calculations.[82]

What is your strategic ambition?

In the face of the growing focus on ESG/sustainability matters and their increasing importance in the boardroom, how do you take the next step, from words to action?

The first step is to identify your overriding strategic ambition. What is driving your ESG discussions in the boardroom, and can you reach consensus on where to take the company? Is your ambition to tackle the waves of regulations as and when they affect you, or embrace sustainability fully in your organisation? Figure 33 shows some typical positions.

Where are you and where do you want to be? Is your top priority compliance, goals or success? Or do you see your business as part of a bigger ecosystem?

Figure 33 – Setting your ambition level for ESG transformation.

Conformist
Compliance-focused positioning

"I focus on **financial return** and consider sustainability as a **regulatory boundary**."

Pragmatist
Goal-focused positioning

"I focus on **optimising financial returns** and have **identified efficient and resource-saving processes** as an effective approach to this, as long as it is profitable."

Strategist
Success-focused positioning

"I realise that the **long-term success** of a company can only be guaranteed if the necessary but increasingly scarce **human and material resources are maintained**."

Idealist
Intrinsically motivated positioning

"I see myself as **part of a global** ecological, economic and social **ecosystem** and reflect this in my processes, steering and systems."

Articulating an ESG-focused vision and mission

Once you have defined your ambitions, and regardless of which tools you use to build a business strategy – a huge range of tools and frameworks are available – you will be able to reflect on the role sustainability plays or will play in your business model.

Most if not all strategy tools cover roughly the same steps:

- vision
- mission
- strategic imperatives
- roadmap design
- strategy execution
- strategy review.

The vision of what your company stands for and the mission you want to accomplish express the core reason for being of the company. Articulating them clearly should enable you to identify a series of key strategic imperatives.[83]

ESG can be part of your mission. Think about the BeyondMeat's mission statement, which clearly defines and steers the brand.

We believe there is a better way to feed our future

By shifting from animal to plant-based meat, we can positively affect the planet, the environment, the climate and even ourselves. After all, the positive choices we make every day – no matter how small – can have a great impact on our world.[84]

While not all companies are (yet) able to articulate how ESG is core to their business, most companies will probably have some strategic imperatives that address ESG challenges and opportunities.

Strategic imperatives are objectives to accomplish, which are time bound, specific and measurable, and thus realise the mission (Table 3).

ESG category	Actual examples of strategic imperatives pursued by various companies	Transformation type
S, G	Gender balance across all levels	Workforce
E	Move to 100% renewable energy by 2025	Operations, Supply chain
S	Lift 5000 farmers out of poverty	Supply chain
E	Quadruple recycled content in our products	Operations, Supply chain
G	Full traceability from farm to fork	Supply chain
E	Net zero by 2030	Operations, Supply chain
E	25% of sales coming from our green product line	Customer
E	25% of sales from new product introduction	Customer
S	No intentionally targeted marketing communications to children under the age of 16	Customer
E	Reducing our emissions across our supply chain by 40% by 2030	Operations, Supply chain
E	Increasing transportation efficiency by 50%	Operations, Supply chain
E	100% recyclable packaging	Operations, Supply chain
E	Zero waste to landfill by 2030	Operations, Supply chain
S	Equal pay	Workforce
S, G	Gender balanced promotions	Workforce
S, G	Gender balanced board	Workforce
E	Divest our traditional business unit by 2028	Finance, Transactions

Strategic imperatives identify what objectives need to be reached. They will eventually have to be structured on a roadmap to execution.

So no matter where you start, be it at the purpose of your company or at the need to have a smaller carbon footprint because of regulation or market pressure, companies are faced with a range of transformations to address. Chapters 9–12 take you through these transformation steps.

But before tackling business transformation, it is important to take stock of where you are now, by assessing your current level of ESG maturity.

How to assess your ESG maturity...

As ESG is discussed more and more at board level, there are key questions to consider, and to reconsider regularly. The list below is certainly not exhaustive, but it's a good starting point, whether from a risk or opportunity perspective (Table 4).

Category	Questions to be addressed
Business strategy	• Has the company clearly articulated a purpose that considers all key stakeholders' needs and aligns with the business strategy? • What are the relevant ESG trends and how might they impact our business model in the coming decade? What are the risks and opportunities (e.g. local for local, geopolitics, cost of carbon, public opinion, electrification, urbanisation...)? • Do we have an accurate stakeholder map and do we engage with them sufficiently to ensure our social licence to operate?
Product and services	• Is the current portfolio adapted to ESG trends? • How can we move to a more circular or regenerative model?
Customers	• Do we need to reconsider customer segmentation based on ESG factors? • How important are ESG topics to our clients? • Can we improve our brand image based on our ESG ambitions, to attract new customers?
Talent	• Do we miss out on talent by not addressing ESG? • Do we have the right capabilities to implement transformations linked to ESG? • Are we sufficiently diverse, inclusive and gender balanced as a company?
Supply chain	• Do we have an accurate view of the impact of our operations on the world at large, as well as the impact on our business (double materiality)? • Is our footprint optimised for cost including CO_2 impact? • Are new technologies available or foreseen that might be an opportunity or a threat? • What do we expect to be the energy source of the future for our operations?
Finance	• Could we have access to cheaper capital by working on ESG? • How do we consider ESG when doing transactions (value lever...)?
Risk management	• Have we done risk mapping for E, S and G? • Do we have sufficient controls in place? • What are the latest ESG-related trends and changes (e.g. legislation, consumer expectation...)? • What are the reporting requirements coming our way in the next few years for all geographies?

...And your ESG reporting maturity

Table 5 provides a means of quickly assessing a company's ESG reporting maturity. It can help board members assess the form of the report, how closely the content of the disclosure is linked to the strategy, whether the right standards are being used, and how accurate the data capture and its supporting technology actually are.

Table 5 – Where does your company fall on the ESG maturity scale?

Grade your company's processes and disclosure to find its ESG maturity level

Topic/Maturity	Limited	Evolving	Optimising	Leading
Form of reporting	ESG report* available on company website	ESG report* on company website and references within proxy statement	ESG report*, disclosures on website, references in proxy statement, discussion of key risks and opportunities included in Form 10-K Disclosures are consistent across platforms	Evidence of an ESG reporting strategy across multiple platforms that are optimised for stakeholders that will be consuming the information there Disclosures are consistent across all platforms
Content of disclosure	No disclosure or traditsional ESG report* that focuses on philanthropy versus strategy	ESG report* that qualitatively addresses material topics for the company but with minimal quantification	ESG report* aligned with material topics that includes metrics, targets and a strategy to achieve them with significant quantitative data	ESG report* that describes a clear link between ESG and strategy Robust quantitative data to support disclosures
Use of standards and/or frameworks	None	Considered	Disclosures in line with one or more common standards or frameworks	Clear data table that illustrates disclosures in line with the standards and frameworks appropriate for the company's industry and size, with cross referencing Disclosure of material issues, relative to the standards and frameworks
Policies and procedures around data collection	Limited use of consistent internally documented policies or procedures	Established policies and procedures	Mature policies and procedures that are documented	Mature policies and procedures that are documented and tested
Reporting technology	Primarily manual accumulation from disparate data sources	Combination of manual accumulation and data automation tools	Data visualisation and transformation tools are used to gather and analyse data into key metrics ESG data used to produce metrics is stored in a centralised location	Data visualisation and tranformation tools are used to gather and analyse data collected largely through integrated system automation and in some cases actively monitored Data stored in a centralised location
Internal controls of ESG reporting	Limited documentation of internal reviews	Documented internal quality reviews by preparers, but without a predetermined control structure and environment	Internal audit involved in defining and performing internal controls Subject to at least limited assurance	Mature and documented processes and controls of ESG data Subject to independent assurance with reasonable assurance on all metrics

Note: An ESG report may also be called a Corporate Social Responsibility Report or Sustainability Report

Pledges — A double-edged sword

Embedding ESG into strategy often entails deciding on some type of time-bound ambitions. A lot of companies have made pledges on a whole range of ESG-related metrics; predominantly in the E space to start with, but also in other areas.

> *"More than 700 of the largest 2,000 publicly traded companies have made net zero commitments, with 59 of the FTSE 100 committing to net zero emissions by 2050."*[85]

It has become almost 'normal' to announce company commitments towards a more sustainable business model and the path towards it. So normal that many have jumped on the bandwagon — sometimes without any viable plan for how to reach their ambitions.

Such pledges are often driven by a desire to meet expectations: employees and the general public want companies to take a stance and show their ambition to 'support the cause'.

Inevitably, as pledge deadlines draw near, many companies will find themselves forced to reevaluate their ambitions and even push back their deadlines, at the risk of finger-pointing and adverse media attention.

Such pledges are being scrutinised: for example, by the Corporate Climate Responsibility Monitor, an annual report produced by the NewClimate Institute and Carbon Market Watch since 2022.[86] This is an assessment of the transparency and integrity of the climate pledges and strategies of 24 major companies — all of whom have endorsed the Paris treaty target of capping global warming at 1.5°C, and aligned themselves with UN-backed campaigns to ensure that business plays its part in decarbonising the global economy.

It covers four areas of corporate climate action:

- tracking and disclosure of emissions
- setting emission reduction targets
- reducing own emissions
- taking responsibility for unabated emissions through climate contributions or offsetting.

The report takes a harsh look at company pledges. The 2023 Monitor noted that *"Climate pledges for 2030 fall well short of the economy-wide emission reductions required to stay below the 1.5°C temperature limit."*

Of course this is headline material: citing the Monitor, BBC News[87] reported that *"Many of the world's biggest companies are failing to meet their own targets on tackling climate change [...]. They also routinely exaggerate or misreport their progress."* And, *"Only 5 companies of the 24 screened came out as clearly committed to deep decarbonisation with their net-zero pledges."*

France24,[88] under the headline *"On climate, most corporations more talk than action"*, stated that *"net zero targets adopted by all 24 multinationals – if met – would barely remove a third of their current emissions"*.

Bloomberg has reported that the world simply does not have enough space to plant the necessary amount of trees for all the companies banking on this kind of carbon capture to reach net zero.[89] A report from Oxfam claimed that we would need to reforest five times the currently-available agricultural land and that this would put heavy pressure on food prices. These land-hungry net-zero schemes could even push an 80% rise in global food prices.[90]

Pledges are not enough

All of this illustrates that making a commitment to net zero may be commendable, showing a company's ambition to improve our world, but it's not enough: pledges need to be backed up by a solid business model and roadmap to get there. Above all, **the 'net-zero' roadmap needs to be credible, and its components realistic and feasible**.

Developing an ESG corporate strategy and a path to execution

There is no shortage in the world of corporate strategy books and other resources: this section does not aim to provide you with a full set of tools and frameworks. The objective here is to highlight that:

- all companies need to take the ESG agenda into account when defining their corporate strategy
- and some companies can even build a competitive advantage out of the ESG and sustainability agenda.

Take automotive companies, for example. Electrification has become a determining factor – even a matter of survival – in their long-term strategy, in terms of product development, launch timelines and the communication strategy. Some companies realised this early on, some need to catch up, while others have woken up too late. But all of them need to adapt.

Some companies have seen the call for a more sustainable business model as an opportunity. Sustainability can be the way to create a 'blue ocean'[91] for your company – a relatively competition-free marketplace – by embedding sustainability into the DNA of your company.

ESG maturity: the path from ESG beginner to ESG champion

Making a net positive impact as a company starts with your corporate strategy. Companies that are successful at incorporating ESG into their top-level corporate strategy will be more appreciated by their clients, have better access to financing at financial institutions, attract more talent and ultimately be more financially sustainable.

One of the difficulties is understanding and defining the ambition level of your ESG transformation programme. While we argue that companies with ESG at the core are better equipped to be sustainable in the long term, there are several ways to start your sustainability journey.

There is also a **logical path towards becoming a mature ESG champion company**, often starting with the pure baselining and metrics which are material to your business (Figure 34).

Figure 34 – ESG maturity path: from ESG beginner to ESG champion.[92]

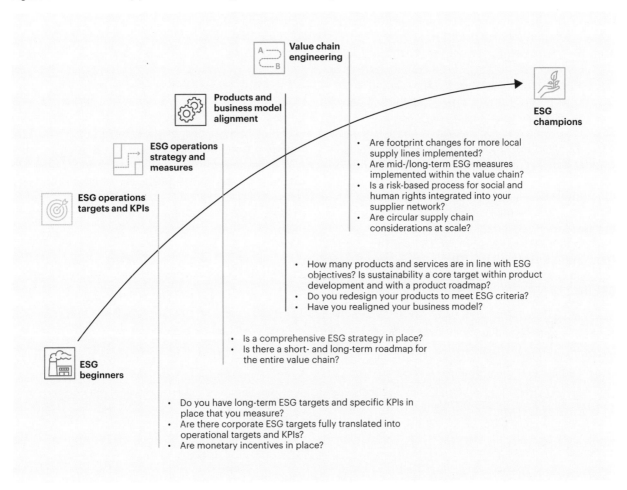

This path begins with identifying the right data points and metrics to set out on an ESG transformation.

- This path begins with identifying the right data points and metrics to set out on an ESG transformation.
- The second stage of maturity is having a clear understanding of the HOW. How will we make this happen? A credible and realistic roadmap is a crucial tool to make the necessary changes.
- In order to become a true ESG champion, one needs to re-evaluate the products and services, and the underlying business model (value chain) that brings these to the customers.

Steps to achieve ESG transformation are described in more detail in *Chapter 10, The 5-phase ESG transformation framework*.

Industry differences

Most companies still have a long way to go to reach ESG maturity. The PwC study mentioned above found that only 6% of the respondents could be classified as ESG champions (Figure 35).

Figure 35 – ESG maturity levels.[93]

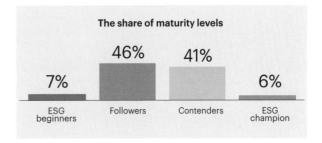

Champions are primarily found in the retail and consumer goods, pharma and medtech, and industrial manufacturing and equipment sectors. This isn't surprising: companies in these sectors by their very nature are more likely to face pressure to act to resolve issues such as human rights, toxins, pollutants and GHG emissions. Governments are ramping up regulatory efforts, and consumers are increasingly likely to choose sustainable, fair-trade and local products (assuming no dramatic cost differences).

For companies in these sectors, ESG measures offer a competitive advantage. Among contenders, the PwC study found that more retailers and consumer goods companies met the criteria than any other industry. That's because retailers are being scrutinised not just by regulators, but also by the public and by their own employees.

The study found noticeably fewer champions among the financial sector and service industries, where companies are under less pressure than in other sectors.

Size matters for ESG maturity

Most champions have revenues of more than €3 billion. Indeed, the higher the sales, the more likely it is that a company will be ESG mature. 43% of champions have gross revenues greater than €20 billion. Companies with high gross revenue are more likely to be under scrutiny, and so are responding by implementing ESG measures more quickly. Obviously, these companies are also more likely to have the necessary means.

Figure 36 – Industry and geographical differences between ESG champions and non-champions[94]

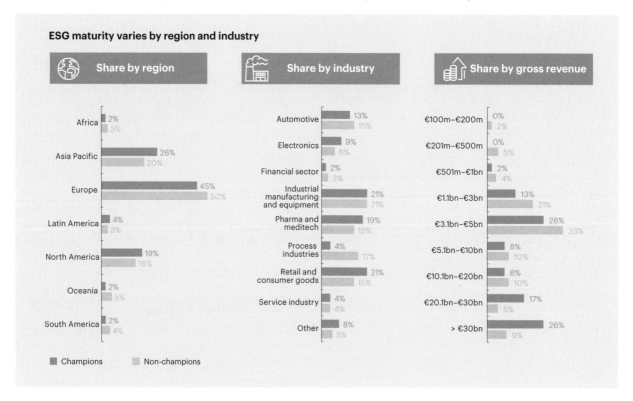

ESG maturity measures

ESG champions are also distinguished from non-champions by the type of measure they have put in place.

Both ESG champions and non-champions have put measures in place to tackle resource efficiency and waste management in production. Again, unsurprisingly, champions implement more measures; these are linked to direct cost benefits.

Other measures that may require more strategic thinking, and structural and organisational changes, are far more prevalent at champions — such as circular product design and use of recycled materials (Figure 37).

Figure 37 – Top 10 measures implemented by ESG champions and non-champions 'Now' and 'In two years'.[95]

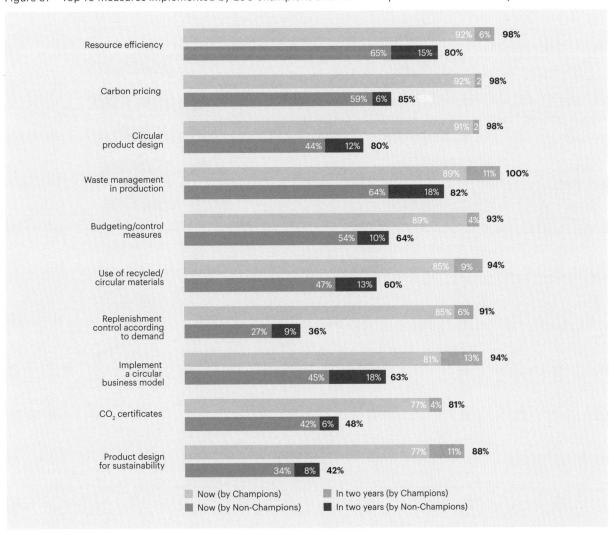

Resource efficiency: 92% 6% 98% / 65% 15% 80%
Carbon pricing: 92% 2 98% / 59% 6% 85%
Circular product design: 91% 2 98% / 44% 12% 80%
Waste management in production: 89% 11% 100% / 64% 18% 82%
Budgeting/control measures: 89% 4% 93% / 54% 10% 64%
Use of recycled/circular materials: 85% 9% 94% / 47% 13% 60%
Replenishment control according to demand: 85% 6% 91% / 27% 9% 36%
Implement a circular business model: 81% 13% 94% / 45% 18% 63%
CO$_2$ certificates: 77% 4% 81% / 42% 6% 48%
Product design for sustainability: 77% 11% 88% / 34% 8% 42%

Now (by Champions) — In two years (by Champions)
Now (by Non-Champions) — In two years (by Non-Champions)

ESG transformation challenges

Overall, ESG champions see 25% fewer challenges than non-champions (Figure 38). But those challenges will be different depending on where you are in your ESG maturity. For champions, access to the correct data is the top challenge (for assessing Scope 3 emissions, for example). Volatile regulatory requirements are also a big challenge: companies face a tsunami of new and upcoming requirements, different per region, industry and company size. Getting a good view on all of them is daunting.

Focus on circular

Given the pressure from so many sides, it is perhaps no surprise that many companies want to create a circular business model. The survey results indicated that implementing a circular business model will be a focus area for a lot of companies in the mid 2020s (Figure 39).

Nearly half of the surveyed companies were working on that when the survey was conducted (2023), while almost two thirds of respondents planned to implement elements of circularity within 2 years.

Figure 38 – Top 5 challenges for ESG champions and non-champions.[96]

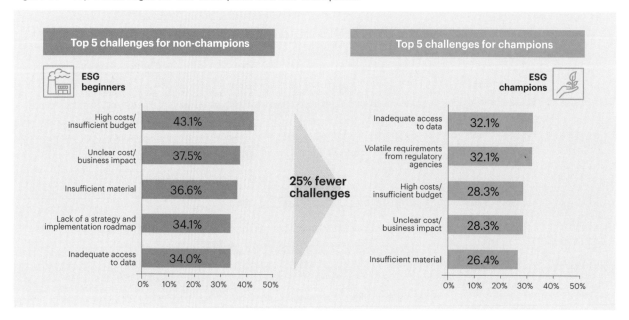

Figure 39 – ESG champions and non-champions aim for a circular business model.[97]

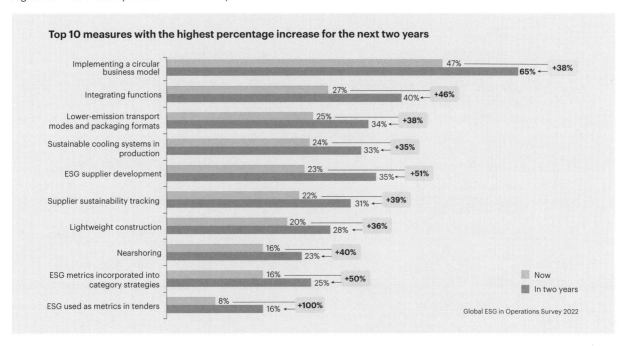

Table 6 – Summary of the key findings of the 2023 PwC study.[98]

1.	ESG is a competitive imperative for companies, with recognised impact on their operations	The majority of companies have set clear targets in all areas and almost all companies (99%) consider ESG criteria in future investments.
2.	Current focus is on the environment	80% of companies have clearly defined long-term targets for emissions, while only 60% have social and governance targets.
3.	Big intentions, small achievements	Only one third of companies have implemented measures for emissions reduction covering Scopes 1 and 2, and only 21% have implemented Scope 3 measures.
4.	ESG leadership starts at the top and filters down	ESG champions enjoy top management support, integration of ESG into their operational strategy and vision, short- and long-term targets by function, and balanced focus on all ESG areas.
5.	ESG maturity varies by region and industry	Comparing the relative share of ESG champions, North America and Asia are ahead of Europe. The industrial manufacturing and retail/consumer goods industries are leading, while the process and service industries are lagging behind.
6.	A majority of ESG champions have revenue greater than €3 billion	Smaller companies have to catch up to not lose competitive ground and to increase resilience to future challenges.
7.	ESG champions have implemented twice as many measures	Primary measures are reengineering of the supplier network and own footprint, product design, and adjusting business models towards circularity.

09.
Reporting

Key takeaways

1. Financial reporting alone provides only a partial view of a company's performance and resilience. The first non-financial reporting was Corporate Social Responsibility (CSR) reporting, which led to the Non-Financial Reporting Directive (NFRD).

2. Sustainability (ESG) reporting is essential for building trust and driving progress towards a more sustainable future.

3. ESG reporting is more than just a compliance requirement: it is the tool for companies to report on their ESG performance in a transparent, comparative, consistent and reliable way.

4. Several ESG reporting standards and frameworks have coexisted, making it difficult to be comparative and consistent. Now, the EU Corporate Sustainability Reporting Directive (CSRD) requires companies to report under the same reporting standards.

5. The CSRD is a comprehensive reporting requirement, and the timelines are very short. It will be a challenge for many companies to be ready.

6. Technology is an enabler for ESG reporting.

The origins of sustainability reporting

Corporate reporting on financial information has grown and matured over centuries. Companies have developed strong management systems to closely monitor financial performance and set up strong processes and controls. Financial information is at the core of business, to manage and measure performance and success. But over time, it became increasingly clear that **financial reporting alone only provides a partial view of a company's performance** and the resilience of the business model. Increasingly, company management, regulators and other stakeholders have been setting demands for more comprehensive data to manage the business and to better understand its resilience and its impact. Companies also started to capture corporate environmental, social and governance impact data, in addition to financial data.

Today, corporate reporting on sustainability information has come a long way in Europe. Corporate reporting began as Corporate Social Responsibility (CSR) a few decades ago. Companies began to report on the positive impact of their business on social- and community-related matters. They notably reported on their voluntary and often philanthropic activities. While CSR reports provided valuable insights, the reporting was often too one-sided, focusing largely on positive impacts, detached from the actual business impact.

In other words, CSR reporting was often insufficiently balanced; the business and other stakeholders wanted better information. They wanted corporate reports that provided *transparent, accessible, consistent and reliable* information.

- *Transparent* data is needed to ensure that business and stakeholders alike can obtain a clear view of the positive and negative impacts. This is an important prerequisite in order to evaluate the resilience of the business, based on transparent reporting of the risks and opportunities and the performance of management.
- *Consistent* data is needed so that information can be compared across performance years, across companies and across sectors, based on the same principles and definitions of

reporting. Consistent data allows management performance to be evaluated and compared over time to enable informed decision making.
- *Accessible* data is needed to ensure that readers can navigate through the complexity of information that is reported and can find the data relevant for them.
- *Reliable* data is needed to ensure that decisions are taken on correct and robust data.

In order to move towards corporate sustainability reporting with these qualities, it became clear that a clear framework for corporate reporting on sustainability information was needed. A framework that would give readers a clear picture of the financial and sustainability impact and resilience of the business.

From CSR to NFRD

Given the clear need for more transparent and comparable reporting on non-financial matters, in 2014 the EU adopted the Non-Financial Reporting Directive (NFRD). Besides providing stakeholders access to non-financial information for affected companies (i.e. large European public interest entities (PIE) — listed companies, banks and insurance companies), it also encouraged these companies to take more responsibility for the ESG impacts of their business. As from FY2017, these companies were required to disclose their sustainability efforts for at least the following ESG domains: diversity, environmental, social and employee matters, respect for human rights, and anti-corruption matters.

For each of these topics, the companies needed to be transparent about the policies applied to address these matters, the results of such policies, the main risks associated with these topics in relation to the business, and key non-financial performance indicators concerning the activities in question.

The NFRD triggered companies to think about their sustainability impact and disclose their ESG-related activities, thereby improving transparency and accessibility for stakeholders. But it still did not bring non-financial information disclosed up to the desired level of consistency and reliability. Moreover, it did not force companies to really think about the true impact of their business on society and the environment, and to translate this into a sustainability strategy fully integrated into the core corporate strategy.

The principal standards and frameworks

In preparing non-financial information, companies are required to base themselves on recognised European and international reporting standards and frameworks. Over the last decades, therefore, companies, non-profit organisations and other stakeholders have developed a wide range of reporting standards, guidelines, frameworks, etc. to address specific sustainability reporting needs.

This unstructured creation of initiatives turned the non-financial reporting landscape into a maze. To help you navigate through the maze, the list below outlines some of the most commonly used ESG reporting standards.

GRI (Global Reporting Initiative)[99]

The GRI defines best practice for how organisations communicate and demonstrate accountability for their impacts on the environment, economy and people. There are three sets of GRI Standards. The *Universal Standards* are designed to deliver an inclusive picture of an organisation's material topics, their related impacts, and how they are managed. They apply to all organisations and include reporting on human rights and environmental due diligence. The new *Sector Standards* enable more consistent reporting on sector-specific impacts. The *Topic Standards* – adapted to be used with the revised Universal Standards – list disclosures relevant to a particular topic.

SASB (Sustainability Accounting Standards Board)[100]

In contrast with the GRI, SASB applies a more financial perspective to determine the material topics for a company and focuses on the sustainability issues likely to have an impact on the company's financial performance and long-term value. A materiality map has been developed by SASB to point out what ESG domains to report on according to the company's industry sector.

SASB reporting is considered to be geared more towards investors and capital providers.

UN SDG (United Nations Sustainable Development Goals)[101]

Besides GRI and SASB, companies frequently also use the SDGs to structure their non-financial reporting and thereby disclose their sustainable business practices aligned with the SDGs. (See *Chapter 6 – From ESG to SDG*.)

CDP (Carbon Disclosure Project)[102]

The CDP helps companies (and cities) to disclose their environmental impact and to address and limit their risks from climate change, deforestation and water insecurity. Companies disclose information to the CDP by completing a questionnaire. Based on a scoring methodology, responding companies are assessed and scored on their replies across four levels, which represent the steps a company moves through as it progresses towards environmental stewardship: from disclosure (D score), awareness (C score), management (B score) to leadership (A score). The resulting CDP score provides a snapshot of a company's disclosure and environmental performance and can be included in a company's external sustainability reporting to inform their stakeholders.

TCFD (Task Force on Climate-Related Financial Disclosures)[103]

The TCFD was created in 2015 by the Financial Stability Board (FSB), an international body that monitors and makes recommendations about the global financial system. Its mission is to help investors, lenders and insurance underwriters understand climate-related risks and opportunities, and their impact on businesses. In 2017, the TCFD published recommendations, providing a framework for companies and other organisations for climate-related financial disclosures included in mainstream financial reporting. In its recommendations, the TCFD determined the disclosure of 11 types of information, divided into four broad categories:

(1) governance around climate-related risks and opportunities

(2) the actual and potential impacts of climate-related risks and opportunities on a company's businesses, strategy and financial planning

(3) identification, assessment and management of climate-related risks

(4) metrics and targets that a company relies on to assess and manage relevant climate-related risks and opportunities.

SBTi (Science Based Targets Initiative)[104]

The SBTi is a partnership between CDP, the United Nations Global Compact, World Resources Institute (WRI) and the World Wide Fund for Nature (WWF). It provides companies with best practices and guidance in defining emissions reductions and net-zero targets in line with climate science. Companies can define their emission reduction targets and have them validated by SBTi, meaning that approved targets are aligned with the objective set out in the Paris Climate Agreement to limit global warming to 1.5°C. This obviously helps to increase the credibility of the plan and to show the intentions are real and sincere. (See also: *Chapter 8, Pledges – A double-edged sword*.)

An extensive list of ESG standards and frameworks can be found at OneTrust.[105]

ESG reporting is no longer optional...

With the increasing regulatory pressure, companies are inevitably focusing more and more on sustainability/ESG reporting. While in the past years a subset of companies already reported on ESG on a voluntary basis, there's an important shift happening to make this reporting mandatory.

Europe has become a front runner regarding ESG reporting requirements: by 2025, most large and medium sized companies will be required to report on their ESG performance; smaller listed companies have until 2027 (FY2026 reporting). This type of reporting will generate a great need for consistent data, metrics and clear standards and definitions. Additionally, ESG reporting will very rapidly need to be at the same level of maturity as financial reporting — and it will also include an external assurance requirement.

It will not be possible for most companies to first embark on an ESG transformation and only then evaluate what ESG information can be disclosed and reported on. The (regulatory) need to develop a fundamental ESG reporting, rooted in a careful (double) materiality analysis, can become a starting point of future ESG transformations and can form the basis for prioritising some elements in this transformation.

...It's a cornerstone for shifting to a sustainable economy

But is sustainability (ESG) reporting merely for compliance? Or is it just the administrative side effect of ESG initiatives? No, it's much more. We would even say that ESG reporting is the cornerstone for making the shift to a sustainable economy actually happen.

However, while many organisations already undertake a multitude of ESG-related initiatives across their operations, the reporting on these initiatives is often still in its infancy.

[Better] ESG reporting is a crucial mechanism for companies and organisations to communicate their environmental, social and governance performance to all stakeholders; from investors, to employees, to customers and the wider public. These disclosures typically include:

- risks and opportunities arising from social and environmental issues
- the impacts of the organisation's activities on people and the environment
- goals, roadmaps and the progress towards achieving them
- policies and achievements.

Disclosing this type of non-financial information is a transparent and accountable way to demonstrate the impact of a company's operations on the environment and society, and to showcase its commitment to sustainable practices. By providing information on ESG metrics such as carbon emissions, waste management and reduction, and diversity and inclusion, sustainability reporting helps stakeholders make informed decisions about the companies they engage with and invest in.

Europe is the sustainability reporting frontrunner

Steps are being taken in the right direction, but it is still very difficult for organisations to see the wood for the trees when starting or continuing their sustainability reporting journey. The wide variety of global reporting initiatives, frameworks and standards make it a daunting process. In addition, while the NFRD was one of the first steps towards a harmonised reporting framework, it did not foster the comparability and reliability of non-financial data that stakeholders were looking for. In order to radically improve the way sustainability information is disclosed and harmonise the muddle of reporting initiatives, the European Commission – as part of the EU Green Deal and its 2020 Work Programme – committed to (amongst other things) revising the NFRD and developing a comprehensive and unified European non-financial reporting standard.

EU Green Deal

The EU Green Deal (Figure 40) is the foundation of sustainability regulation and reporting within the European Union. The purpose of the EU Green Deal is to transform the European Union into a modern, resource-efficient and competitive economy.[106] Achieving this will require massive public investment and increased efforts to direct private capital towards climate and environmental action, while avoiding lock-in into unsustainable practices.[107] It means companies will need to be more resilient in the wider context of environmental and social challenges, and shows that the business world is also playing a key role in society to drive positive change.

Figure 40 – The European Green Deal[108]

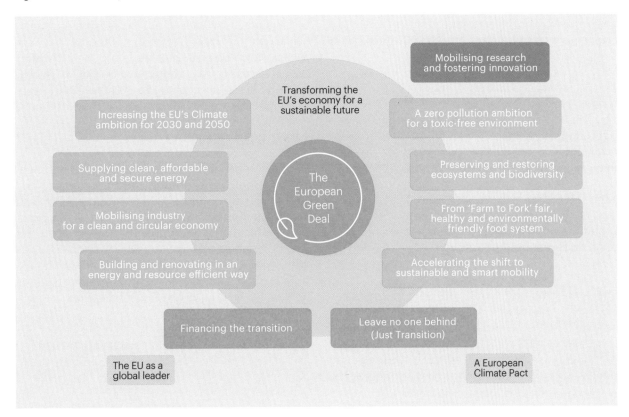

Finally, let's not forget that sustainability reporting is above all intended to drive positive change within a company by encouraging it to set ambitious sustainability goals and to continuously improve its performance.

The European Green Deal aims to transform the EU into a modern, resource-efficient and competitive economy – as already stated – with no net emissions of greenhouse gases by 2050. It wants to decouple economic growth from resource use, and ensure that all EU regions and citizens participate in a socially just transition to a sustainable economic system. It also aims to protect, conserve and enhance the EU's natural capital, and to protect the health and well-being of citizens from environment-related risks and impacts.

In order to achieve these ambitious goals, an action plan was developed to reorient capital flows towards sustainable investments by drastically improving the transparency, accessibility, consistency, compatibility and reliability of non-financial information disclosed by organisations. The European Commission developed a set of consolidation initiatives by building on existing international sustainability reporting initiatives.

The Sustainable Finance Disclosure Regulation (SFDR)[109]

The SFDR mainly applies to financial institutions operating within the EU and is intended to increase transparency on sustainability among financial institutions and market participants. The regulation consists of disclosure requirements at organisational, service and product levels to standardise sustainability performance, thereby preventing greenwashing and enabling comparisons for sustainable investment decisions.

The EU Taxonomy Regulation[110]

The Taxonomy Regulation sets up a classification system for environmentally sustainable economic activities, with the aim of scaling up sustainable investments and combating the greenwashing of 'sustainable' economic activities. It requires companies within the scope of the NFRD (and later the CSRD) to disclose certain indicators about the extent to which their activities are environmentally sustainable according to the taxonomy. At a later stage the Taxonomy Regulation will be further expanded to also include social and governance taxonomies.

The Corporate Sustainability Reporting Directive (CSRD)[111]

The CSRD is the revision of NFRD; it drastically increases the ESG reporting requirements and the number of companies affected. Companies in scope will need to prepare an extensive reporting of qualitative and quantitative disclosures related to environmental, social and governance topics. A set of reporting standards – the European Sustainability Reporting Standards (ESRS) – provides an extensive list of more than 80 disclosures, each of which contains additional underlying disclosure requirements and application guidance that need to be considered.

It's clear that this wide-ranging set of EU directives and regulations is designed to encourage change in business behaviour. It aims to ensure that companies are transparent about the progress they are making towards a sustainable future, and that they are addressing the information needs of stakeholders. It's also expected to increase scrutiny on businesses' sustainability strategy and performance.

Integrated reporting

Perhaps most importantly, this legislation mandates 'integrated reporting', putting financial and non-financial reporting at the same level and to provide a holistic and integrated view of a company's performance and impact. This will affect the way companies do business, who they do business with, and how capital is allocated towards sustainable business activities, thereby working towards achieving the EU's Green Deal objectives.

Figure 41 shows the timeline, with the first CSRD reporting due in 2025, for FYs starting in 2024.

Figure 41 – Timeline for CSRD reporting.[112]

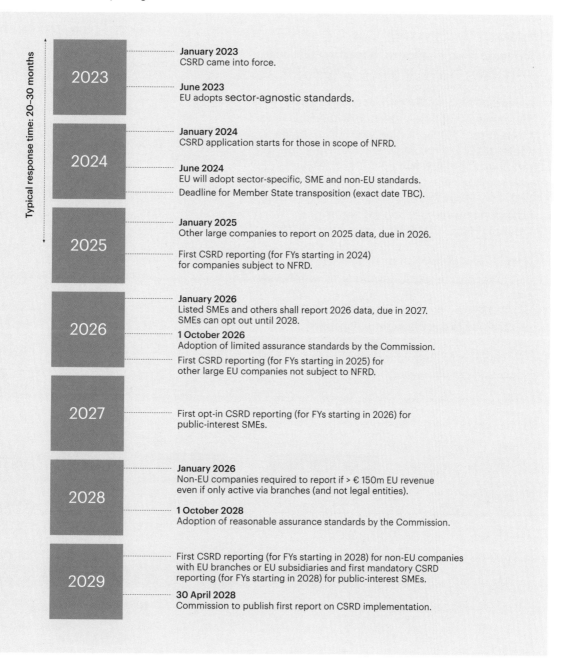

Typical response time: 20–30 months

2023

January 2023
CSRD came into force.

June 2023
EU adopts sector-agnostic standards.

2024

January 2024
CSRD application starts for those in scope of NFRD.

June 2024
EU will adopt sector-specific, SME and non-EU standards.
Deadline for Member State transposition (exact date TBC).

2025

January 2025
Other large companies to report on 2025 data, due in 2026.

First CSRD reporting (for FYs starting in 2024)
for companies subject to NFRD.

2026

January 2026
Listed SMEs and others shall report 2026 data, due in 2027.
SMEs can opt out until 2028.

1 October 2026
Adoption of limited assurance standards by the Commission.

First CSRD reporting (for FYs starting in 2025) for
other large EU companies not subject to NFRD.

2027

First opt-in CSRD reporting (for FYs starting in 2026) for
public-interest SMEs.

2028

January 2026
Non-EU companies required to report if > € 150m EU revenue
even if only active via branches (and not legal entities).

1 October 2028
Adoption of reasonable assurance standards by the Commission.

2029

First CSRD reporting (for FYs starting in 2028) for non-EU companies
with EU branches or EU subsidiaries and first mandatory CSRD
reporting (for FYs starting in 2028) for public-interest SMEs.

30 April 2028
Commission to publish first report on CSRD implementation.

CSRD timeline details

- **Financial Year 2024 (for reporting in 2025)** for large public interest entities (PIEs) with more than 500 employees (companies that are already subject to the NFRD).
- **Financial Year 2025 (for reporting in 2026)** for companies that meet two out of the following three criteria: (i) more than €20 million balance sheet total; (ii) more than €40 million net turnover and (iii) more than 250 employees on average over the financial year (applicable to both EU companies and EU subsidiaries of non-EU companies respecting the thresholds).
- **Financial Year 2026 (for reporting in 2027)** for listed small and medium sized enterprises (SMEs), including small and non-complex credit institutions and captive insurance, which can decide not to provide sustainability reporting until 2028 (but have to include a justification of its absence in the management report).

The EU Taxonomy Regulation will further add to the reporting requirements (Figure 42).

Figure 42 – EU taxonomy-relating reporting timeline.[113]

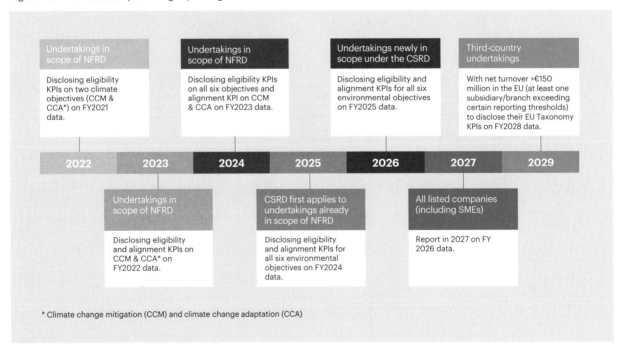

US and international standards

In parallel with the CSRD and ESRS, two other international standards are being developed with the purpose of harmonising the sustainability reporting landscape.

US Securities and Exchange Commission

In March 2022, the US Securities and Exchange Commission (SEC) proposed a rule[114] to disclose climate-related information in annual reports as from fiscal year 2023. This includes disclosure in financial statements of detailed information about climate-related financial risks, metrics (such as GHG emissions), targets and net-zero transition plans. The main purpose of this new rule is to ensure that investors have consistent, comparable, and reliable information to enable them to make informed judgments and decisions related to the impact of climate-related risks on current and potential investments.

International Sustainability Standards Board

In 2021, the IFRS Foundation announced the formation of a new standard-setting board: the International Sustainability Standards Board (ISSB). In developing their International Sustainability Reporting Standard (ISRS), the ISSB will initially start with a climate standard (thereby further building on the principles of TCFD) and later broaden their scope to cover the broader spec-

trum of ESG. Similar to the US SEC's climate disclosure rule, the ISRS is focused on disclosures mainly material for investors (i.e. the impact on the enterprise value) and will therefore give a more restricted view on a company's sustainability effort compared to the double materiality point of view applied in the CSRD (in which a company's impact on society and the environment are also taken into account, regardless of whether it affects enterprise value).

The reporting requirements landscape is complex

These three non-financial reporting standards (CSRD, IFRS-ISSB, SEC, also referred to as the 'big three') are considered to set the foundation for future ESG reporting and improve the completeness, comparability, and accountability of corporate (sustainability) reporting. The reliability of the published non-financial information is further enhanced by the assurance requirement included in the CSRD and the US SEC climate disclosure rule.

Figure 43 provides an overview of the connections between the various reporting standards and reporting requirements. It illustrates the significant complexity and the challenges this may bring to companies to monitor and manage the requirements.

Figure 43 – Connections between different reporting standards

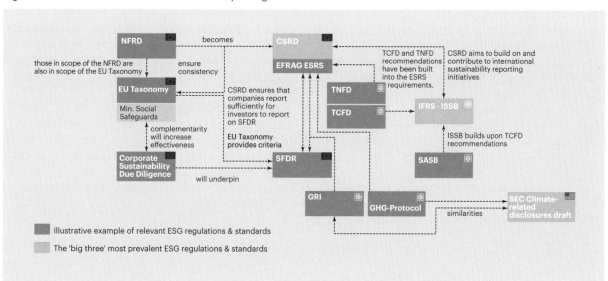

How ESG rating agencies play their role

Similarly to the development of various sustainability reporting standards and initiatives, the high demand for [comparable and reliable] ESG information has inspired several players to develop ESG ratings. Today, the ESG rating industry contains a wide variety of different methodologies and approaches, but they all share one common objective: measuring the sustainability performance of a company.

A recent survey (Ninety One[115]) amongst investment professionals in Europe found that most respondents (88%) are using third-party ESG ratings to support investment decisions or as part of their investment process. An overwhelming majority (92%) said they expect to increase their use of ESG ratings in the future.

One of the root causes of this high reliance on ESG is most certainly the EU Green Deal, with its goal to relocate capital towards sustainable business activities. ESG ratings transform the muddle of voluntary non-financial reporting by companies into easily accessible, transparent, consistent and comparable data. However, besides these benefits, there are also some downsides in using ESG ratings as a source of information.[116]

For example, the ESG ratings that companies obtain diverge across the different providers depending on the applied scoring methodology and scope of ESG topics analysed. In addition, a 2021 review (Bloomberg) showed that upgrades in ESG ratings were very often due to governance improvements and *"rudimentary business practices"* rather than to substantive improvements in social or environmental matters:

> *"Upgrades were often driven by check-the-box practices, such as conducting an employee survey that might reduce turnover, and rarely for substantial practices, such as an actual reduction in carbon emissions. Half of the companies were upgraded for doing nothing—the result of methodological changes."*[117]

This again emphasises the importance for companies to develop robust sustainability reporting to meet the information needs of their stakeholders, and to not focus purely on their ESG ratings.

Building a robust sustainability reporting framework

Given the rapidly changing regulatory environment and related sustainability reporting requirements, companies are currently focusing on building the underlying sustainability reporting frameworks.

While financial reporting frameworks have been built and matured over the past decades, one of the main challenges for the sustainability reporting frameworks is the timeline. Even if the ESRS still needs to be transposed into national laws by the EU Member States, the CSRD has set tight timelines for reporting, as shown earlier in Figure 41.

The timelines are very challenging, considering the wide range of information that will need to be disclosed which, depending on the company, can expand to about 80 disclosure requirements across different domains, over 1000 data points typically coming from various sources and systems across the different plants and sites, etc. Solid and consistent reporting of all of this information will require a well established system to identify, collect, calculate, transform, consolidate and report the relevant data. This will need to include the establishment of adequate policies and procedures, internal controls, and roles and responsibilities. For many companies these processes may need to be supported by data and technology solutions.

Double materiality analysis

In elaborating a sustainability reporting framework, an important starting point is the double materiality analysis, which also constitutes one of the qualitative disclosures requirements as part of the ESRS 1[118] (Figure 44).

Figure 44 – Double materiality analysis

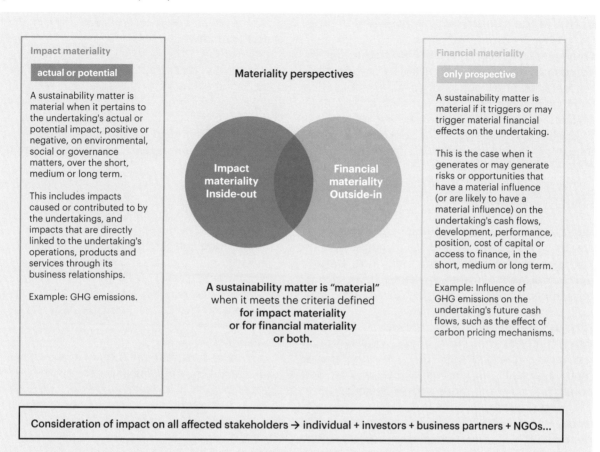

Impact materiality

actual or potential

A sustainability matter is material when it pertains to the undertaking's actual or potential impact, positive or negative, on environmental, social or governance matters, over the short, medium or long term.

This includes impacts caused or contributed to by the undertakings, and impacts that are directly linked to the undertaking's operations, products and services through its business relationships.

Example: GHG emissions.

Materiality perspectives

Impact materiality Inside-out

Financial materiality Outside-in

A sustainability matter is "material" when it meets the criteria defined **for impact materiality or for financial materiality or both.**

Financial materiality

only prospective

A sustainability matter is material if it triggers or may trigger material financial effects on the undertaking.

This is the case when it generates or may generate risks or opportunities that have a material influence (or are likely to have a material influence) on the undertaking's cash flows, development, performance, position, cost of capital or access to finance, in the short, medium or long term.

Example: Influence of GHG emissions on the undertaking's future cash flows, such as the effect of carbon pricing mechanisms.

Consideration of impact on all affected stakeholders → individual + investors + business partners + NGOs...

This (double) materiality analysis is the starting point for companies to determine what sustainability topics really matter for them. It is referred to as a double materiality analysis as it evaluates both:

- the impacts caused by the company on the people and the environment that are directly linked to its operations, products and/or services, and
- the financial impact of sustainability matters on the company.

This materiality approach is an important starting point when elaborating a sustainability reporting framework; it will drive the scope of your reporting. If, according to the materiality analysis, a sustainability matter is determined to be immaterial to a company, it may be possible to omit the related disclosure requirements or data points in their sustainability reporting. The double materiality assessment thereby helps ensure that a company's sustainability report is sufficiently focused on material topics only.

ESRS 1 details the concept and the approach to take when conducting materiality analyses. Note that the materiality analysis must cover all topics, and that some of the ESRS and specific data points cannot be excluded from reporting (e.g. for ESRS 2, ESRS E1). It's important to carefully analyse what can be excluded and what should be included in the reporting before elaborating the sustainability reporting framework.

The people are watching. Or why compliance should not be your key driver

While stakeholder pressure is increasing on companies to report sustainability information, reporting is often approached as a compliance exercise to meet legal requirements, satisfy information needs of key stakeholders and as a means to shed a positive light on a company's impact. Reporting should, however, be approached as a means to an end — with the end being that companies are transparent about the resilience of their business and the impact that they create.

Reporting should be an interactive process that serves as the **starting point for a company to be transparent about its vision, ambitions, targets and performance** related to the reduction of negative impacts and the increase of positive impacts.

It is also the process through which a company can show that they have actually delivered on the ambitions and targets. This is becoming ever more important as readers of ESG claims and commitments grow more knowledgeable — not only about good practices but also about greenwashing practices. Increasingly, companies are denounced – by the media, shareholders, other stakeholders, or activists – for not managing the business responsibly and for not integrating important ESG considerations into the core of the business. And it's becoming ever easier to track the commitment and performance of companies. For instance:

- the Yale Chief Executive Leadership Institute (CELI)[119] is an easily accessible online platform to track responses from major companies to continue or curtail operations in Russia after the invasion of Ukraine
- Climate TRACE[120] is an online platform to track human-caused GHG emissions using AI and satellite imagery down to the level of individual factories.

In this context, stakeholders expect companies to publish relevant and reliable information about the impact and resilience of the business. Impactful sustainability reporting should reflect that the information reported is deeply relevant for the company, enabling it to manage the business for its financial well-being and for its responsibility towards stakeholders, as per the concept of double materiality.

Sustainability reporting is therefore not just a compliance exercise for the sake of meeting regulatory requirements. It should be embedded into the core of the company's business model and strategy. And it should capture both double materiality impact dimensions: financial impact and stakeholder impact.

Furthermore, sustainability reporting covering both these impact dimensions should be:

- embedded into the management practices whereby the business model and strategy are implemented at all levels of the company (i.e., *first line of defence*]
- integrated into the risk management and compliance practices [i.e., *second line of defence*]
- part of the mandate of internal and external auditing [i.e., *third line of defence*].

Such proper integration of sustainability reporting into the core of the company management practices is the only way to ensure that the business is resilient and has a positive impact in the long run. And isn't this what every company ultimately aims for? To be a 'net positive company', as defined by Paul Polman and Andrew Winston, that:

"improves well-being for everyone it impacts and at all scales—every product, every operation, every region and country, and for every stakeholder, including employees, suppliers, communities, customers, and even future generations and the planet itself."[121]

Is this not a worthy concept for every company that aspires to be relevant in our market economy and to be resilient enough to navigate through increasingly uncertain times?

In short, sustainability should be embedded into every company. And sustainability reporting should focus on the information that is closely linked to the company's impact. It's easier said than done, and requires significant change compared to how business was traditionally led.

Technology as an enabler for reporting

Adhering to the different ESG reporting requirements can be a complex and challenging task. While the number of reporting frameworks, standards and regulations is evolving, companies need to find ways to navigate through the constantly changing landscape.

As ESG data is scattered across business operations, the main challenges arise from getting the right information from different sources, whether from within the company itself or from external sources and stakeholders. Fortunately, technology can play a crucial role in supporting companies in their ESG reporting journey.

It boils down to a few simple key requirements:

- pull the right data from the right sources into a 'single source of truth'
- smoothly integrate solutions with existing software solutions that contain ESG data, using templates, data models and automated mapping
- present information in a user friendly, tangible and actionable way.

Implementing the right technologies helps companies in many ways.

- **Data collection and data management solutions** help companies to streamline and simplify their ESG reporting. This often translates into the setup of a specific ESG data-integration layer that collects all relevant ESG data into one single source of truth. ESG data can be collected from multiple sources, including internal systems and databases, external databases and supply chain partners, to name just a few.
- **The right tools and software solutions** can facilitate compliance with the various reporting frameworks and standards thanks to templates, data modelling and automated mapping capabilities that align with the different reporting frameworks and standards.
- **Online portals, interactive dashboards and digital communication** tools help enhance transparency and stakeholder engagement.

In today's world, communicating about doing the right thing in a transparent way is just as important as actually doing the right thing. Open communication and transparency fosters trust amongst employees, stakeholders and shareholders.

- **Aggregating and analysing large volumes of ESG data** enables companies to monitor and track ESG performance over time. Technology plays a crucial role to support ESG performance benchmarking, both internally over defined time periods and externally against peers.

Figure 45 shows the IT architectural components that are relevant for ESG reporting and monitoring. ESG data can come from multiple sources and needs to be centralised in order to meet the reporting needs. The framework illustrated in Figure 45 can be used as a 'go-to' model for companies, but the actual implementation of ESG technology solutions will depend on the business context, the maturity of the current ESG reporting and the companies' existing technology landscape. Each company can define its preferred IT architecture[122] in order to meet the mandatory and voluntary reporting needs.

It's important that the selected technology is complementary to the existing landscape, and doesn't cause any unwanted disruption to current business processes.

Figure 45 – IT architectural components that are relevant for ESG reporting and monitoring.

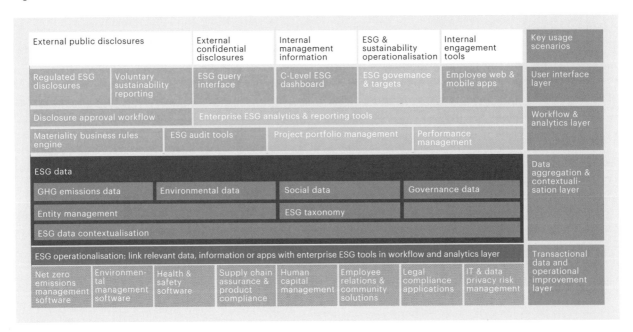

The ESG technology landscape

A key element within the ESG IT architecture is the operationalisation layer between the different software solutions that aggregate the relevant ESG data into a single source of truth for ESG reporting use cases.

For example, a company's key ESG data might be composed of GHG emissions data and broader environmental data, social data (e.g. diversity and inclusion numbers, employee retention rate, etc.) and governance data (e.g. management structure, health and safety policies, etc.). On top of that, the necessary disclosure approval flow can be implemented to meet the regulatory and voluntary ESG reporting requirements.

In parallel with the constantly evolving regulatory landscape, technology providers are speeding up their efforts to bring technology solutions to the market to support companies in their ESG journey. While the supply on the market is very extensive, there is no one solution that fits all reporting needs.

Some of the large technology companies offer solutions to help companies in their ESG transition. These solutions have various functionalities, all with the aim of bringing together the right data and making it available in manageable reports, both for internal and external reporting.

Table 7 outlines some of the main technology players and their offer.

Table 7 – Overview of some of the main ESG technology providers and solutions

Category	Vendors	Offer
Broad range of ESG solutions and applications	• Microsoft • SAP • Salesforce • Workday • Oracle	These vendors offer a variety of ESG tools and solutions, each for a specific purpose, that allow companies to measure, analyse and report on environmental, social and governance practices. Typical functionalities include, for example: measuring and reporting on Scope 1, 2 and 3 emissions impact and savings; enabling energy management; setup of a sustainability control tower (i.e. a single source of truth interface); measuring diversity and inclusion of the workforce.
Cloud solution providers	• AWS • Google • Microsoft	These vendors offer a sustainable cloud infrastructure to support their clients in achieving their sustainability goals and enable ESG reporting. They also offer specific tools, for example to track and measure carbon footprint and identify areas of improvement.
Specific ESG reporting solutions	• Workiva • Sphera • Icertis	Tools from these vendors have a specific focus within the broader ESG landscape. Workiva offers ESG reporting tools to collect, analyse and report on ESG data. Sphera is more focused on risk assessment from an EHS&S (Environmental, Health, Safety & Sustainability) perspective, and Icertis is specialised in managing sustainability clauses. Given their specific purpose, these tools are often combined with other tools.

The ESG technology landscape is constantly evolving and it can be challenging to obtain a comparable overview of the different technology solutions and their functionalities. Table 8 (see Appendix 1) provides a more extensive comparison of existing ESG software vendors, for the categories 'Reporting and Disclosures' and 'Data Management and Analysis'. While this list is not exhaustive, it's a solid first high-level indicator of the main functionalities offered by the vendors.

The future of ESG/ sustainability reporting

So what does the future hold? How can we get to a state where corporate reporting provides a clear view on (1) how the business creates financial and stakeholder value and (2) how resilient it is in these increasingly challenging times?

With the recent changes to the sustainability reporting landscape, there is a clear **ambition to bring sustainability reporting** to the level of financial reporting.

For this to be achieved, sustainability reporting needs to be *transparent, accessible, consistent and reliable,* as outlined already on p. 118. In order for business to implement the CSRD reporting obligations, significant business transformations are needed to properly embed sustainability management practices into the core of the business model, the core of the business strategy and management practices. This is by no means an easy exercise.

Corporate reporting over the next few years will show how successful business is in making those transformations.

The coming years will show how well business can rise to the challenge of meeting the CSRD requirements in the limited time that is left to prepare. Future corporate reports will show whether and how business has been able to scale up sustainability reporting to the level of financial reporting, and how sustainability management practices have become integrated into the core of the business.

ESG reporting is a means to an end: business transformation

While the corporate reports will show the outcome of business transformations, it's much more significant to comprehend the extent to which businesses will have become more [positively] impactful and more resilient. This is essentially what is driving corporate ESG reporting and performance improvements, and defining performance targets. Let's not forget; reporting is a means to an end. If done right, reporting can be a powerful means to transform the business into a responsible business that's resilient in the short, medium and long term, and accountable for the positive and negative impact that it creates. Is this not in essence the role of business in society? To contribute to solving important problems in a resilient and impactful manner.

The changes in corporate reporting and the transformation that it requires have the potential to move businesses closer to being 'net positive'.

By meeting the CSRD requirements, or even going beyond them, Europe can set a strong precedent for business, regulators and other stakeholders around the world, and demonstrate the value that corporate reporting can provide. The coming years will show if this will result in successful transformations, with corporate reporting driving positive impact and greater business resilience — hopefully also beyond the EU borders.

10.
ESG transformation in practice

Key takeaways

1. **ESG can be addressed within different functional areas, but the same framework for sustainable transformation can be applied to each: the sustainable business transformation framework.**

2. **Some pitfalls to avoid:**
   - **not embedding ESG into the top-level corporate strategy**
   - **failing to connect to all stakeholders**
   - **inability to measure and track ESG metrics.**

3. **A good transformation starts with a definition of the objectives, the baseline metrics, the ambitions or targets and a credible roadmap.**

4. **A compliance programme is a core requirement in many regulations. An effective compliance programme needs both ownership and reach.**

5. **Governments are shaping national net-zero strategies, amid broader plans for a sustainable society, and paying more and more attention to policy levers, including incentives, to support the energy transition and ESG transformation.**

ESG is driving the sustainable transformation agenda

Companies that prioritise ESG considerations tend to experience better financial outcomes. Studies by McKinsey[123] show that companies with strong ESG performance are more likely to have stable earnings and are considered less risky investments. A strong ESG proposition can drive value creation in different ways: top-line growth (e.g. attracting more customers, better access to resources, brand spillover), cost reductions (e.g. lower energy costs), productivity uplift (e.g. improved employee motivation, talent attraction and retention), and investment and asset optimisation (e.g. enhanced investment returns, improved access to capital).

However, realising this value requires much more than just compliance with ESG requirements. The potential of ESG transformations can only be fully realised when a company moves beyond box-ticking and incorporates ESG considerations into its day-to-day operations, strategies, and processes. This requires a thorough, company-wide transformation in which ESG permeates all aspects of a business, including its business units, functions, operating models, and processes (See also, *Chapter 5 – G for Governance* and *Chapter 8 – A framework for ESG strategy*).

The significance of ESG measurement and employee engagement cannot be overemphasised. Effective measurement from top to bottom within a comprehensive framework lays the foundation for continuous improvement and helps evaluate the progress and accountability of the transformation. Furthermore, involving employees and fostering a sense of ownership is crucial in promoting a company culture of sustainability. These two elements are not just standalone but need to be constructed in such a way that they reinforce each other. The right measurements at the right levels drive employees in the right direction and contribute to creating engagement. Not doing so can lead to the belief on the floor that it's all talk and no (coordinated) action. Vice versa, the right engagement can be channelled and coordinated in the right direction by means of a robust measurement framework. Not doing so leads to a lot of good intentions and loose initiatives on the floor.

In short, ESG transformations must be approached holistically to provide value, competitive advantage and resilience. Integrating ESG is not only about maintaining a company's licence to operate, but also about ensuring its long-term success. This chapter explores ESG transformation, including its definition, why it's important, and how companies can begin implementing it. Before that, let's examine two real-life examples of ESG transformations.

Case study: DEME

Belgian-based dredging, environmental and marine engineering company, DEME Group,[124] is an example of how a successful ESG transformation can create value. The company has a long-standing commitment to sustainability and a distinguished track record in ESG performance, with its ESG strategy deeply ingrained into its overall business strategy and operations, backed by a dedicated team of experts.

One of the hallmarks of DEME's ESG transformation is its emphasis on renewable energy. The company is making substantial investments in technologies such as offshore wind, with the goal to become a leader in the renewable energy space. As a result, DEME has already succeeded in making a notable contribution to reducing greenhouse gas emissions, positioning itself as a frontrunner in the sector.

One example of DEME's success in new markets is its involvement in the construction of offshore wind farms in Europe. With the shift towards renewable energy, DEME has been able to leverage its expertise in marine engineering to become the leading player in the offshore wind industry – today accounting for around 35% of DEME's total revenue. The company has also expanded its business into the sustainable development of ports and coastal infrastructure, helping to mitigate the effects of climate change and protect local communities.

The benefits of DEME's ESG transformation are evident in its operations. By streamlining processes, reducing waste, and enhancing efficiency, the company has realised cost savings and improved productivity, creating a more sustainable business model.

DEME has an extensive ESG reporting system in place, allowing it to closely monitor and assess its progress on ESG matters. The company also actively engages with its stakeholders to better understand their concerns and align its ESG strategy with their needs.

Furthermore, the company's ESG transformation has bolstered its reputation, strengthening relationships with its stakeholders. DEME is widely acknowledged as a leader in ESG performance, consistently ranking among the top performers in ESG indices. For instance, in 2022, the company won the first Trends Impact Award, a prestigious Belgian award for companies that create sustainable value for society.[125]

Figure 46 – DEME's sustainability themes.

DEME'S 8 KEY SUSTAINABILITY THEMES AND THEIR CONNECTION WITH THE RELEVANT SDGs.

Case study: Bekaert

Bekaert,[126] a Belgium-based global market and technology player in material science of steel wire transformation and coating technologies, is another example of a company that is undergoing a transformation to incorporate ESG principles into its business model.

The company's ESG journey started with a thorough assessment of its markets and operations' ESG impact, which allowed it to identify opportunities for improvement. In line with Science Based Targets, Bekaert set ambitious ESG targets and developed a comprehensive ESG strategy that covered all domains of ESG.

One of the key initiatives implemented by Bekaert was the introduction of a closed-loop production process, which has resulted in reduced waste, emissions and energy consumption. The company has also invested in energy efficiency and renewable energy sources and worked with suppliers to improve their ESG performance. Moreover, Bekaert places a strong emphasis on employee engagement, diversity and inclusion, and community involvement.

Bekaert's ESG focus has enabled the company to innovate and develop new products that cater to the needs of sustainability-conscious customers. For instance, the company has developed advanced steel cord products that are used in wind turbines, an industry that is booming as the world shifts to renewable energy sources. The demand for Bekaert's products has increased as more companies adopt ESG-driven strategies, which has in turn driven the company's growth and expansion into new markets. Bekaert has also been able to enter new markets and industries, including hydrogen production and electric vehicles, where the company's products are used in the production of green hydrogen, cabling for fast charging batteries and other components.

Bekaert's commitment to ESG has not only resulted in improved environmental and social impact, but has also had a positive impact on the company's financial performance. The ESG initiatives have resulted in cost savings and increased efficiency, and have enhanced the company's reputation with customers and stakeholders. Bekaert's integrated approach to ESG, combined with a focus on continuous improvement, has enabled the company to drive real and measurable change that benefits both the company and society as a whole.

Bekaert can serve as a role model for companies seeking to embed ESG principles into their business operations. The company's efforts have been recognised through a number of ESG awards and certifications, including the gold recognition level from EcoVadis, a sustainability rating agency.

As of 2023, Bekaert is one of the 20 companies in the BEL ESG index, which comprises the leading sustainable, Belgian listed companies and tracks those demonstrating the best environmental, social and governance practices. The index also highlights the market's growing demand for sustainable investments.[127]

Embarking on an ESG transformation

The need for an ESG transformation in a company can be sparked by various internal and external factors and should be part of your strategic review.

External triggers may come in the form of market pressure from investors calling for decarbonisation, shifts in consumer preferences, supply chain demands, and regulatory requirements such as the many regulations and directives under the EU Green Deal. On the internal front, the drive for ESG transformation can be catalysed by technology upgrades, management changes, strategic shifts, risk reduction efforts, audit findings and the failure of previous ESG initiatives.

To ensure the success of an ESG transformation (see also Chapter 8), companies must have strong leadership commitment and understanding of the importance of ESG. A materiality assessment should be conducted to identify the most critical ESG issues, while specific, measurable and ambitious ESG performance indicators need to be established. ESG should be integrated into all aspects of the business, and the company's performance should be continuously monitored and reported transparently to stakeholders.

Common mistakes in ESG transformations

While ESG transformations can be highly beneficial for companies, *common mistakes* are often made during the process.

Not embedded in the corporate strategy
One common mistake is failing to fully integrate ESG into their top-level corporate strategy and target-setting, treating it as a separate initiative rather than a core aspect of their operations. This can result in a lack of accountability and commitment to sustainable practices.

Not engaging stakeholders
Another pitfall is not engaging stakeholders effectively, including investors, customers and employees. Companies may prioritise short-term financial gains over the long-term benefits of ESG, which can lead to reputational damage and loss of trust from stakeholders. It's crucial to establish open and transparent communication channels to build trust and credibility with stakeholders.

Insufficient monitoring and reporting
A third mistake is failing to track and report on ESG performance effectively. Companies must establish clear metrics and targets to measure progress and report on their ESG efforts. Failure to do so can result in missed opportunities to improve ESG performance, as well as damage to the company's reputation and loss of investor confidence.

Misleading claims
Finally, companies must avoid greenwashing, or making false or misleading claims about their ESG performance to appeal to stakeholders. Instead, they should focus on taking genuine and meaningful actions to improve their ESG performance and communicate their progress transparently.

Not walking the talk
A recent case serves as a cautionary example of the consequences of such failed ESG transformation. Despite having an ESG programme in place, and despite having identified alternative operational options, an international mining company damaged a heritage site of exceptional archaeological and cultural significance in order to access resources. The company subsequently faced significant financial penalties, reputation damage and leadership changes. This highlights the need for a comprehensive ESG transformation that goes beyond mere lip service and integrates sustainability into all aspects of a company's operations, including its risk management processes.

The 5-phase ESG transformation framework

Undertaking an ESG transformation is a complex and multi-dimensional process that demands a deep-seated commitment to change throughout an organisation. **A well-structured ESG transformation framework is vital** to ensure that the transformation is implemented effectively, stays focused on its ESG goals, and establishes accountability and ownership within the organisation.

One example of such a framework is PwC's Sustainable Business Transformation framework (Figure 47). It consists of five crucial phases and provides a roadmap for organisations to successfully bring ESG transformation to life.

Figure 47 – 5-phase sustainable business transformation framework.[128]

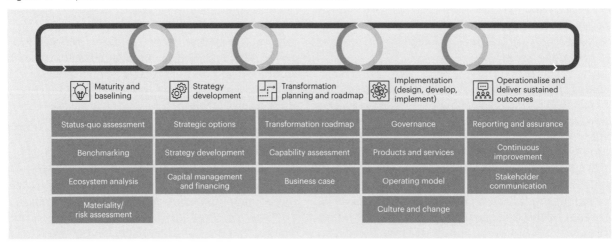

Phase 1: Maturity and baselining

A strong foundation for ESG transformation lies in the maturity assessments and baselining exercises that determine the current ESG performance of a company and its ecosystem, and prioritise ESG goals. The process includes **benchmarking** against peers and best practices, determining the **materiality** of ESG issues and developing a **roadmap** for the transformation that aligns with the company's priorities and stakeholders.

Chapter 3 outlined why climate change is the most urgent issue the world faces. It's the most pressing risk, with the most potential to irrevocably alter our future. The Sustainable Business Transformation framework can be used to define the action plan for your carbon footprint, in parallel with other ESG metric improvements.

Phase 2: Strategy development

Effective ESG transformation requires a strategic approach that combines capital management and planning to deliver long-term value. Companies should consider a range of strategic options to improve their performance, such as reducing emissions and waste, increasing the use of renewable energy, improving sustainability in the supply chain, and enhancing diversity and inclusion. In addition to embedding ESG in the corporate strategy, a comprehensive ESG strategy should be developed, informed by assessments and benchmarking, defining the **goals, targets and initiatives**, and providing a roadmap for the transformation. Capital management and financing play a crucial role, ensuring that the necessary resources are available to implement ESG initiatives.

Phase 3: Transformation planning and roadmap

A clear and concise **transformation roadmap** is critical for a successful ESG transformation. The roadmap should outline the implementation timeline, steps required to achieve ESG goals, and the ESG journey ahead. The roadmap should be informed by the corporate (ESG-based) strategy and regularly reviewed and updated. **A capability assessment** should determine the resources required to deliver ESG initiatives effectively, including the skills, knowledge and experience of the workforce, as well as the systems, processes and technology needed. Finally, the **business case** should provide a compelling argument for the ESG transformation, outlining the benefits, costs and risks.

Phase 4: Implementation

Achieving profound measurement and employee engagement are crucial elements of a successful ESG transformation. These should get sufficient attention during the implementation phase.

Companies should focus on defining **clear and measurable ESG goals and policies**, cascaded into all products and processes. By linking these KPIs to change management efforts, employees can be guided in the right direction through a shared sense of ownership and company culture of sustainability.

Phase 5: Operationalise and deliver

The final phase of an ESG transformation involves **monitoring the progress** towards ESG goals and targets, and continuously improving performance. Regular assessments and benchmarking against peers and best practices help to track progress, identify areas for improvement, and maintain the relevance and alignment of the ESG strategy with the company's ESG ambitions.

By taking a systematic approach to ESG integration, companies can unlock the full value potential of this transformation and secure a sustainable future for themselves and future generations. In the following sections, we will explore how **this concept translates to different functional domains**, including the transformation triggers, value potential and proposed implementation approach.

Sustainable governance transformation

Towards an ESG-based governance model

As described in *Chapter 5 — G for Governance,* an ESG-based governance model is not about governance of environmental and social matters. It is about building an overarching corporate governance model founded on E+S principles. Where E+S are not relegated to separate verticals or 'limbs' of the organisation; instead, they encompass ethical principles that inform and guide how the business is run.

It is an aspirational approach to doing business. But achieving your ESG/sustainability ambitions is very concrete, and starts with regulatory compliance. This is a shared responsibility, but it will only work when there is clarity on roles, responsibilities and accountabilities.

Typically, responsibility is generally allocated in the appropriate verticals in the organisation, as decided/approved by, and reporting to, C-level and the board of directors. But **hierarchical accountability in the organisation is not necessarily the same as legal responsibility or liability**. It's all very well to say, for example, that labour matters are 'owned' by a governance committee, compliance matters by a risk committee or financial matters by an audit committee — and that 'they' are accountable. In reality, as already mentioned, individuals at top level may be held legally liable.

Transformation means taking ownership across the value chain

That's why top management needs to take full ownership of and ultimate responsibility for the complete value chain. And that means ensuring that they know what is happening right down the line.

There's nothing new in this chain of accountability or liability. What's [relatively] new is the burgeoning amount and scope of legislation to be complied with, particularly in the sphere of ESG, as well as the increase in the amount of scrutiny, not just by regulators but by society at large. In a governance model founded on environmental and social principles, ESG will naturally be embedded in the top-level corporate strategy, and not be a sub-category.

How to integrate ESG/sustainability into corporate governance

There's no single way to instantly embed sustainability principles into your business. But the higher it is in the chain of command, the more impact it will have on the business.

Figure 48 shows three models for sustainability integration into governance.

Figure 48 – Comparison of three sustainable corporate governance models.[129]

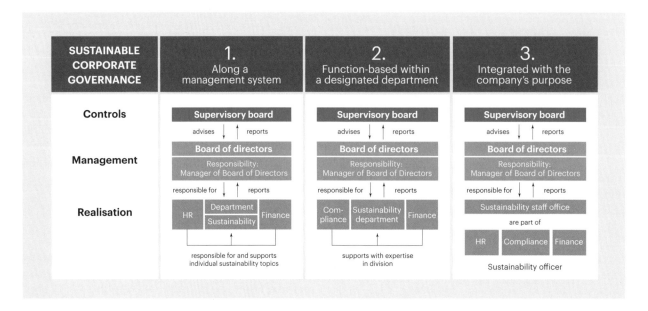

Model 1 is typical of most companies today, where sustainability is a management function dealing with sustainability topics. In model 2, sustainability is a department or division on a par with compliance and finance, providing expertise to the whole organisation on sustainability issues. In model 3, sustainability is at a top level of the organisation, embedded in the corporate strategy and in a steering position in relation to other functions.

In a model 3 governance structure, sustainability is fully integrated with the company purpose. It is positioned to have broad oversight, responsibility and accountability.

The starting point: know what's happening

You don't know what you don't know, but ignorance is no excuse
One of the biggest governance challenges companies face is actually knowing what's happening

across the complete value chain. The bigger the company, the bigger the risk that the board or CEO is not aware of non-compliant practices — practices that they could someday be held personally accountable for. Compliance failures may result in penalties: fines, sanctions, loss of licence to operate, reputational damage or even liability charges against individual officers or directors.

Given the increasing national- and regional-level scrutiny of corporate practices and impacts, particularly in areas relevant to ESG, the importance of risk prevention cannot be overstated.

Establishing a comprehensive compliance programme is the best – perhaps the only – way to properly identify, evaluate and mitigate your risk.

This **compliance programme ideally sits within the framework of a broader governance model**.

Doing the right thing. Or why you need a compliance programme

A compliance programme is not just a nice to have: it's a core requirement in many regulations. If something goes wrong, your compliance programme should provide evidence of proof of effort. Regulators – such as the European Commission, the European Securities and Markets Authority, the US Department of Justice (DOJ), the US Securities and Exchange Commission (SEC), etc. – will evaluate your corporate compliance programme when determining fines, penalties, convictions, etc.

Furthermore, many regulations include director and officer liability provisions and the lack of a programme or adequate reporting to the board will impact liability.

In addition to regulatory obligations, a compliance programme sends a strong signal to employees and other stakeholders about your ethical approach and how you want to do business. It should include a compliance function that provides independent oversight over the compliance programme.

Compliance programmes are cost effective. They allow you to focus on the areas that matter most, based on risk assessments that help you define where inherent and residual risk exists. Executing audits and reviews in-house, for example by in-house health and safety experts, saves on hiring expensive external service providers. And you can execute multiple different audits following the same standard methodology, thus increasing comparativeness.

Crucially, a compliance programme ensures there is clarity around roles and responsibilities, with no unexpected loopholes and gaps.

An effective compliance programme needs both ownership and reach.

The four fundamentals of an effective compliance programme

A well-designed, ethical compliance programme is based on four fundamentals.

The **compliance or regulatory universe** is the overview of compliance domains that apply to the company. Having a clear understanding of the compliance universe or, in other words, of all of the different (regulatory) domains that apply to the business, is critical to the design of the overall compliance programme's target operating model and the governance model for compliance oversight.

The **operating model** defines the responsibilities and accountabilities for (regulatory) compliance within the organisation. It is clear that not all compliance domains can be the responsibility of one function; it is a shared responsibility across the business. But what is the operating model currently implemented? Who in the organisation has ownership over the different compliance domains? What should change going forward to reinforce compliance and to make it stronger? And what changes are required in the compliance department itself to enable it to fulfil its role in the future target operating model? In other words, what competencies are required? How many FTEs are required?

The **governance structure** defines how the organisation structures its oversight function over the compliance programme, both at the board and management level. How are the board and management currently overseeing the compliance programme? What are the reporting lines that have been established? Is this model working and are the regulatory owners (i.e. people in the business that have a responsibility and accountability for compliance) held accountable?

Lastly, the design of an effective compliance and ethics management system is based on a **compliance framework**. The framework is the key tool that the compliance function and the owners of the compliance domains will use to establish and design their compliance management system. In accordance with best-practice compliance standards, such a framework would consist of: vision and culture; governance, autonomy and resources; regulatory universe and regulatory inventory; risk management; policies and procedures; third party (risk) management; training and communication; testing, monitoring, investigations and remediations; and reporting and enforcement.

Sustainable finance transformation

The increasing importance of ESG has led to a shift in the way companies approach investments and decision making. The aim is to redirect investment capital towards a more sustainable, inclusive and equitable economy, while maintaining financial stability and profitability. This trend towards more sustainable finance models has been driven by several factors.[130]

Triggers

One of the key triggers for sustainable finance transformations is the increased attention being paid to the environmental impact of business and investment activities. The growing concern about climate change has made ESG considerations a critical part of investment decisions. This has led to an increased demand for ESG data and analysis, which can help investors understand the potential risks and rewards associated with different investment options.

Another trigger is the increased regulatory pressure being placed on financial institutions. Governments around the world are adopting sustainability policies and regulations that require companies to take ESG factors into account when making investments. This has led to a growing focus on ESG disclosure and reporting, as well as a need for investment products that are aligned with these new regulatory requirements.

Benefits

The potential benefits of ESG-driven finance transformations are significant.[131] By considering ESG factors, financial institutions can identify and invest in companies and projects that are better equipped to withstand environmental, social and governance risks, and are therefore more likely to generate long-term, sustainable returns. This can help to reduce investment risk and improve overall investment performance. Additionally, ESG-driven investments can contribute to a more sustainable and equitable global economy, by promoting business practices that are aligned with the long-term interests of both investors and society.

Implementation

Realising the full potential of ESG-driven finance transformations requires a systematic approach that encompasses all aspects of investment processes and decision making.

Risks and opportunities assessment

In order to successfully implement ESG integration within finance, companies should start by assessing the ESG risks and opportunities associated with each investment [Phase 1: Maturity and Baselining]. This involves gathering and analysing ESG data, such as a company's carbon footprint or labour practices, and incorporating this information into investment decisions. This helps to identify potential ESG risks, such as exposure to climate change or human rights violations, as well as opportunities to invest in companies that are leading the way in sustainability.

ESG in processes and culture

Companies must also embed ESG considerations into their internal finance processes and culture. This includes establishing and implementing ESG policies and practices, training employees on ESG best practices and setting ESG performance targets. This way, ESG will become an integral part and priority area of the finance organisation and operations. Furthermore, the finance function in many companies acts as the spider in the data web, so it's a good place to drive the sustainability agenda.

Case study: Allianz

A recent example of a successful ESG transformation in finance is the case of Allianz,[132] one of the largest global insurance and asset management companies.

Allianz has made significant investments to embed ESG principles into its core business operations and investment processes. This has involved changes to its governance and decision-making structures, as well as to the products and services it offers.

One key initiative has been the creation of dedicated ESG task forces to integrate sustainability matters across the core processes in the (finance) organisation. These task forces are led by senior executives and staffed with team members from different functions to ensure top-level alignment and buy-in as well as true integration in these functions.

In addition, Allianz has taken steps to improve the transparency of its ESG data and reporting, through the use of leading ESG ratings and benchmarking providers, as well as through the establishment of new internal systems and processes to capture and report ESG data.

The results of these efforts have been impressive, with Allianz seeing a significant increase in demand for its ESG-focused products and services, and achieving a top-tier ESG rating from leading ratings agencies. This has helped to enhance the company's reputation and credibility with stakeholders, as well as to position it as a leader in the ESG investment space.

Sustainable supply chain transformation

In order to move the world towards a more sustainable future, companies are looking for ways to optimise their operations and minimise their environmental impact, to secure market access and attract capital. One area that has come under increased scrutiny is the supply chain, which can significantly impact the environment and society. The integration of ESG considerations into supply chain management is emerging as a key driver of transformation in this space.

Triggers

The triggers for sustainable supply chain transformations come from various sources, including regulatory pressure, resource scarcity, investor and customer expectations, the strategic intent and principles of companies and organisations, geopolitical pressure, trade wars, climate change impact, and so on. The EU Green Deal legislative initiatives aim to create transparency and traceability of resources, goods and services.

The introduction of the Inflation Reduction Act in the US in 2023 provides a good example of the upcoming fight to attract capital. Those forces are creating waves that are leaving a large share of industries with two choices: surf on the waves to secure sustainable economic performance and competitiveness or collapse under the increasing weight of the waves.

Benefits and costs

One of the misconceptions is that sustainable transformation only drives higher costs for limited value creation. However, sustainable supply chain transformations can generate substantial financial and non-financial top- and bottom-line benefits.

Cost-saving opportunities can be achieved through levers such as circular economy or new processes that can improve resource efficiency, reduce waste, etc. Taking the example of so-called 'hard to abate' companies – such as the steel or cement industry, which are highly dependent on fossil-based technology – a surge in energy prices and carbon prices directly threatens profitability.

To navigate through the storm, such companies can reduce short-term costs through material and process efficiency improvements and long-term costs through the strategic deployment of new processes, such as hydrogen-based processes.

On the revenue side, research has shown that almost all consumers (>80%) would be willing to pay 5% extra for their products if they were more sustainable (Figure 49). Around half would even be willing to pay 15% extra. However, there are limits to how much of a premium people will pay. For all but one category (packaging), less than

10% of consumers said they would choose green products if the premium rose to 2%.

The reason is simple: consumers are becoming increasingly concerned about the social and environmental impact of the products they purchase and are therefore willing to pay more for products that fit their vision of the world. Therefore, companies that demonstrate a commitment to sustainability through their supply chain operations are more likely to attract and retain customers and build brand loyalty — if it is not perceived as greenwashing.

Figure 49 – Many people will pay a premium for green products. If it's not too much.[133]

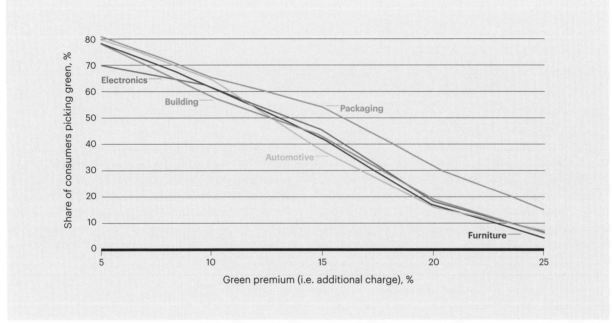

Resilience and costs

The ability of a company to be **future-proof** is also considerably challenged. To remain competitive, companies must be able to face supply chain disruptions, energy crises and structural market evolution. Events such as the Covid-19 crisis or the war in Ukraine dramatically highlighted the interdependencies in our global supply chains. By focusing on **resilient supply chains** through partnerships and realistic mitigation plans, sustainable companies have proven better equipped to face unpredictable disruptions. As emphasised in

Bill Gates' book 'How to Avoid a Climate Disaster', companies must evaluate the premium cost of more sustainable operations against the potential savings in the long term. He suggests that companies should take a long-term view and consider the benefits of sustainable operations beyond just reducing emissions. These benefits include increased efficiency, reduced resource consumption, and improved brand reputation, which can lead to a competitive advantage in the market.

Implementation

Realising the full potential of ESG-driven supply chain transformations requires careful implementation. The trade-off between cost and value is not an easy beast to tame. The magnitude of the risk and opportunities are highly correlated with the industry and geographic position of the company. Companies must overcome any lack of transparency, of support or of execution potential in their supply chain while securing the success of their corporate strategy.

One size does not fit all

Different supply chain levers can help materialise the short- and long-term ESG strategy. The selection of the right levers however, will depend on the company's corporate strategy and baseline ESG maturity (See Chapter 8). The industry in which the company is operating also affects what areas are material and thus a focus for the sustainable transformation. The United Nations SDG Industry Matrix is a very useful reference to inspire companies: it showcases industry-specific examples and ideas for corporate action related to the SDGs.[134]

The first step in supply chain transformation is, therefore, to identify the ESG areas, beyond compliance, that offer potential for transformations that would support the corporate strategic sustainability ambitions. To identify these areas, it's important to understand the different levers of action regarding ESG and the different benefits that could result from their applications.

For example, consider a corrugated board producer focusing on customer intimacy (i.e., alignment with their customers' needs and values), in a niche market. It might be useful for this organisation to secure access to materials by vertically integrating access to a forest. This would provide a steady service to its customers for a premium price; over time, it could allow better carbon and social management.

The same approach couldn't be used for a copper refinery. Indeed, to achieve the same outcome, the refinery would have to work closely with its raw materials suppliers to support them (the suppliers) to achieve an equivalent environmental or social impact in line with its (the refinery's) strategy.

How to do it

To identify the best supply chain transformation strategy, a company needs to:

- create visibility on its ESG impacts
- identify optimisation strategies
- select the path that reflects the corporate strategy
- engage with key stakeholders
- create sustainable ecosystems under an empowered organisation.

This baselining exercise (along with the double materiality analysis; see Chapter 9) is crucial and is performed in the first phase of the sustainable business transformation framework.

Creating visibility in the supply chain is all about data. The key challenge is to **gain transparency and traceability** over your supply chain to identify your baseline and analyse data to spot relevant optimisation opportunities. More challenging, how do you internalise data considered as externalities in your decision-making process to spot sustainable relevant opportunities?

The setup of such a system requires a mix of the **top-down identification of opportunities and the bottom-up setup of the data collection points** required across your supply chain.

Supply chain transformation Phase 1: Maturity and baselining

A top-down approach allows you to set a rough baseline from existing data in your control. Combine operational data (Scope 1) with your spend data (Scopes 2 and 3) and map your data to a life-cycle inventory database (database of emissions per product and process) per country: this will provide a rough indication of the average split of Scope 1, 2 and 3 emissions for your organisation per category and region.

A bottom-up approach would focus on the setup of a supply chain that is able to provide you with the equivalent information with the right level of assurance. Doing so requires convincing your stakeholders to provide the right information — through collaboration or enforcement.

To internalise CO_2 emissions in your decision-making process, you could decide to put a price on carbon or identify areas where cost and carbon reduction overlap. Regardless of your choice, the right trade-off between cost, value, and ESG impact must be found in order to achieve the most favourable outcome.

Supply chain transformation Phase 2: Strategy development

Once your baseline is established and the areas of action identified, the next step is to identify what to do by assessing ESG optimisation opportunities. Depending on the area in your supply chain in which you want to focus and your corporate strategy, different sustainability levers will have different strategic impacts in terms of cost, attractiveness, or service level. A careful understanding of **sustainability levers such as business model redesign, sourcing strategy or process redesign** will be key to assessing the strategic proximity of those levers and the magnitude of their impact. Such an analysis can allow you to segment which part of your supply chain is critical for achieving your strategy and what is the best path to achieve the best strategic outcome at the lowest cost.

A marginal abatement (i.e. 'reducing') cost curve – or MACC – can help you identify which levers of action are able to support your net-zero transition and what is the best path from a cost efficiency perspective. A MACC presents the **costs or savings expected from different opportunities, alongside the potential volume of emissions that could be reduced if implemented**. MACCs measure and compare the financial cost and abatement benefit of individual actions.

Having the right expertise both in terms of industry and sustainability levers is key to selecting the reduction opportunities in line with the corporate strategy.

For example, a construction company could balance the costs of transition to net zero over time, by introducing – across the supply chain – a wide range of material and process efficiency measures to reduce CO_2 emissions, such as:

- procurement
- renewable power for aluminium
- mechanical recycling of plastic materials
- renewable heat for cement production
- etc.

By contrast, a freight company would have a limited number of options available. They could achieve some reductions at relatively low cost though route optimisation, but the most significant reduction method would be long term, expensive and require a drastic change of strategy or supply chain design: a fuel switch to, for example, fuel cell trucks or synthetic aviation fuel. Such a company would be considered as 'hard to abate'.

Supply chain transformation Phase 3: Transformation planning and roadmap

For many companies, realising the full value of the sustainability levers will require engagement with relevant suppliers. The outcome of your baseline and MACC (i.e. identification of optimisation opportunities) should better understand which suppliers are critical to achieving your strategy and which are not. Critical partners will have to be aligned with your overall target to support the development of action plans for improvement. When relevant, the ability of your stakeholders to be onboarded in your transformation journey should be ignited by close support in their own transition journey. This can involve providing training and support, as well as setting joint ESG goals and tracking progress over time. For Scope 3 reductions, such actions are critical if you want to stimulate transformation outside of your control zone.

Beyond bilateral engagement, sustainability transformation also requires engagement in relevant ecosystems. Joining forces – for example in sectoral coalitions – can help companies overcome lack of governmental support or market maturity. Being part of such initiatives can help you to secure an early transition at the lowest cost possible.

Supply chain transformation Phase 4: Implementation

To translate the above elements into an actionable roadmap, it's key to understand the internal changes required to unlock their potential. Which governance fits best, with which process, and with which rewards? While answering those questions may seem trivial, it has been proven that organisational efforts are as critical and challenging as operational changes. Securing support from the very top of the organisation and establishing a strong governance structure is the cornerstone to achieve the intended transformation. A **transformation office** can sometimes help to assign the right profiles to the transformation, using best practices for internal communication, change and programme management.

Supply chain transformation Phase 5:
Operationalise and deliver

Once the roadmap is implemented, close monitoring is needed to ensure the objectives of the transformation are met.

Typically, this often means revisiting the maturity and baselining step to assess whether additional actions are required.

Technology plays an important role in making sure the follow-up can be done accurately and effectively: setting up a good data collection and analytics system gives people fast access to the right data and insights without querying and manipulating huge data sets.

Finally, all the changes resulting from the transformation need to be integrated into the communication plans and reporting.

In conclusion, **applying the steps of the sustainable business transformation framework to the supply chain enables companies to achieve long-term sustainability goals** and reap the rewards of being at the forefront of responsible business practices. ESG-driven supply chain transformation is a proactive and strategic approach that is not only a matter of corporate responsibility but, perhaps even more importantly, a strategic investment in the future success of any company.

Case study: Nestlé

Nestlé,[135] the world's largest food and beverage company, has made significant strides in its ESG transformation journey over the past decade and has taken important steps to integrate sustainability throughout its supply chain.

For example, the company has worked to reduce the environmental impact of its packaging and committed to making all Nestlé packaging recyclable or reusable by 2025. The company has made significant investments in sustainable packaging solutions, such as using biodegradable materials and reducing the overall amount of plastic used in its products. Nestlé has also implemented programmes to encourage recycling and reduce waste in its operations.

Beyond packaging, Nestlé has also implemented initiatives to improve the sustainability of its agricultural supply chain. They have set ambitious targets to reduce greenhouse gas emissions from farming operations, while also promoting sustain-

able farming practices such as soil conservation and water management. Nestlé has also launched programmes to promote the economic empowerment of smallholder farmers, such as offering training and financial support to help them improve their farming practices.

Nestlé has made significant strides in promoting ethical and responsible business practices throughout its supply chain. They have implemented strict standards for labour rights and ethical sourcing, and worked to eliminate child labour and other forms of exploitation in their operations. Nestlé has also taken steps to promote gender equality and diversity throughout its workforce.

Finally, Nestlé has been leveraging technology and innovation to drive its ESG transformation. This includes the use of big data and analytics to better understand their environmental impact, and to make informed decisions about how to reduce it.

Carbon trading

'Carbon' is now traded, and the price of carbon credits fluctuates as if it were a market commodity. This means that the price of carbon credits can contribute to a positive ROI for potential investments related to decarbonisation in companies. The higher the price of carbon credits, the higher the attractiveness of investing in green solutions for your company rather than paying for credits.

The World Bank publishes a comprehensive overview of carbon trading and taxation mechanisms, the Carbon Pricing Dashboard (Figure 50). It's a good place to start looking at how carbon is being addressed in the parts of the world you are operating in as a company.

Figure 50 – World Bank's Carbon Pricing Dashboard.[136]

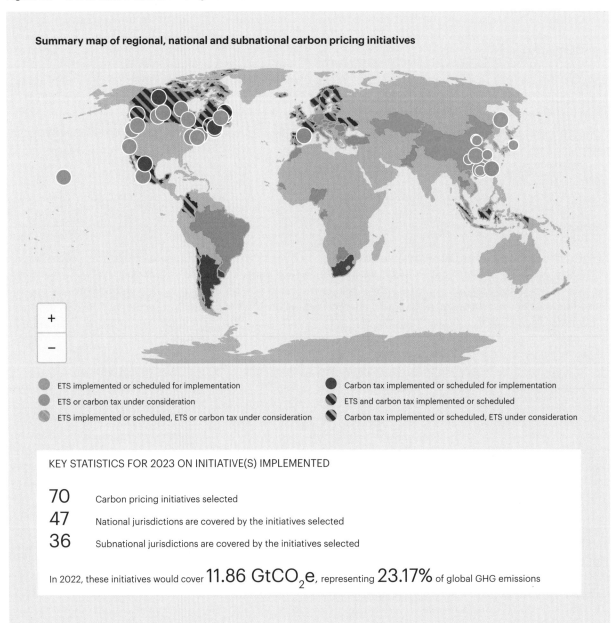

Summary map of regional, national and subnational carbon pricing initiatives

● ETS implemented or scheduled for implementation
● ETS or carbon tax under consideration
● ETS implemented or scheduled, ETS or carbon tax under consideration

● Carbon tax implemented or scheduled for implementation
◕ ETS and carbon tax implemented or scheduled
◕ Carbon tax implemented or scheduled, ETS under consideration

KEY STATISTICS FOR 2023 ON INITIATIVE(S) IMPLEMENTED

70 Carbon pricing initiatives selected

47 National jurisdictions are covered by the initiatives selected

36 Subnational jurisdictions are covered by the initiatives selected

In 2022, these initiatives would cover **11.86 GtCO$_2$e**, representing **23.17%** of global GHG emissions

Decarbonisation in practice

Energy sources used across the entire operations and supply chain play an important role in developing a path to net zero, especially in manufacturing industries. Companies are expected to communicate on their ambitions and timeline. This section explores setting ambition levels and provides a framework to develop your own decarbonisation programme.

'Carbon neutrality' versus 'net zero'

While both terms refer to combatting GHG emissions and are used interchangeably, there's an important difference in ambition and direction. Although the precise language and terminology can differ by region, the core principles are always different.

- A company achieves **carbon neutrality** by purchasing sufficient carbon offsets to compensate for all its emissions. In practice, some companies will commit to offsetting Scopes 1 and 2 only, some to all Scopes. As a consequence, the concept of carbon neutrality does not really give you an insight into the performance of a company. It might even be that emissions of a 'carbon neutral' company keep increasing. This might lead to accusations of greenwashing.
- **Net zero** implies that a company commits to reducing its emissions in line with the science based targets trajectory (see *Chapter 9, SBTi*). Offsets are used for the current and the remaining emissions. With SBTi, Scope 3 is within the coverage if it is over 40% of the emissions.

It is clear from this that the term 'net zero' indicates a stronger commitment to emissions reduction than 'carbon neutral' (Figure 51).

Figure 51 – Comparing carbon neutral with science based targets and net-zero ambitions.

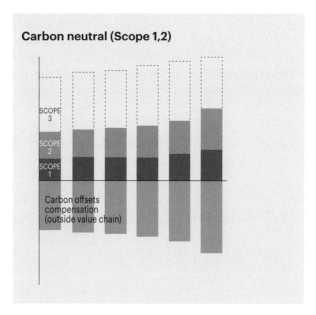

Carbon neutral (Scope 1,2)

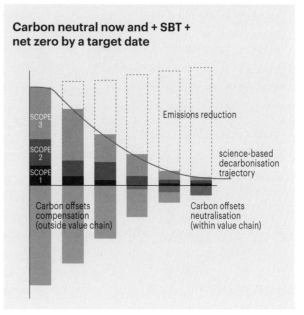

Carbon neutral now and + SBT + net zero by a target date

The current landscape of ambitions and timelines
Research from PwC (Figure 52) shows the ambition and timeline to achieve carbon neutrality and net zero by a given year. Nearly two thirds of companies want to achieve carbon neutrality, meaning using offsets, by 2040, while **nearly 80% commit to net zero by 2050**, in line with the ambition of the EU, the US and many other countries. It's worth noting that more than **18% of companies have no target at all** for either carbon neutrality or net zero by 2050.

Achieving net zero is not an easy task. Figure 53 sets out a 7-step programme to develop your own roadmap. It entails not only looking at the energy sources used to reduce your carbon footprint, but also elements such as product design, reuse of products and optimised supply chains. Companies need to work on all elements of the value chain to be able reach the net-zero goal — the sooner one starts, the higher the chances of reaching it.

Figure 52 – Timeline to achieve carbon neutrality and net zero by a given year.[137] Companies aim to achieve net carbon neutrality earlier than net zero, focusing first on emissions compensation, then on reduction.

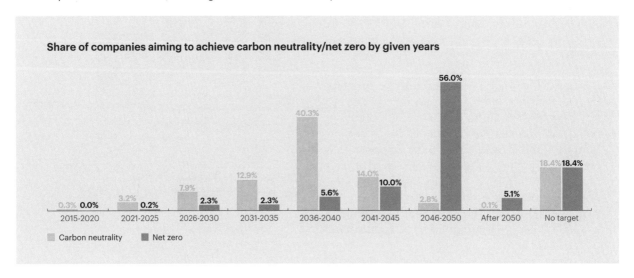

Energy transition as part of supply chain transformation

Many companies have been committing to decreasing their GHG emissions, especially facing the emission trade schemes and the carbon border tax mechanism which is coming into play. Basically, this means that every tonne of CO_2 has a certain value. The higher the cost of 1 tonne CO_2 equivalent, the faster the transition towards a more renewable energy landscape will happen.

Figure 53 – 7 steps to achieving net zero.

1.
Vision and strategy
- Translate corporate net-zero strategy into specific goals
- Achieve transparency on emissions generated
- Identify operations areas with GHG reduction potential along the value chain

2.
Product design
- Translate net-zero goals for product portfolio
- Consider alternative plans and materials or production processes
- Assess GHG emissions for developed products; prioritise and derive measures
- Conduct life cycle assessments

3.
Optimised supply chain
- Translate net-zero goals into supply chain planning guidelines
- Consider supply chain planning and transport plans
- Translate net-zero goals into transport guidelines
- Modify procurement strategies to align with net-zero goals
- Set up GHG-driven supplier network management
- Implement, track and optimise supply chain network, supplier measures and transport management

4.
Manufacturing
- Design factory with reference to net zero: carry out, track and optimise factory construction
- Align factory infrastructure regarding construction materials, energy supply, IT and internal logistics
- Translate net-zero goals into KPIs for production
- Operational excellence for net zero, focusing on energy efficiency and in-house logistics in production
- Set up predictive maintenance to ensure energy efficiency

5.
Reuse processes
- Translate net-zero goals into reuse guidelines
- Set up net-zero reuse processes
- Implement, track and optimise reuse processes

6.
IT/OT infrastructure
- Set up IT infrastructure to achieve transparency on generated emissions according to product portfolio and production footprint
- Set up IT/OT infrastructure to collect and aggregate GHG data from all relevant areas (2-7), starting from shop floor level
- Enable analytics-based and data-driven decision making in operations

7.
Operating model
- Translate net-zero goals into job descriptions and derive required roles and competencies
- Implement change management and training

Corporate GHG reporting
Align top-down SBTi targets and EU regulations with operational emissions reduction measures

Sustainable customer/ commercial transformation

Customer/commercial transformation is about improving the brand experience and attracting customers while driving growth, improving sustainability and mitigating risk. All this in an ever-changing business landscape where customers' (and regulators') sustainability expectations are constantly increasing. ESG has emerged as a key driver of customer/commercial transformation, allowing companies to create value and differentiate themselves in the market through responsible and sustainable business practices.

Triggers

A growing awareness of the impact of business operations on the environment and society, combined with increasing regulatory requirements, has led many companies – and customers – to prioritise ESG considerations. The key trigger for companies to begin a sustainable customer/commercial transformation is often a recognition of the potential benefits. Companies that have successfully implemented ESG-driven transformations in their customer experience and commercial practices have seen improved financial performance, enhanced brand reputation, and a more engaged and motivated workforce.

Benefits

Indeed, ESG-driven customer/commercial transformations can deliver significant value in many areas.

First, companies that prioritise ESG considerations and run ESG-friendly operations can lower costs, improve resource efficiency, and reduce risks such as regulatory penalties, legal action and reputation damage.

Secondly, ESG-conscious companies are often more attractive to investors, customers and employees, who are increasingly drawn to companies that align with their own values and contribute to a better world. By demonstrating their commitment to sustainability, companies can gain a reputation for being socially and environmentally responsible, which can help to build trust and credibility with consumers and other stakeholders.

Thirdly, focus on ESG can drive innovation, allowing companies to take advantage of new business opportunities in sustainable markets. The increasing global awareness of the importance of sustainability has led to a growing demand for products and services that align with ESG values, providing new opportunities for companies to differentiate themselves and capitalise on this trend. By integrating ESG principles into their supply chain customer/commercial operations, companies can **create a competitive edge when entering new markets or novel industries**. A Bain survey of 29 executives from top Belgian companies[138] found that 54% of Belgian companies see ESG as a way to develop new businesses beyond their core.

"Gains come when the company can mimic the speed and entrepreneurial energy of a start-up and combine these with the benefits of being a large, well-established organization. [This] can take one of three forms: reinventing the core; moving into a distantly adjacent area; and/or launching a totally new business."[139]

Implementation

One way that companies can leverage ESG to enter new markets is through responsible sourcing. This involves evaluating and mitigating the environmental and social impacts of the supply chain, and implementing practices that promote sustainability.

Another way is by developing new, sustainable products and services. This can involve investing in research and development to create innovative solutions that address environmental and social challenges, such as renewable energy technologies, sustainable transportation systems and waste reduction solutions. Companies that are leaders in developing these types of solutions are often seen as experts in their respective fields, and can gain a competitive advantage in new markets.

In addition to entering new markets, companies can also use ESG to enter novel industries. For example, a company that specialises in sustainable agriculture could leverage its ESG expertise to enter the sustainable fashion industry by producing eco-friendly clothing made from novel sustainable materials. By capitalising on its existing strengths and applying them to new industries, a company can differentiate itself from competitors and create new business opportunities.

Case study: Aspiravi

Aspiravi[140] is a leading Belgian energy company specialising in the development and operation of green power and heat facilities, including wind and solar energy projects, and processing of non-recyclable wood waste.

The company is deeply committed to sustainability and social support, with an ambition to help drive the transition to sustainable energy sources. For example, Aspiravi works hand in hand with communities, in partnerships with local cooperatives through which local residents can co-invest in wind energy projects in their neighbourhood. The gains for local residents are threefold: access to local, green energy; growth towards a more sustainable living environment and greater support for wind energy in one's own neighbourhood; and a return through an expected annual dividend.

Each customer of Aspiravi Energy automatically supports a local social project. For each megawatt hour consumed, Aspiravi Energy donates an amount to a charitable organisation aiming to combat energy and child poverty.

Aspiravi considers the energy transition towards a more sustainable production capacity as irreversible and ever more relevant. To meet the needs, and contribute towards achieving governments' and citizens' many climate objectives, various forms of renewable energy production are required. Moreover, they focus on increasing the amount of energy produced locally to reduce dependency on suppliers in other countries. Aspiravi is expanding its foothold in the Belgian green energy market as well as operations abroad and offshore.

Aspiravi aims to make a fundamental contribution to the energy transition, while playing its part in the implementation of the policy choices and commitments made by authorities at international, national and local levels.

The company is convinced that well-informed citizens demonstrate a great sense of responsibility that renewable energy is the future and that we must take action together. They therefore dedicate significant resources to communicating the benefits of the energy transition to investors, employees, customers and local communities, being transparent about their sustainability challenges and successes. These activities include open days, press activities and initiatives with local schools to teach children about wind turbines, green energy and the importance of the energy transition.

Sustainable HR transformation

It's essential for companies to consider the role of ESG principles in their HR transformation. This covers not only the social commitments embedded in ESG, but a wider consideration of the environmental and governance aspects affected by the transformation.

Triggers

One of the key triggers for a sustainable HR transformation is the increasing demand from employees and stakeholders for ethical and responsible business practices. In today's competitive job market, employees are seeking out companies that align with their values and provide a positive work environment. Implementing ESG principles in HR can help companies to meet this demand and create a workplace culture that's both sustainable and attractive to top talent.

Benefits

The value that can be derived from integrating ESG principles into HR practices is significant. Such a transformation not only aligns with the company's commitment to sustainability and ethical business practices but also helps to attract and retain talent, foster a positive workplace culture and enhance the company's reputation.

Companies that prioritise ESG can differentiate themselves from their competitors and create value for their employees, suppliers and other stakeholders, and the environment. They can expect to see a boost in employee morale, engagement and productivity. A positive workplace culture that values diversity, inclusivity and sustainability can also help to reduce staff turnover and attract top talent. Moreover, such companies are also likely to enjoy a better reputation in the community, which can help to build trust and establish strong relationships with stakeholders.

Implementation

ESG-driven HR policies and practices can include, for example, flexible work arrangements (such as remote work) to reduce carbon emissions, promote well-being and improve work/life balance. Or programmes to promote diversity, equity and inclusion in the workplace.

To unlock the value of ESG in HR transformations, companies need to:

- develop HR policies and practices that reflect ESG principles
- provide training and resources to employees to support their understanding of ESG and help them adapt to new practices
- establish metrics to measure the success of ESG initiatives
- explore the value and feasibility of novel HR strategies and practices
- engage employees in the process and encourage them to actively participate in the ESG efforts.

Case study: Patagonia

A recent example of a company that successfully transformed its HR practices with a focus on ESG is Patagonia,[141] an outdoor clothing and gear company.

Patagonia's commitment to ESG is reflected in its mission statement: 'Build the best product, cause no unnecessary harm, and use business to inspire and implement solutions to the environmental crisis.' Over the years, Patagonia has cofounded or joined numerous progressive coalitions to change the industry, including the Fair Labor Association,[142] the Sustainable Apparel Coalition[143] and B Lab.[144] These coalitions collectively focus on improving the lives and workplaces for people across the globe, using data to identify the industry's most pressing challenges, and ensuring a balance between the needs of business and those of society.

As part of its ESG transformation, Patagonia has taken several steps to ensure its HR practices align with its values. For instance, the company offers a number of benefits to its employees that support environmental sustainability, such as paid time off for environmental volunteer work, and financial incentives for reducing carbon emissions.

In addition, Patagonia has created a diverse and inclusive workplace, with a focus on hiring and promoting individuals from under-represented groups. The company provides its employees and their families with a range of healthcare, well-being and mental health benefits.

By prioritising ESG in its HR practices, Patagonia has not only improved the well-being of its employees, but has also built a strong reputation as a responsible and sustainable company, which has helped to attract and retain top talent.

This case study highlights the importance of integrating ESG, as it not only benefits employees, but also has a positive impact on the company's reputation and bottom line. In a rapidly changing business landscape, HR leaders that prioritise ESG are more likely to attract top talent and remain competitive in the long term.

Technologies supporting ESG implementation

Advanced data analytics, blockchain, artificial intelligence (AI), satellite technology, robotics and the Internet of Things (IoT) are reshaping the business landscape, offering a wealth of possibilities to support the ESG agenda, both in terms of compliance and business transformation.

For example, data technology and AI provide new tools that empower organisations to go beyond mere compliance. Companies can seamlessly collect, analyse and interpret vast volumes of information, uncovering patterns and connections. They can use this information to assess and mitigate risks, identify opportunities, and measure their environmental footprint, social progress and governance excellence. They can extract data-driven, meaningful insights to make informed decisions that balance profitability with ESG ambitions.

Blockchain[145] may offer opportunities to revolutionise supply chain management, ensuring responsible sourcing and reducing fraud by making every transaction traceable and accountable. While still in its infancy, blockchain could potentially allow companies to establish verifiable chains of custody for raw materials, offering full visibility into their origin and sustainability credentials. This would enable informed decisions about suppliers and foster a culture of transparency and accountability throughout the value chain, creating a virtuous cycle where responsible practices are rewarded and trust is nurtured.

AI and machine learning can, for example, help companies to monitor and analyse information from social media, to better understand public sentiment – perceptions, concerns and expectations – regarding ESG issues. This can empower organisations to proactively address emerging challenges, engage in dialogue and tailor their strategies to align with stakeholder values. Such tools also help companies to empower stakeholders, by crowdsourcing ideas, collecting feedback, and fostering co-creation and shared responsibility. Online platforms and mobile applications can invite customers, employees, investors and communities to actively participate in sustainability initiatives.

Technology at the service of ESG is not only about data and digital tools; it's also about equipment and systems. Clean energy solutions and energy management systems. Smart grid technologies, combined with energy storage solutions. Waste management technologies. Satellite tracking. And more...

Robotics and automation have evolved from a sci-fi fantasy to an everyday reality. Robots are now working in hospitals, warehouses, restaurants, offices and homes. Robotics has consequences – both practical and ethical – with many concerning implications for employment, privacy, security, etc. It also offers opportunities to support ESG transformation, by using robots to carry out dangerous work in factories, mines and warzones, for example, or under untenable conditions (heat, cold, underwater...).

Incentives as a catalyst for ESG transformation

Across the globe, governments are shaping national net-zero strategies, amid broader plans for a sustainable society. They are paying more and more attention to policy levers, including incentives, to support the energy transition and ESG transformation. Incentives such as cash grants, (soft) loans and tax credits play an important role in driving ESG investments and in the reallocation of capital towards more environmentally and socially sustainable outcomes.

Incentives encompass a wide variety of measures: renewable energy production, circularity, energy efficiency, habitat preservation, deforestation prevention, upskilling employees, etc. This section offers a high-level overview on what's happening within the larger regions.

European Union

EU Green Deal Industrial Plan
In order to enhance the competitiveness of Europe's net-zero industry and support the fast transition to climate neutrality, in 2023 the European Commission launched the Green Deal Industrial Plan.[146] The plan is based on four complementary pillars: 1) simplified regulatory environment; 2) mobilising private and public funding; 3) upskilling

workforce; and 4) diversification of the critical raw material supply chain. It includes financial measures to support the EU's manufacturing capacity for net-zero technologies and products, aiming to simplify and align incentives.

The EU's strategy on access to finance for its companies is based on a multitude of financial instruments, taxes and incentives coming from both new and existing funds such as REPowerEU, InvestEU, the Innovation Fund and the Social Climate Fund. The European Commission has approved new measures via the Temporary Crisis and Transition Framework in support of the transition towards a net-zero economy. The combination of an amended General Block Exemption Regulation (GBER) on state aid and the latter Framework will assist in speeding up investment and finance for clean tech production, and allow Member States more flexibility to design and implement support measures in sectors key for the transition to climate neutrality.

As part of the European Green Deal, the **Innovation Fund** (IF) aims to support innovative projects to reduce greenhouse gas emissions and serves the goal to make the EU the first climate neutral continent by 2050. The IF provides grants and other forms of financial support to a wide range of large- and small-scale projects focusing on renewable energy, energy storage, carbon capture, utilisation and storage, and energy-intensive industries. The IF is the **world's largest funding programme for innovative low-carbon technologies**. The fund will also broaden its scope of action to include maritime, aviation, buildings and road transport sectors as potential beneficiaries.

The European Parliament and the Council also agreed on establishing a **Social Climate Fund** (SCF) by 2026. This programme aims to combat energy and mobility poverty and will be set up following the adoption of the EU Emissions Trading System. The SCF will be funded by part of the revenue from this new EU ETS, and will include project-based investments, at national level, promoting zero-emissions mobility, energy efficiency and building renovations, and direct payments for low-income households.

The Green Deal Industrial Plan is a temporary EU programme subject to frequent changes.

European Social Fund Plus and Interreg
The European Commission's social incentive opportunities include the European Social Fund Plus[147] and Interreg[148] programmes. These support collaborative investment projects focusing on reducing disparities in the development and quality of life in certain European regions and striving to improve the economic, environmental, social and territorial development. Social inclusiveness and sustainability are key priorities in these programmes.

For an up-to-date overview of currently existing and upcoming grant programmes, including Horizon Europe, LIFE and the Innovation Fund, see the European Commission funding and tenders portal.[149]

Grant application is via an online portal and is supported by comprehensive guidelines on the administrative formalities (including templates, project budgets, evaluation process, etc.) depending on the call.

United States

US Inflation Reduction Act

Billed as the largest climate legislation in US history, the IRA[150] includes tax credits, incentives and other provisions intended to help companies tackle climate change, increase investments in renewable energy and enhance energy efficiency. While the legislation also addresses healthcare and corporate taxes, the climate-focused elements are especially significant. The IRA has provisioned nearly $370B in climate and clean energy and is expected to advance decarbonisation in many ways, including:

- driving more demand for electric vehicles (EVs), low-carbon materials/construction and clean technologies
- increasing growth of renewable energy through extensions of tax credits and increases in funding
- spurring innovation through research and development (R&D) of clean technology and low-carbon materials
- creating demand for low-carbon products in construction of federal buildings and transportation projects.

The law presents opportunities for companies across multiple industries to deliver on sustainability and carbon reduction commitments, while further defining the path to get there. As with the EU's Green Deal Industrial Plan it's also an opportunity – that may impact tax, finance and sustainability – to drive growth in operations, supply chain, risk management and product development.

The IRA is a temporary US Government programme subject to frequent changes.

Asia Pacific

The momentum to address climate and sustainability challenges is building across Asia-Pacific (APAC): more than 15 countries and 670 companies have set (or are committed to setting) emission-reduction targets.

A 2021 OECD report[151] noted that *"small and medium enterprises (SMEs) make up the vast majority of firms in the Association of Southeast Asian Nations (ASEAN) Member States (97-99%) and provide the majority of employment. They are also responsible for a significant portion of industrial pollution, not least because they are less heavily regulated than large enterprises. The environmental performance of SMEs will thus be critical to putting ASEAN economies (and most others around the world) onto a more sustainable development path."*

Africa

Across the African continent, the shift to ESG criteria is more and more crucial. Foreign investors, donors and even international development aid organisations are increasingly basing their decisions on environmental, social and governance criteria when deciding whether or not to invest.

The dominance of the extractive industries is an obvious barrier to the growth of ESG investment strategies in Africa, in particular from an environmental perspective. But while investors in developed economies are increasingly eliminating or reducing their future investments in fossil fuels, these sectors remain undeniably important contributors to revenues in Sub-Saharan Africa, with the export of oil products, coal, metals and minerals.

At national level, African countries offer both tax incentives and cash grants for a variety of activities such as waste and pollution (Ghana, Angola, Sierra Leone), and energy efficiency, GHG reduction and renewable power generation (Uganda, Zimbabwe). South Africa offers multiple incentives in each of the activities mentioned.

Middle East

The market for green and sustainable bonds in Gulf Cooperation Council (GCC) economies has been rising rapidly, with increased participation from banks and government-related entities. Total GCC green and sustainable bond and sukuk issuances[152] rose to $28.5 billion in 2022, from just $605 million in 2021.[153] Major issuers in the region include Saudi Arabia's sovereign wealth fund, and the Public Investment Fund, which in October 2022 listed a debut $3 billion green bond on the London Stock Exchange. In the United Arab Emirates (UAE), the Abu Dhabi National Energy Company, PJSC (TAQA), a government-controlled energy holding company, and Masdar, a government-owned renewable energy company, have successfully issued green securities.[154]

Overview of incentives across the globe

Figure 54 provides an overview of the different ESG-related incentives in different regions. This analysis is based on the input of 96 countries[155] and categorised in six major ESG-related themes relevant in each region: energy efficiency, GHG emissions reduction, recycling and waste management, renewable power generation, resource efficiency and water savings. It is intended to show comparative rather than precise values. Europe is ahead of the curve on all themes because of its Green Deal (since 2019) and Green Deal Industrial Plan. Renewable power generation and energy efficiency are leading investments in all regions.

Figure 54 – Overview of the volume of different ESG-related incentives in different regions. Source: PwC.

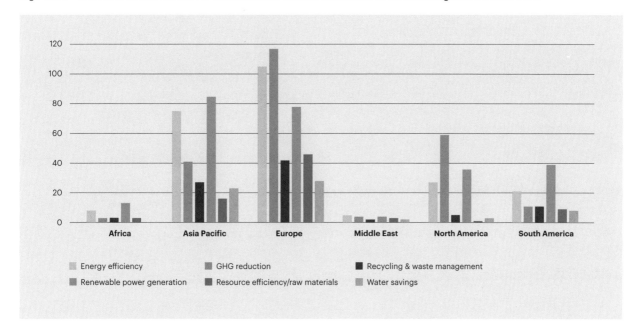

Accelerate decarbonisation by using grants and incentives

As the world moves to combat climate change, decarbonisation has become a priority for governments and companies alike. Understanding how to achieve environmental goals cost-effectively should be paramount. As outlined above, one way that governments around the world are spurring progress is through thousands of green taxes and incentives. Taxes form a major plank of companies' contributions to productive societies and, as such, need to be effectively incorporated into strategy. For businesses, the use of grants and incentives will become an important differentiator in their competitive position in the market.

Yet too often, and in too many organisations, **tax leaders are insufficiently involved when key strategic decisions are made**. These companies are missing opportunities, facing unexpected costs, and leaving benefits on the table that otherwise might help them accelerate their decarbonisation journey.

To summarise briefly, the integration of ESG into different functional domains is now more important than ever. It's not only a responsible business practice but also a strategic opportunity for companies to create value, improve their competitive position and better serve the needs of their stakeholders.

By embracing ESG principles, companies can mitigate risks, improve brand reputation, attract investment and build a more resilient business. ESG can also drive innovation and create new market opportunities.

Implementing ESG transformation requires a multifaceted approach, represented in the sustainable business transformation framework. This includes setting clear goals and targets, establishing effective governance structures, engaging with stakeholders, and measuring and reporting on ESG performance.

ESG transformation is not without its challenges. Common mistakes companies make during an ESG transformation include lack of leadership commitment, inadequate resources and insufficient stakeholder engagement.

The use of data analytics and technology can help companies measure and report on ESG performance, identify areas for improvement and drive innovation.

Finally, there are opportunities to benefit from different incentives created to support a more sustainable business landscape.

The journey towards ESG transformation may not be easy, but the benefits are clear for companies that are willing to make the necessary changes.

11.
ESG in transactions

Key takeaways

1. ESG is clearly gaining importance in the deals cycle. It should be given the same attention as other areas such as finance, tax, legal and HR.

2. When evaluating or preparing for a deal, take the six orange flags into account.

3. ESG is about more than just compliance. Don't just think in terms of costs and investments: consider ESG factors as value drivers and adjust the business plan accordingly.

4. When competing in a bid, take into account that ESG maturity is different in different parts of the world; this might create competitive [dis]advantages.

5. ESG does not stop with the closing of a deal. It remains essential in post-deal actions to ensure the actual value is realised.

Given the growing attention to ESG paid by many stakeholders – investors, governments, clients, suppliers, employees and the general public – it's no surprise that ESG is also affecting many aspects of merger and acquisition (M&A) transactions. Moreover, it's a stepping-stone process: the impact is surging, and what was exceptional and rare a couple of years ago is becoming standard.

What are private equity, pension funds and venture capital doing?

An increasing number of limited partners are pushing private equity (PE) towards more sustainable assets. This has led, amongst other things, to the creation of The Net Zero Asset Management initiative,[156] an international group of asset managers committed to supporting the goal of net-zero GHGs by 2050 or sooner, in line with global efforts to limit warming to 1.5°C, and to supporting investing aligned with net-zero emissions by 2050 or sooner.

The initiative was launched in 2020 and, on 31 December 2022, assembled 301 signatories with $59 trillion in assets under management. Similar pressure is observed from authorities, financial institutions and pension funds.

A 2021 PwC survey[157] showed that emphasis on ESG has increased significantly in all areas, from performance valuation to monitoring and reporting (Figure 55).

In broad terms, for PE, pension funds and venture capital (VC) – altogether, financial investors (FI) – there are three drivers of different strategies.

1. ESG turnaround: brown to green

   FI invest in activities that are significantly lagging behind compared to their peers or are in sectors that are worst of class in terms of sustainability. The investment rationale is to transform the business and create value as a consequence.

   The first movers in these areas were investors focusing on real estate and on redeveloping industrial sites into commercial or residential properties. Brownfield investments are often faster compared to greenfield mainly because of easier permits. The clean-up costs can obviously be very high.

2. ESG leaders: buy cleaner, outperform

   PE invests in activities that are clearly ahead of the pack and create value by increasing the gap.

   One of the many examples of this strategy is the acquisition of Desotec by Blackstone in 2021. Desotec is a European environmental service company active in circular filtration solutions. The drawback of such investments is that they are often highly priced.

Figure 55 – Private equity firms are placing greater emphasis on all areas of ESG.[158]

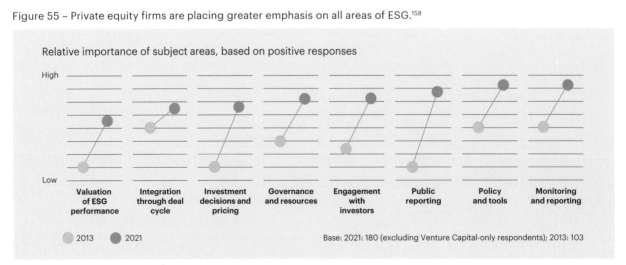

3. ESG disruption: buy ESG
solutions early, take to scale

FI, and especially VC, select truly innovative activities, anticipating that they will conquer large markets through their technological advancement. The target market in early stage ESG solutions is a veritable mushroom field, with activities ranging from ESG-enabling software, to innovative customer solutions, to new materials.

The challenge is to pick the winners that will survive. A good example amongst many is the acquisition of Sphera by Blackstone in 2021. Sphera is a software (SAAS), data and consulting services company helping clients to surface, manage and mitigate ESG related risks.

What is industry doing?

When companies transform their strategies and operations to become more sustainable, this also impacts the allocation of capital. Assets need to be carved out and disposed of, and others to be acquired and integrated. Very often, industrial players do both at the same time, selling activities that have a poorer perspective from an ESG angle, to raise funds to acquire greener activities.

As a result, this rapid change often outpaces organic change and internal R&D can't keep up. Corporate venturing comes to the fore as established industrial companies create vehicles to acquire minority stakes or other financing in start-up companies active in the field of new technologies. Taking minority stakes reduces the risk associated with start-up activities and at the same time the start-up retains sufficient room for manoeuvre to keep on being ground-breaking.

ESG is increasingly part of M&A processes

All of the above has a significant impact on how M&A processes evolve over time. Up to a few years ago, ESG was not addressed in the due diligence. Then it became common to include a small amount of ESG information included as an ancillary section to the overall reports.

Today, however, more and more often, 'pure play' ESG due diligences are carried out covering broad scope analyses, focusing not only on risk, but also on opportunities for value creation.

Understanding the shifting approach and scope of ESG due diligence is paramount to properly prepare M&As, and to ensure that they unlock value, resilience and impact.

A typical ESG due diligence is modular (Figure 56) and can be tailored to align with the company's overarching sustainability policy, the ambition of the target and the specific nature of the potential acquisition in itself.

Where avowedly green assets are acquired, ESG performance is key and discrepancies should be assessed against best of class. For industrial complementary activities, rather high level risk assessments of red and orange flags might suffice.

The topics around ESG are maturing, and today more and more factors related to ESG are being considered relevant and included in M&A due diligence processes. Given the upcoming EU regulations, we expect ESG due diligence to increase in importance: there will be more ESG information and a need to objectively compare performance with competitors, and to assess the feasibility of the ESG strategy and underlying commitments.

Figure 56 – A modular ESG due diligence approach.

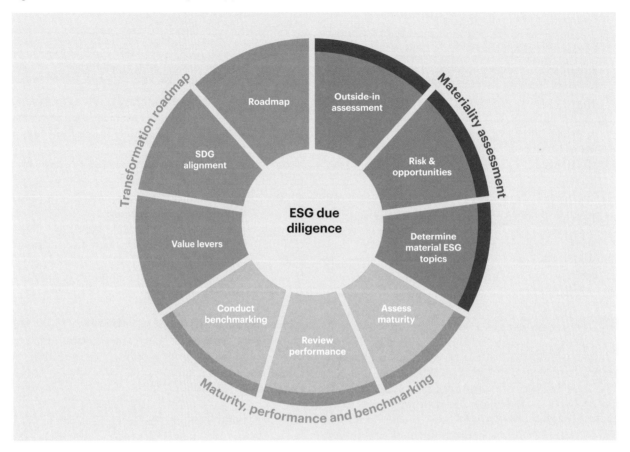

Materiality assessment

Where a company is targeted for a merger or acquisition, an ESG materiality assessment can identify and prioritise critical ESG-related factors and the level of residual risk or opportunity they may represent. This is the foundation of an ESG due diligence analysis and of the ESG due diligence report. It typically addresses questions such as those below.

Are there any red flags regarding the company?

Identification of integrity-, reputational- or ESG-related risks associated with the target, key individuals or suppliers.

What are the main ESG-related risks and opportunities for the company?

Assessment of specific ESG-related factors which could have a value impact on the target in the deal thesis.

What are the ESG topics material to the target?

Identification of material ESG topics based on target sector, geography and size, according to the assessor's expertise as well as industry recognised standards and frameworks such as SASB.

Table 9 provides an overview of typical themes and issues to consider in ESG due diligence, highlighting whether they are high-, medium- or low-materiality issues.

Table 9 – ESG due diligence materiality assessment themes and issues.

GENERAL THEMES	Vision & Governance	Business Ethics	Human Resources	Environment	Value Chain	Societal Relations
SPECIFIC ESG ISSUES	Corporate & CSR goverance	Prevention of bribery & corruption	Occupational health & safety	GHG emissions & climate transition	Supply chain management	Social licence to operate
	Values & corporate culture	Competition	Diversity, inclusion & equal treatment	Exposure to physical climate change risks	Human rights	Local economic and social impact
	Business model resilience	Relations with public authorities	Talent attraction & retention	Operational eco-efficiency	Scarcity of sourced materials	Thought leadership
	Risk management	Personal data protection	Training & development	Environmental pollution	Environmental & social impact of supply chain	Philanthropy
	Compliance	Behavioural ethics	Employee engagement	Environmental compliance	Selling practices & product labelling	
			Work-life balance	Circular economy	Product quality	
			Labour relations	Biodiversity & land use	Access & affordability	
					Customer health & safety	
					Innovation & product CSR alignment	

High-materiality issues   Medium-materiality issues   Low-materiality issues   June 2023

Many parameters, ranging from business model to business relations, geographies and industry, will play a role in this initial ESG materiality assessment; these can be discussed and validated with the management of the target company. These parameters will affect the selection of ESG material topics, themes and issues. For example:

- the industry in which the target company operates: e.g. the clothing industry would trigger supply chain and human rights risks
- the country in which it operates or sells its products: e.g. dealing with third parties in a country identified by the Corruption Perceptions Index as being high risk would trigger the ABAC risk
- the business model of the company: e.g. if it relies on cargo flight to move its goods across its supply chain, then Scope 3 emissions would be a high attention point.

On the opportunity side, a business model could also be a signal of an opportunity, e.g. to reflect on the circularity of the business model, through a reuse, recycle product line, etc.

Maturity, performance and benchmarking

The material topics form the basis of the evaluation of the target's overall maturity and KPI performance (depending on available data). This can then be benchmarked using a range of metrics: peers, regulatory requirements, customer commitments, leading practices and so on. The most appropriate analysis will depend on the individual target. A comprehensive evaluation will address questions such as the following.

What is the maturity level of the target's current ESG programme?

Identification of the policies, processes and other elements in place at the target to ensure that ESG risks and opportunities are appropriately identified and addressed.

How does the target perform on important ESG-related KPIs?

Regardless of maturity, how does the target perform in material ESG topic areas when considering KPIs and other performance data?

How do the target's maturity and performance compare to key metrics?

Analysis of how the target is positioned with regards to, for example, current and upcoming sustainability-related regulation, investor policy and expectations (climate commitments, etc.), peers, leading practice, and more.

Transformation roadmap

A transformation roadmap is built on the output of the previous analyses (materiality, performance and benchmarking). Its purpose is to identify value creation levers and a roadmap of the investments needed for sustainable outcomes, and to create resilience in the target's business. The transformation roadmap addresses:

- actions needed to ensure sustainable value creation and a resilient business model
- planning to implement leading practices, respond to market trends and maximise value creation, based on input from all previous modules within the wheel
- identification of the UN SDGs applicable to the target
- assessment of the target's positive and negative contribution in relation to the applicable SDGs, considering both value to society and to the business
- assessment of the financial value to the target of addressing ESG topics
- identification of potential levers to create value post acquisition.

Where possible, the potential financial impact of ESG changes on cash flow is also assessed, which allows a value bridge to be prepared. Figure 57 shows an example of such a value bridge.

Figure 57 – Example of a value bridge in an ESG transformation roadmap. (EBITDA: earnings before interest, taxes, depreciation and amortisation).

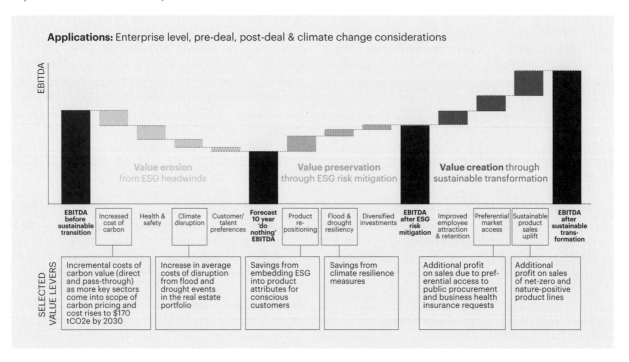

Six orange flags for dealmakers

In a 2023 article (reproduced below), Miriam Pozza[159] identified six orange flags for dealmakers that are relevant in every step of the deal: the preparation, the execution and the integration. The flags are orange to signal to dealmakers to proceed with caution and take careful steps to limit risk and enhance value. They are usually not red flags that would stop a deal from happening.

The six orange flags are:

- unethical marketing
- reputational risks
- high-risk supply chains
- disengaged employees
- transformational deals that don't deliver on wider outcomes
- inadequate non-financial disclosures.

Unethical marketing

Unethical marketing is problematic for dealmakers, because it means messages are inconsistent with reality—they don't align with regulation, stakeholder sentiment, or public positions taken by acquirers. When acquirers sought to buy a vocational education provider, their due diligence took a close look at public statements and found that certain claims about its courses and outcomes for students were wrong. In such instances, regulatory and other penalties can be factored into deal costs, a consideration that underlines the importance of casting a wider net on marketing claims. We see that such claims are related not only to environmental commitments, but increasingly to operations and governance.

To manage value risks arising from marketing mismatches, it is essential to build a robust corporate control framework, covering compliance with applicable laws, regulations, and reporting requirements—especially those that are due to come into force. Diligence should also evaluate the strengths of processes and controls designed to prevent unethical claims from being made. Dealmakers need to be attuned to inconsistencies in public messages and the efficacy of products, especially in industries where marketing regulation is loose. For instance, words like clean and organic

do not have an internationally agreed meaning throughout the cosmetics industry. Value may be enhanced in targets that achieve compliance with agreed standards at an early date and, conversely, may be damaged in targets that miss deadlines.

Reputational risks

The reputational risks linked to ESG performance are not new. As has been well established by recent high-profile "greenwashing" accusations in the corporate world, failures to meet regulations, internal targets, and stakeholder expectations can lead to negative attention, knocks to consumer and client confidence, and loss of revenue. Forward-thinking diligence on reputation involves gaining a more robust understanding of a firm's value proposition in terms of market focus and potential, and verifying a wider set of ESG claims. It's worth examining what competitors are emphasizing most. Is it, for example, their green credentials, their diversity, or other principles aligned to their value proposition?

Reputational due diligence can also be helpful at revealing and addressing deeper issues at a company. ESG can provide a framework—and sometimes the air cover—to handle potentially thorny issues that fall outside standard diligence. In one recent deal opportunity, an acquirer learned about legal issues surrounding sitting members of the target company's executive committee. By homing in on social and governance issues via due diligence of employee views and organizational culture, dealmakers assembled information that helped them decide to move executives out of the business. Because they were able to rectify governance issues, the sponsors were able to continue with the investment and achieve outcomes in line with their ESG commitments.

High risks in supply chains

High risks in supply chains are emerging more frequently, as wars, conflicts, and trade tensions persist across global routes—and these risks are heightened by threats from physical climate events. However, the demand for diligence around contracts and the formality of supply chain relationships is growing. Modern slavery, health and safety, and labor rights have also grown in importance, alongside continued awareness of the sourcing of raw materials [...]. For example, due diligence on the supply chain of one apparel manufacturer revealed issues with factory conditions, including subpar health and safety, and poor air quality. To address these issues, parties agreed to raise operating standards in factories and to pursue environmental, health, and safety initiatives. The costs of these measures were factored into deal valuations, and a legal framework was written into the deal terms stipulating that workforce obligations—including further improvements to working conditions—would be taken up by the seller.

Buyers are also looking at the stability of supply chains, with some investors taking steps to add resilience when they recognize geopolitical and ESG vulnerabilities. A firm exploring the acquisition of a target in the sports market learned through supply chain due diligence that roughly 80% of the target's manufacturing was done at only two factories. That finding revealed a challenge the otherwise successful company had in keeping up with demand. Other social and governance orange flags cropped up related to the factories' host countries and global trade tensions. Getting the deal done involved establishing five-year plans to diversify and build resilience in the target's supply chain, and, further, to align the company's sourcing footprint with its social and governance credentials.

Disengaged employees

Employees, who are often an important voice for the legitimacy of a company's ESG credentials, continue to be a critical asset at the center of most deals. And workforce issues, such as evidence of disengaged employees, are gaining prominence in M&A. Greater scrutiny of governance, employee development and retention, workforce diversity, and equal pay are now more likely to be factored into diligence. Dealmakers are increasingly looking to diagnose staffing losses through specific assessments of social and governance issues, examining areas such as company culture and employee satisfaction, including input from staff surveys and one-on-one interviews. If an acquirer's talent practices cause workers in the target company to leave, that destroys value. On the other hand, if an acquirer can impart its good talent practices to a target with subpar talent management, it can create more value. [...]One company looking at a

target where turnover was higher than the industry average estimated that it could achieve an incremental cost savings of up to US$8 million per year by investing in social factors, such as staff engagement, to bring the target's employee retention rate up to industry averages.

Orange flags can also crop up because of issues that may not have been part of past workforce diligence, such as staff development. In industries like healthcare, where skilled technicians and professionals are difficult to recruit and retain, dedicated investment, good governance, and a supportive company culture are often critical for learning and development. Acquirers know this, and so they are paying careful attention to the impact of talent management on deal valuation. One acquirer of a healthcare company, for example, chose to have senior stakeholders at the target pledge support and investment for development programs serving junior staff as a way of improving retention.

The transformative deal that isn't

The challenges to delivering sustained ESG outcomes as a society are large and complex. Dealmakers have an important role to play in ensuring a Just Transition by balancing complex trade-offs among social, economic, and environmental issues with carbon-reduction goals. The opportunities for venture capital and PEs are well understood, given the appetite to help portfolio companies reach sustainability goals and to invest in new and high-growth business models supporting the ESG transition. But progress brings risks, if outcomes are overpromised or underdelivered. As we navigate toward a low-carbon world, technological disruption is generating enormous upheaval, challenging the strategy of companies, their business models, and how they operate.

Against this backdrop, the nature of dealmaking is changing, from largely static to proactive plays. [...] Players that can manage this disruption through heightened due diligence around "future proofing"—for instance, early planning for carbon taxes, cash grants, and other environmental initiatives—will be best placed to protect and create value while making meaningful contributions to a Just Transition. They will maximize their impact materiality, in addition to their financial materiality.

Take the creation of "green jobs" as part of the wider Just Transition. In OECD countries that are undergoing a construction and infrastructure boom and will drive global spending in this area, the construction workforce is predominantly male. As the energy transition occurs and roughly 20 million new green jobs are created, more green jobs will likely be filled by men than women. Without intervention, the gender mix in the green workforce could be even more imbalanced than in today's labor market.

When dealmakers incorporate ESG into their decision making, it can go a long way to changing the mindset across an industry. However, achieving ESG outcomes is a collective challenge—these goals won't be reached with a single deal. Although meeting stakeholder expectations for performance is still the main goal for many dealmakers, the most forward-looking among them are exploring how they can incorporate an ESG agenda to boost both impact and financial materiality.

Inadequate nonfinancial disclosures

What is reported and what is not is an ongoing issue, as is the transparency and validity of data. For dealmakers, inadequate nonfinancial disclosures are an important orange flag. We've noted that some companies are reporting physical climate risks and the impact these will have on their businesses as part of their nonfinancial disclosures. However, in some cases they have used climate scenarios that are unrealistic and perhaps favorable to their business. [...]Certainly, inadequate disclosures create regulatory or reputational risk. But if an acquiring company fails to envision that a high-warming scenario would create serious physical risks for a target, or an accelerated-decarbonization scenario would create significant transition risks, it could miss out on a lot of value.

Ultimately, companies will need to disclose more information, as stakeholders demand greater transparency and regulatory thresholds are heightened. But in the meantime, dealmakers who see orange flags around disclosures will be wise to value targets under multiple ESG scenarios.

Dealmakers have known for some time that external ESG issues can influence a company's ability to create value. Now, the most forward-thinking players are also recognizing that a business's impact on the world can be material, and they are creating accountability, often at the board level, for such impact. By incorporating an orange flag process to highlight concerns related to both financial and impact materiality, dealmakers will be better positioned to unlock value and create resilience through their M&A.

And one red flag...

Of course any ESG assessment may reveal any number of red flags related to the target company's ESG credentials. But one that should not be overlooked is how information is provided. An important challenge in ESG assessment in deals is when target companies provide a lot of detailed information but in an incoherent and piecemeal fashion. This is a red flag in itself, signalling a negative impact on the business plan.

Preparing the deal: due diligence

Clarity, transparency and predictability have a very significant impact on the value of companies. This is particularly important regarding new challenges related to ESG. It's paramount to carefully prepare for the ESG aspect of a deal right from the start. Good deal preparation that takes ESG into account optimises value, and is likely to be very helpful for potential buyers to attract financing for the transactions.

Step 1 — Focus on what's important

The first step is to get a clear view on what's actually important. To establish this, it's helpful to work with a predefined framework. Here we show an example of a framework that looks at materiality from two different perspectives, or views. View one indicates materiality under the various ESG categories (Figure 58). View 2 indicates materiality depending on position in the supply chain (Figure 59).

Figure 58 – Example of key ESG issues for a chemical company in food supplements. View 1: Materiality by ESG category.

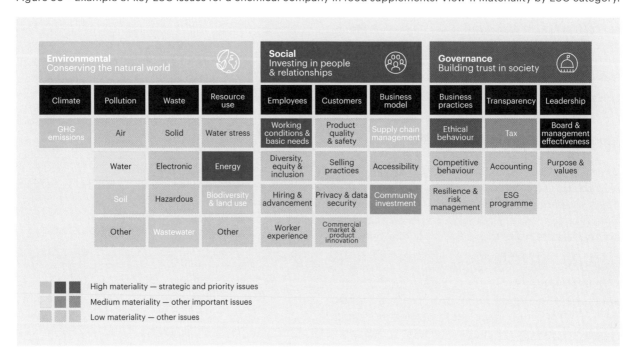

Figure 59 – Example of key ESG issues for a chemical company in food supplements. View 2: Materiality in the supply chain.

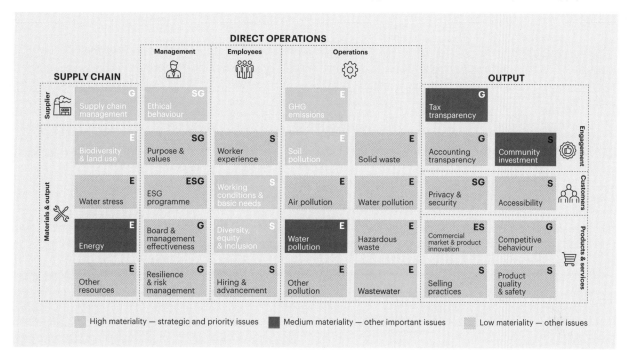

Step 2 — Evaluate impacts

The next step is to evaluate the most material ESG factors, to identify which may have a predictable impact on business plans, both from a cost or investing (capex) point of view and from a predictable business plan point of view. This assessment includes five parts, to identify:

1. the strategy

2. the steps to get there — the roadmap

3. the objectives and which KPIs underpin them

4. how the KPIs are measured and how they evolve

5. the (estimated) positive and negative impacts on the business plan (preferably set apart from the general business plan).

Many companies have some kind of net-zero commitment by a certain year. In a transaction context, it's essential to assess the strategy and roadmap to meet that commitment. If not, cost and needed capex may be overstated by anyone interested and no positive impacts (such as preferential access to markets) will be added.

With further economic headwinds and energy price challenges ahead, businesses have important decisions to make if they are to place decarbonisation efforts at the heart of their economic futures.

An incomplete assessment is better than none
Chapter 8 includes the full trajectory to create a holistic ESG strategy. Within the context of a transaction, there's often not enough time to do this. The pay-off will be bigger through focusing on a limited number of items: it's certainly better than doing nothing at all because the full process is deemed too laborious.

Even if there's no overall strategy, it's definitely worthwhile to go through the steps for the most important segments prone to ESG impact — for example, for selected production sites, groups of products or specific territories.

Executing the deal: acquisition strategy

Whereas 'Preparing the deal' put the spotlight on the seller in a transaction, in this section, we focus on the buyer. ESG has not created a whole new deals world, but has added a new overarching dimension to the world as we know it. Business plans are still business plans, but will be affected by ESG matters that were largely unconsidered in previous decades.

The ESG impact on target evaluation

Any due diligence process will highlight issues in the target company that will need to be resolved, such as non-compliance or expected business challenges. Buyers face this in the midst of the sometimes cut-throat competitive environment of the bidding process. The party that cares least about the past and most about the bright future is most likely to win…

In that context, ESG needs to be part of your acquisition strategy. The more prominent the ESG factor is in a particular transaction, the more you will need the comfort of knowing what the issues are and anticipating how to handle them.

For example, consider an acquisition where the value will derive from geographical expansion with local-for-local production. In this case, compliance with local applicable regulations might be sufficient. By contrast, in an acquisition where the value will derive from expansion with production and/or distribution in different parts of the globe, mere local compliance won't be enough. Compliance with ESG regulations in all of the target's potential markets will be necessary.

In an ideal world, getting all the information you need for comfort might be possible, but it seldom happens. More often, the buyer faces a dilemma: do you dig deep (and risk diluting your focus on matters that prove to be of minor importance) or dig less deep (and risk bad surprises on matters that turn out to be crucial)?

Obviously, if you are a PE fund building a green fund, the scope of the ESG due diligence will be much more extensive and more likely to influence the deal, even to the point of delivering show-stoppers.

Once your own key ESG metrics for a potential deal are clear, the follow-up step is to assess where the target stands now and how much effort it might take to get them where you would want them to be. Your strategic goals should determine the key questions to be raised; the due diligence should answer them. Merely highlighting the black spots is often a sign of insufficient due diligence.

Throughout the due diligence process, the initial step is obviously to identify the non-compliances to fix and the associated cost. But even so, defining the target's baseline and the roadmap towards aligning with the buyer's baseline is important. Equally important is assessing how well prepared the target is for the expected upcoming challenges related to, for instance, sustainable sourcing, the EU Corporate Sustainability Due Diligence Directive (CS3D)[160] and so on. At this stage, it will probably not yet be possible to lay out a full value creation plan for all value levers in the area of ESG. Nevertheless, identifying the main value levers and their potential will bring the positive angles to light, make your offer more competitive or create more headroom to absorb some of the risks. Analysing the impact of some of your best practices on the target is likely to shed further light on the transactions and on the ways to unlock value.

The post-acquisition ESG impact on the buyer

After the acquisition, the newly acquired entity will be consolidated into the buyer's group or portfolio. This might create a temporary setback in ESG impact requiring distinct actions and reporting.

The actors in this field are used to monitoring the impact of acquisitions on their debt profile, debt covenants and financial performance based on their main KPIs. Reporting on ESG KPIs is much more recent, which makes it quite an endeavour to assess the impact of substantial new activity added to the existing whole, particularly if the new activity is less advanced in the ESG area.

Reputation

The target's level of ESG maturity and performance affects the buyer's image and brand perception. If the target company is substantial in comparison to the buyer, their corporate images will blend, potentially affecting how stakeholders such as consumers and employees perceive the combined entity. It's somewhat comparable with corporate cultures that melt and merge into a new post-integration culture. This can obviously go both ways — it's essential to assess what the impact could be and to take appropriate actions including communication.

Reporting

Getting the reporting aligned might prove to be more cumbersome than first expected. Although KPIs might look the same, the devil is always in the details of the definition, and in the methodology used to gather information and to calculate the measure.

For instance, take CO_2 emissions. Even if only considering Scope 1 (own) emissions, it's necessary to align the granularity at which emissions are measured and the tables used to convert emissions or energy data to the equivalent amount of CO_2 emissions. In other words, to use the same basis, same scope and same conversion for both the acquirer and acquiree. It's a laborious exercise but essential, as the new CO_2 emissions outcome might be significantly different from the initial sum of the unaligned acquirer and acquiree data.

A buyer should foresee a considerable effort to get reporting aligned, and this simultaneously with all other integration matters. It goes without saying that the effort is even bigger if the target is less evolved or located in areas where ESG reporting is not top of mind.

Financing

A surging number of finance agreements contain ESG-based measures to determine interest rate intervals. Better performance and KPIs on which assurance is expressed bring down interest costs. Adding new activities may distort a positive trend or may, at least in a first stage, make assurance problematic. There are no magic solutions for this.

Ideally, existing financing agreements should contain a steady scope provision or a grace period for built-on acquisitions. In case a steady scope financing exists, new acquisitions could be financed through new financing, including a new set of ESG KPIs to be measured at the level of the new acquisition, and a path ahead determined for that specific activity.

Of course if no KPIs are available for the target, this increases the risk enormously as to the assessment of the impact on current financing and on the possibilities to secure new financing.

ESG impact on deal dynamics: competitiveness

ESG is driving a new shift in competitiveness, because not all sellers are subject to the same requirements or operate under the same conditions.

In the short term, sellers that are subject to more stringent regulations are at a disadvantage. They come with risks that others don't have. They will be faced with more concerns about financing than others. In the race to a greener world, they have a head start, but risk losing out on acquisitions in the short run. In today's business climate, for example, in the case of US based buyers competing with EU based buyers over a US business that's subject to comparatively few ESG constraints, it's clear that the US buyers are at a distinct advantage.

Post-deal integration

It seems a recurrent refrain, but ESG makes the post-acquisitions process different. Not totally different, perhaps, but it adds a layer to many aspects of the whole process. It also creates new opportunities. The assessment of day 1 readiness, the determination of a target operating model and a 100-day plan to start realising synergies, are all still very much pertinent.

As in any acquisitions or integrations, the paradigm remains: fix, align and shift higher.

Fix

The fix part is all about mitigating risks identified during the due diligence process. This seems an obvious part, but often the focus shifts so quickly to synergy realisation that developing an action plan to mitigate risks, and following up on this plan, are forgotten. The actions to fix risk are likely to be more short term and part of the day 1 readiness and the 100-days plan.

Align

Aligning means ensuring the target's and buyer's baselines are aligned. It's not simply a matter of moving forward in areas where the target lags, but also of identifying areas where the buyer lags and needs to step up. In other words, it's about creating the best of both worlds. Alignment is included in the target operating model, where ESG is very important as it will also determine, along with other factors, the pace and degree of integration. The purely local-for-local situation might be extended to allow more time to align with ESG requirements in other territories.

Shift higher

The most exciting part is definitely the shift higher part. Shift higher is about unlocking value through (re-)defining the strategy by taking into account the opportunities offered by ESG. Figure 60 is an example for a packaging company for cosmetics.

The merger and acquisition market is maturing as it begins to consider ESG in the transaction process more systematically. This is driven by pushing factors such as the wave of EU regulations forcing transparent reporting by companies in Europe. However, as the Green Deal ambitions are translated into additional regulations, it's important that governments also reflect on how to further support business in transitioning their business models and adapting to a changing world.

Figure 60 – Shift higher example for a cosmetics packaging company.

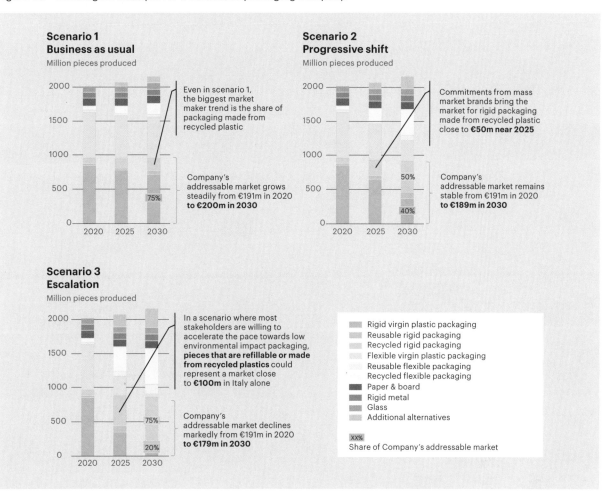

Scenario 1
Business as usual
Million pieces produced

Even in scenario 1, the biggest market maker trend is the share of packaging made from recycled plastic

Company's addressable market grows steadily from €191m in 2020 **to €200m in 2030**

75%

Scenario 2
Progressive shift
Million pieces produced

Commitments from mass market brands bring the market for rigid packaging made from recycled plastic close to **€50m near 2025**

Company's addressable market remains stable from €191m in 2020 **to €189m in 2030**

50%
40%

Scenario 3
Escalation
Million pieces produced

In a scenario where most stakeholders are willing to accelerate the pace towards low environmental impact packaging, **pieces that are refillable or made from recycled plastics** could represent a market close to **€100m** in Italy alone

Company's addressable market declines markedly from €191m in 2020 **to €179m in 2030**

75%
20%

Rigid virgin plastic packaging
Reusable rigid packaging
Recycled rigid packaging
Flexible virgin plastic packaging
Reusable flexible packaging
Recycled flexible packaging
Paper & board
Rigid metal
Glass
Additional alternatives

XX%
Share of Company's addressable market

12.
The legal
framework for ESG

Key takeaways

1. Businesses are navigating an increasingly complex legal environment, especially within the ESG framework.

2. The European Union is leading the world in ESG legislation, with the most ambitious and comprehensive legal framework for ESG matters. It sets the standard for legislation that may follow in other parts of the world. While ESG has long been considered a matter of 'soft law' and auto-regulation, it now has clearly entered the field of 'hard' law.

3. Compliance with ESG regulations ensures responsible behaviour, mitigates risks and safeguards stakeholder interests.

4. The legal dimension of ESG goes beyond mere compliance. It empowers companies to proactively integrate ESG considerations into their operations, driving positive social and environmental impact.

5. The wealth of legislation can be considered not so much as a burden for companies, but rather as a tool — a framework on which to build ethical conduct, transparency and accountability.

6. The legal framework also facilitates disclosure and reporting, enabling informed decision making by shareholders, investors and other stakeholders.

ESG legislation provides a framework for action

As businesses begin to recognise the crucial value of sustainability and responsible business practices, they are navigating an increasingly complex legal environment, especially within the ESG framework. It's becoming essential for these businesses, in close collaboration with their internal and external legal teams, to understand the relevance of the growing number of regulations and legal issues they may be facing. This is also an opportunity to seize the ESG momentum: to revisit the legal organisation of the business across the group, such as risk control and reporting policies, and to rethink the contractual strategy, from sourcing to delivery and beyond.

Current and new ESG legislation is putting increasing pressure on companies to comply with a burgeoning number of hard regulations. It will indeed be challenging for companies over the coming years to keep up with it all.

However, the legal dimension of ESG goes beyond mere compliance. It empowers companies to proactively integrate ESG considerations into their operations, driving positive social and environmental impact. The wealth of legislation can be considered not so much as a burden for companies, but rather as a tool — a framework on which to build ethical conduct, transparency and accountability. Compliance with ESG regulations ensures responsible behaviour, mitigates risks and safeguards stakeholder interests, which ultimately leads to value creation, as described below. The legal framework also facilitates disclosure and reporting, enabling informed decision making by shareholders, investors and other stakeholders.

Compliance benefits and risks

Compliance with relevant laws and regulations not only ensures ethical behaviour but also brings a multitude of indirect benefits. First and foremost, **legal compliance is fundamental for companies seeking to integrate ESG practices effectively**.

- E – Environmental regulations govern the impact of business operations on ecosystems, air and water quality, and natural resources. Compliance ensures that companies mitigate environmental risks, reduce pollution and promote sustainable resource management.
- S – Labour laws protect workers' rights, ensuring fair employment practices, safe working conditions, and fair wages. By adhering to labour regulations, companies foster a harmonious work environment and uphold the dignity and well-being of their employees.
- G – Governance holds paramount importance in the legal ESG context. While the E and S have a larger number of specific regulations to comply with, the G is not only a third pillar of ESG but is overarching the three. It encompasses the legal framework that ensures transparency, accountability and ethical conduct within a company.

Compliance with ESG regulations safeguards a company's reputation and shields it from legal and financial risks. Violations of environmental, social or governance laws can lead to reputational damage, public scrutiny, and costly litigation. Compliance minimises the potential for fines, penalties and legal disputes, thereby protecting a company's financial stability and shareholder value.

Beyond direct compliance, the legal framework also indirectly benefits companies by fostering trust, attracting investors and enhancing brand value. Investors increasingly consider ESG factors when making investment decisions, as they recognise the material impact of environmental and social risks on financial performance. Compliant companies are more likely to access sustainable investment funds and attract responsible investors who seek long-term value creation. Additionally, consumers, employees and other stakeholders are increasingly conscious of a company's ESG practices, and legal compliance serves as a testament to a company's commitment to ethical conduct. This, in turn, strengthens brand reputation, boosts customer loyalty, and attracts top talent, contributing to long-term business success.

Legal compliance also facilitates access to markets and partnerships. Many countries and regions impose ESG-related requirements for companies to enter their markets or engage in public procurement. Regulatory compliance opens doors to new opportunities, expands market reach, and enables collaboration with like-minded organisations. By embracing legal obligations, companies position themselves as responsible and trustworthy partners, fostering mutually beneficial relationships with governments, NGOs and other stakeholders.

Focus on European legislation

The European Union is leading the world in ESG legislation. This chapter focuses on the European legislative framework: it is to date the most established, ambitious and comprehensive legal framework for ESG matters. And it sets the standard for legislation that may follow in other parts of the world. Moreover, EU legislation is already impacting industry in the rest of the world by affecting EU imports and the operations of global companies.

Most hard laws are issued at a European Union level by either a directive or a regulation.

- **Regulations** have binding legal force throughout every Member State and enter into force on a set date in all the Member States (e.g. the SFDR).
- **Directives** lay down certain results that must be achieved. Unlike a regulation, which is directly applicable in Member States after its entry into force, a directive is not directly applicable in Member States; it must first be transposed into national law before it is applicable and each Member State is 'free' to decide how to transpose it into national law. The directive can determine the amount of freedom the States have.
- Both regulations and directives can be supplemented by **delegated acts**: non-legislative acts adopted by the Commission to supplement or amend certain non-essential elements of a legislative act.[161]

It is the European Commission's task to monitor the conversion status of directives and apply its infringement procedure when necessary. When a Member State does not transpose a directive (in time), the Commission may initiate infringe-

ment procedures and bring proceedings against the country before the Court of Justice of the EU (the non-enforcement of the judgement on this occasion can lead to a new conviction, which may result in fines).

So in the context of ESG, notably the CSRD and CS3D, it's important to note that, in principle, these directives only take effect once transposed into national law.

However, the Court of Justice considers that a directive that is not transposed can yet have certain effects directly if the:

- transposition into national law has not taken place or has been done incorrectly
- terms of the directive are unconditional and sufficiently clear and precise
- terms of the directive give rights to individuals.

When these conditions are met, individuals may rely on the directive against a Member State in national courts. However, an individual may not rely on it to make a claim against another individual with respect to the direct effect of a directive if it has not been transposed.

E from a legal perspective

The environmental aspect of ESG is often given the most emphasis by politicians, legislators and businesses due to the substantial environmental threats both to society and businesses. Climate risk, water scarcity, extreme temperatures and GHG emissions are among the many environmental issues that now jeopardise economic growth. The state of the environment directly affects a company's competitive position, making environmental management a core component of ESG.

To address these environmental risks, regulatory responses have emerged across the globe. In Europe, this resulted in the Green Deal in 2019.[162] The Green Deal comprises a series of policy initiatives aimed at guiding the EU towards a sustainable transition, with the ambitious objective of becoming the first climate-neutral continent by 2050. Its goal is to foster a modern and competitive economy while mitigating environmental impact.

As an interim target, the Green Deal aims for a 55% reduction in GHG emissions by 2030 compared to 1990 levels. To achieve this, the Fit for 55 package seeks to translate the Green Deal's ambitions into legally binding legislation. This process started with the adoption of the European Climate Law in 2021, which imposes a binding target on EU Member States to reduce their global emissions by 55% by 2030 and achieve climate neutrality by 2050. By establishing legally binding targets, the European Climate Law reinforces the commitment to combat climate change, and sets a clear trajectory towards a greener future.

Climate change and energy

Climate change represents one of the most pressing global challenges, necessitating urgent action to mitigate its impacts. The energy sector, being a major contributor to GHG emissions, has a direct influence on climate change. Therefore, evaluating and addressing the environmental impact of energy-related activities is essential to reduce the carbon footprint of the energy sector.

Additionally, focusing on the energy performance of buildings is essential, as buildings account for a significant portion of energy consumption. Implementing energy-efficient design, insulation and technologies can significantly lower energy demands and associated emissions.

Likewise, transport plays a significant role in the energy transition. Transportation is a significant source of GHG emissions, contributing to air pollution and climate change. Encouraging sustainable transport options, such as electric vehicles, public transportation and cycling, will be crucial.

Energy sector

As 75% of EU GHG emissions come from energy use and production, decarbonising the energy sector is a crucial step towards a climate-neutral EU. By adopting sustainable and low-carbon energy sources, such as renewable energy, and improving energy efficiency, the EU can significantly mitigate its carbon footprint.

Promoting and developing cleaner energy sources is a key priority, and achieving this objective will involve revising the current legislation on energy efficiency and renewable energy.

Revision of the Renewable Energy Directive (RED)[163]

Boosting the share of renewables will be essential to reach the climate goals set by the EU. The revised RED will set more ambitious targets, increasing the share of renewables in the energy mix. The new target for 2030 will require that at least 40% of total energy consumption is from renewable energy. Each Member State will be required to contribute by preparing national energy and climate plans. Additionally, the revision will introduce new EU-wide sector-specific sub-targets. Measures for areas such as buildings, industry, heating and cooling, renewable hydrogen, and transport and fuels have their own sub-targets. Furthermore, the new rules will include measures to accelerate permitting procedures of renewable projects.

A provisional political agreement was reached in March 2023, with formal adoption by the EU institutions due soon after.

Revision of the Energy Efficiency Directive (EED)[164]

The revision of the RED alone will not be sufficient to achieve the swift and ambitious energy transition required. Saving energy and reducing its consumption will be equally important. Energy savings are considered the most cost-effective solution for a more climate-friendly energy system. The revision of the EED includes targets for energy consumption, introducing a mandatory target of a 38% reduction in final consumption, which relates to the amount of energy consumed by end users. Under the new rules, Member States will be required to increase their energy savings from 2024 to 2030. Additionally, the public sector will effectively contribute by reducing its annual consumption by 1.9% each year and renovating its buildings to improve their energy performance.

A provisional political agreement was reached in March 2023, with the formal adoption by the EU institutions due soon after.

Revision of the Energy Taxation Directive (ETD)[165]

To facilitate the energy transition, the ETD plays a crucial role by implementing a tax system where the most environmentally harmful fuels are subject to higher taxation. This approach aims to create incentives for producers, users and consumers to embrace sustainable practices.

The revision of the directive seeks to accurately reflect the environmental impact of motor and heating fuels in their pricing. The proposed update primarily concentrates on restructuring the tax rates based on factors such as energy content and environmental performance, rather than solely considering volume. Furthermore, the revision aims to broaden the taxable base by including a wider range of products and eliminating exemptions and reductions, ensuring a more comprehensive and equitable taxation system.

As of June 2023, EU institutions have not yet reached a provisional agreement.

Revision of the Energy Performance of Buildings Directive (EPBD)[166]

The buildings sector is one of the largest energy consumers in Europe and is responsible for more than one third of the EU's GHG emissions. Buildings represent a huge potential for emissions cuts, since 75% of existing buildings are inefficient in terms of energy.

The revision of the EPBD will help make buildings in the EU more efficient. The revised directive sets up new energy efficiency standards for both new constructions and renovated buildings in the EU. Additionally, it sets a long-term target requiring all buildings to be net zero by 2050. The revised directive is constructed around three pillars: new and existing buildings, green energy and electrical infrastructure.

Starting from 2030 (2028 for publicly owned buildings), all new constructions will have to be net zero and must obtain an energy performance certificate. For existing buildings, specific minimum energy performance standards need to be met within certain timelines, depending on whether the building is residential or non-residential. For instance, residential buildings will have to meet a D energy performance class level by 2030 and be net zero by 2050. Some exceptions are obviously provided for specific types of buildings (historical, armed forces, etc.).

Another significant change introduced by the new directive is the requirement for new or renovated buildings to install solar energy infrastructure. The installation timelines for solar energy infrastructure differ based on the building's function (residential or non-residential) and the owner (public entity or private entity), with specific deadlines set between 2027 and 2030. Finally, more charging points have to be installed for electric vehicles or bikes.

Transport

Cars and vans

Cars and vans contribute approximately 15% of total EU CO_2 emissions. To address this issue, a new EU regulation on CO_2 emission standards for cars and vans[167] was implemented, and revised in 2023, imposing emission reduction targets for new cars and vans.

The revised legislation increases the targets for 2030 and sets a new target of achieving 100% reduction in emissions by 2035. This means that all new cars and vans placed on the market in the EU from 2035 onwards should be zero-CO_2 emissions vehicles.

Implementation of the regulation is expected to bring many benefits. First, it will lead to improved air quality and health for citizens. Secondly, consumers should benefit from more affordable net-zero emissions vehicles. The automotive industry will benefit by taking a strong leadership position in the market.

Alternative fuels infrastructure

In addition to the CO_2 emissions standards, the EU has also introduced a new Regulation for the Deployment of Alternative Fuels Infrastructure (AFIR),[168] which repeals the Directive on Deployment of Alternative Fuels Infrastructure. The objective is to ensure the deployment of sufficient infrastructure for the charging or refuelling needs of cars, trucks, planes and ships using alternative fuels, with adequate coverage across the EU.

Currently, the EU estimates that there are approximately 13.4 million alternative fuel cars in the EU, accounting for 5% of the car fleet. This number is expected to grow tenfold by 2050. Therefore, the regulation sets requirements to deploy sufficient electricity recharging and hydrogen refuelling stations for cars, vans and heavy-duty vehicles, from 2025 to 2030. By ensuring a maximum distance between stations, and enough stations in urban nodes, the goal is to provide easy public access and a sufficiently dense network to travel across the EU.

Moreover, the newly developed road infrastructures will have to be consumer-friendly and easily accessible. As for maritime ports, the busiest will have to provide access to shore-side electricity supply for at least 90% of container ships.

In March 2023, the EU institutions reached a political agreement, with formal adoption due to follow soon after.

Aviation and maritime transport

Within the EU's overall emissions from the transport sector, aviation and maritime sectors account for 14.5% and 13.5% respectively. Two proposed regulations, namely ReFuelEU Aviation[169] and FuelEU Maritime,[170] are aiming to promote the use of sustainable fuels in the respective sectors.

In the aviation sector, aircraft fuel suppliers at EU airports will be required to gradually increase the share of sustainable fuels that they distribute. Additionally, EU airports will be required to guarantee the necessary infrastructure for sustainable fuels. To enable consumers to make informed choices, a European Union label for sustainable performance of aircrafts will be implemented.

In the maritime sector, the proposed regulation will require large vessels to reduce the GHG intensity of the energy used on board. They will also be required to connect to onshore power supply for their electrical power needs, unless they employ other zero-emissions technology.

Carbon pricing

Introducing a carbon price in the EU

Introducing a carbon price on the emissions generated by industrial activities serves as an economic signal, internalising the true cost of carbon emissions. By doing so, it provides economic **incentives** for businesses and individuals **to actively reduce their carbon footprint** and transition towards cleaner and more sustainable

alternatives. Moreover, it creates a market-based mechanism that fosters the efficient allocation of resources and encourages innovation in low-carbon technologies.

Without such a price, individuals and businesses would essentially be 'free riding', as they wouldn't bear the true cost of their activities. By setting a price on a given amount of CO_2 emitted, the actual cost of products is accurately reflected in the final price. This fundamental understanding has driven the EU's initiative in establishing an emissions trading market for specific industries. This market-based approach offers flexibility in achieving emission reductions. More comprehensive insights on this approach are detailed below.

However, the introduction of a price on carbon does present some risks. One potential risk is that the costs of production may increase, leading producers and suppliers to consider relocating their activities outside the EU. If the transportation costs of bringing goods into the EU are lower than the carbon price imposed, it becomes economically favourable for them to do so. Consequently, this would result in a shift of GHG emissions from a jurisdiction with carbon constraints to one with fewer or no constraints — commonly referred to as 'carbon leakage'. To prevent a significant transfer of production and emissions, measures have been taken to address this concern. The EU has introduced a border tax – the **Carbon Border Adjustment Mechanism (CBAM)**[171] – to ensure that goods entering the EU are subject to an equal carbon price. This mechanism aims to avoid creating a competitive disadvantage for EU-based industries by levelling the playing field. By implementing the CBAM, the EU intends to discourage carbon leakage and protect domestic industries while also incentivising non-EU producers and suppliers to adopt cleaner practices.

Revision of the EU Emissions Trading System (ETS)[172]

The ETS is a cap and trade mechanism covering certain industrial sectors. It sets a limit or a cap on the total amount of GHG emissions permitted from operators within the system. Over time, this cap is gradually reduced to ensure a decline in global emissions. Operators receive or can purchase emissions allowances, which they can trade with one another. Annually, operators must submit a number of allowances covering their emissions, facing important fines if they do not.

Initially, the ETS framework focused primarily on CO_2 emissions. It encompassed sectors such as electricity and heat generation, energy-intensive industry sectors (e.g. oil refineries, steel work, iron production…) along with aviation in Europe. However, as part of the Fit for 55 package, the EU recently adopted a revision of the ETS. The revision includes several changes.

First, there is an accelerated reduction rate for the cap, demonstrating a more ambitious approach towards emission reductions. Stricter regulations regarding the free allocation of allowances have also been introduced. Furthermore, the scope of the ETS has been expanded to include maritime transport, recognising the significant emissions associated with this sector.

Additionally, a new separate ETS has been introduced specifically targeting the building and road transport sectors. The new ETS now encompasses emissions from fuel combustion in buildings, road transport and other smaller sectors. The system, starting from 2027, is designed to operate in an organised, efficient, and seamless way. Monitoring and reporting emissions will commence in 2025. These updates reflect the EU's commitment to tackling emissions across multiple sectors and driving towards a more sustainable future.

Carbon Border Adjustment Mechanism (CBAM)[173]
Operating as a mechanism to address carbon leakage risks, the **CBAM applies a carbon price to EU imports of specific goods that are considered carbon-intensive**. This includes products such as cement, iron, steel, electricity, hydrogen and fertilisers.

The primary objective is to ensure that imported goods align with EU climate goals, by discouraging carbon-intensive production practices and incentivising the adoption of cleaner industrial practices in non-EU countries. Ultimately, it serves as a measure to promote a level playing field and encourage global partners to adopt sustainable practices in line with the EU's commitment to combat climate change.

The **CBAM holds importers accountable for the carbon emissions associated with the goods they bring into the EU market**. They must obtain certification as declarants. They are required to report annually on the quantity of goods imported into the EU during the previous year, along with the embedded GHG emissions. Based on these reports, declarants must surrender a designated number of certificates. The price of these CBAM certificates is equivalent to the carbon tax.

The CBAM establishes a framework where transparency and reporting play a crucial role in assessing and addressing embedded carbon emissions. It was officially adopted in May 2023, with a transitional phase from October 2023 to December 2025 to ensure gradual implementation.

Circular economy and resource depletion

A fundamental element in attaining EU climate neutrality by 2050 is the decoupling of economic growth from resource use, accompanied by a transition towards circular systems in production and consumption. In 2020, the EU adopted a new **Circular Economy Action Plan** (CEAP),[174] a pillar of the European Green Deal. (See also: *Chapter 7 – From SDG to circular economy.*)

The CEAP represents a comprehensive roadmap for action, encompassing various sectors and policy areas, including waste management, product design, resource efficiency and sustainable consumption.

Waste management
The **Waste Framework Directive**[175] establishes a general framework for managing waste within the EU. It promotes waste prevention, recycling and recovery, rather than disposal. By establishing clear requirements and guidelines, the directive ensures that waste is properly classified, managed and regulated throughout its lifecycle.

One of the key aspects of the directive is the **emphasis on waste prevention**, encouraging measures that reduce the overall generation of waste.

Additionally, the directive sets requirements for waste classification, waste management plans and the establishment of a permit system for waste facilities. It also encourages the reduction of hazardous substances in waste.

The directive is very general and broad, recognising the need for specific regulations and measures tailored to different waste streams and sectors.

Plastic waste

Many legislations have been proposed or updated to address the problem of plastic, one of the main types of waste in the EU (and the rest of the world). Their focus is to promote reuse and refill practices, increase the use of recycled plastics and facilitate the transition to a circular and resource-efficient plastics economy. The EU's plastic strategy includes several specific actions.

A notable initiative is the enactment of the **Single-use Plastic Directive (SUPD)**.[176] It imposes a ban on specific single-use plastics that are the most commonly found in the EU, including cotton bud sticks, beverage stirrers, cups and containers, cigarette butts, hygienic wipes and plastic bags. These items are deemed to have reasonable and affordable sustainable alternatives. For other single-use products, the EU focuses on limiting their use through less-constraining measures such as awareness raising, design requirements, labelling requirements, and waste management and clean-up obligations. The directive came into force in 2021 and is being transposed into national legislation.

Another initiative is the **Packaging and Packaging Waste Regulation** (PPWR), proposed by the European Commission in 2022 as a revision of the Packaging and Packaging Waste Directive (PPWD),[177] which covers both packaging design and packaging waste management. The proposed regulation applies to all types of packaging and packaging waste. It sets stringent requirements for substances in packaging, such as restrictions on lead, cadmium, mercury and hexavalent chromium, and mandates that all packaging be recyclable. Specifically, all packaging should be designed for recyclability by 1 January 2030 and be recyclable on a large scale by 1 January 2035. The proposal also introduces minimum recycled content in plastic packaging, as of 1 January 2030. For instance, single-use plastic beverage bottles would need to have a minimum recycled con-

tent of 30%, with certain exemptions for medical devices. These percentages would be progressively increased over time.

Batteries

Batteries and accumulators are a key technology in the transition to climate neutrality, and to a more circular economy. Global demand for batteries is increasing rapidly and is set to increase 14 times by 2030.

Because of the environmental impact of this exponential growth and in light of new socioeconomic conditions, technological developments, markets and battery usages, the EU proposed a new **Batteries Regulation**, replacing the Batteries Directive. The aim is to make batteries sustainable throughout their entire life cycle, from the sourcing of materials to their collection, recycling and repurposing. It would apply to all types of batteries sold in the EU.

The regulation represents a significant reform and includes more stringent removability and replaceability requirements, as well as marking, labelling, information and supply chain due diligence requirements.

The proposed final text of the regulation was published in 2023.[178]

Right to repair

Three EU initiatives have been proposed, which together aim to cover the full life cycle of goods and jointly deliver on the 'right to repair'.

- **Directive on Common Rules Promoting the Repair of Goods:**[179] focused on the after-sale context; the directive promotes sustainable consumption through repair initiatives, **introducing a 'right to repair' for consumers**. During the legal guarantee period, sellers will have to offer repair for the goods they provide unless it is less expensive to replace the item. Beyond the legal guarantee period, consumers will be granted a new set of rights and tools to make 'repair' easier and more accessible. These include a right to claim repair, a right to information, the provision of an online platform, transparency obligations and quality standards.

OPERATING WITH POSITIVE IMPACT

This directive is complemented by two other proposed pieces of legislation promoting sustainable consumption.

- **Regulation on Ecodesign for Sustainable Products:**[180] promotes the reparability of products from the production phase
- **Directive on Empowering Consumers for the Green Transition:**[181] enable consumers to be informed about the reparability and durability of goods when they purchase them.

Substantiating green claims

The European Union has made greenwashing a priority within the framework of the new CEAP. The EU wants to foster consumer confidence and protect consumers, allowing them to make informed purchasing decisions.

To this end, in March 2023, the EU proposed a **Directive on Green Claims,**[182] seeking to ensure that environmental labels and claims are credible, comparable, verifiable and reliable. The directive would establish a level playing field for products through standardised criteria for green claims and labels. It would establish clear criteria for companies, making them accountable for substantiating their green claims and labels, defining requirements for such claims and labels, and implementing a robust third-party verification process. Additionally, the proposal includes rules on the governance of environmental labelling systems to ensure transparency and reliability. The focus of this proposal is voluntary claims made by businesses to consumers.

Ecodesign

By setting clear and robust ecodesign requirements, the EU aims to promote the development and availability of more sustainable products throughout the market. The aforementioned proposed **Regulation on Ecodesign for Sustainable Products** replaces the existing Directive on Ecodesign.[183] The regulation outlines a framework for establishing ecodesign requirements for specific product categories, with the overarching goal of significantly enhancing their circularity, energy performance, and overall environmental sustainability. It will set performance and information standards for nearly all types of physical goods that are made available on the EU market.

Under this regulation, a wide range of requirements will be implemented, including requirements on product durability, reusability and reparability, as well as energy and resource efficiency. Additionally, consideration will be given to incorporating recycled content, reducing carbon and environmental footprints, and other relevant factors. To date, EU institution negotiations on the proposal have not yet begun.

Biodiversity restoration

The European Green Deal includes a biodiversity strategy — a comprehensive plan to restore biodiversity by 2030. It encompasses specific commitments and actions aimed at **safeguarding nature and reversing the degradation of ecosystems**. The strategy builds upon existing nature laws and serves as a key framework for protecting and restoring biodiversity within the European Union.

The proposed **EU Nature Restoration Law**[184] reflects the urgent need for collective action to combat biodiversity loss and promote sustainable land and sea management practices across the EU. It combines an overarching restoration objective for the long-term recovery of nature in the EU's land and sea areas with binding restoration targets for specific habitats and species.

EU countries are expected to submit National Restoration Plans to the Commission within two years of the regulation coming into force, showing how they will deliver on the targets. They will also be responsible for monitoring and reporting on their progress. The ambition is for the measures to **cover at least 20% of the EU's land and sea areas by 2030, and ultimately restore all ecosystems in need of recovery by 2050.** This includes various sectors such as forests, agriculture, urban areas and other ecosystems requiring attention.

The proposal stirred political reactions in Member States. Some countries expressed concerns about the challenging timeframe, deeming it to be extremely demanding. There were also claims that some Member States were not comfortable with the scope of the proposal.[185] Despite the concerns, the law was passed by the EU parliament in July 2023.

Forests, deforestation and land use

Forests play a crucial role in maintaining human health, and it is essential to strike a balance between the environmental, social and economic aspects of sustainable forest management. The **Regulation on Land Use, Land Use Change and Forestry (LULUCF)**,[186] is a key component of the EU's environmental strategy.

The regulation, revised in 2023, establishes rules for emissions reductions and carbon removals in the LULUCF sector, which encompasses activities related to land use, land conversion and forest management. Carbon removals refer to the process by which forests and land absorb CO_2 from the atmosphere, making them invaluable in mitigating GHG emissions. In fact, EU forests alone absorb approximately 10% of the EU's total GHG emissions.

Under the previous rules, emissions from land use and land-related activities had to be offset by an equivalent removal of CO_2 within the sector. The revised rules increase the EU-wide target for CO_2 removals by 150%, by 2030, and set binding targets to be implemented at national level. The process will unfold in two phases: the first phase, until 2025, will bring minimal changes, while the second phase (2026–2030) will see both the EU and national targets becoming binding and enforceable.

Tsunami of E-related legislation

It's a significant challenge for Member States to transpose environmental directives and apply environmental regulations. The process of transposition often requires coordination among different government departments and agencies, further adding to the complexity. Meeting the tight transposition deadlines can be demanding, requiring swift action and efficient collaboration between stakeholders. Failure to comply with the transposition obligations can result in infringement procedures and legal consequences.

The EU has launched its ESG transition, taking the initiative on many fronts, as demonstrated by the many legislation examples detailed above. The number of new environmental regulations is only increasing, and the implications they will have will require a lot of adaptation, both for businesses and individuals. **The challenge will therefore be for national authorities to keep up with this wave of new legislation**.

S from a legal perspective

The social aspect of ESG plays a pivotal role in shaping responsible and sustainable business practices. There is a broad legal framework dealing with these matters, including international, European and national or local legislation, covering human rights, equality and well-being.

Human rights

One of the multitude of factors covered within the social spectrum is human rights, including the **respect of (minimal) labour and employment standards, the abolishment of modern slavery and the right to dignity**. For many people, respect for the human rights of workers seems obvious, but unfortunately the data[187] shows otherwise. This section explores the European legislative framework and the importance of incorporating human rights into your ESG strategy, to create added value not only for society but also for your business and towards stakeholders.

Human rights as a foundation of legal instruments
Human rights are a fundamental part of (European) legislation and are embedded in various legal instruments at both the national and supranational level. Both the Council of Europe and the European Union play a compelling role in safeguarding human rights within its Member States.[188]

Although the first international standards for workers' protection date back to the beginning of the 20th century, it's fair to say that the concept of human rights was first introduced with the **Universal Declaration of Human Rights** proclaimed by the General Assembly of the United Nations on 10th December 1948.

In 1950, this was translated into **the European Convention on Human Rights**[189] — a core human rights treaty concluded within the Council of Europe. Although the treaty has a broad scope in terms of human (civil and political) rights, it also includes various rights that we hold high in the workplace today, such as the prohibition on forced labour and slavery, freedom of conviction and religion, freedom of assembly and association and the prohibition on discrimination. As the counterpart of the European Convention on Human Rights, the **European Social Charter**[190] (also referred to as the Social Constitution of Europe) was adopted in 1961 (revised in 1996) within the framework of the Council of Europe. It is a treaty that guarantees a broad range of everyday social and economic human rights, mainly related to employment, such as the right to fair remuneration, the right to safe and healthy working conditions, etc. The Charter gives special attention to the protection of vulnerable persons such as elderly people, children, people with disabilities and migrants, and emphasises the need to guarantee the rights without discrimination.

Additionally, the **Charter of Fundamental Rights of the European Union** (CFR)[191] came into force in 2009, and consolidates the most fundamental personal freedoms and rights enjoyed by citizens of the European Union, including workers' right to information and consultation within their organisation, the right to bargain and act collectively, protection against unjustified dismissal, fair and just working conditions and the prohibition of child labour.

These international instruments, as well as related national or local legislation, are familiar in most businesses and guide us through the workplace on a daily basis.

Human rights are also explicitly embedded in numerous European 'sustainability' directives and regulations. (See also: *Chapter 9 – Reporting*.)

- The **Sustainable Finance Disclosure Regulation** (SFDR)[192] aims to improve transparency in relation to sustainable investments products and sustainability claims made by financial market participants (banks, insurers, asset managers and investment firms). The SFDR consists of disclosure requirements at organisational, service and product levels. The SFDR explicitly labels respect for social and employee matters, as well as human rights, as 'sustainability factors' that these financial actors need to take into consideration when making investment decisions and disclose how they have done so.

- The **Corporate Sustainability Reporting Directive** (CSRD)[193] is very relevant to the S. It substantially increases reporting requirements on companies' progress towards a sustainable future. These rules ensure that stakeholders have access to the information they need to assess investment risks arising from sustainability issues. The directive prescribes that companies within its scope are (amongst others) required to report on (i) equal treatment and opportunities for all (ii) working conditions and (iii) respect for the human rights, fundamental freedoms, and democratic principles and standards established in various international standards. It is without a doubt that this will encourage a change in business behaviour by ensuring that companies are transparent about their sustainability endeavours. Avoiding human rights violations – not only by companies but also throughout their entire supply chain – has become a hot topic on the European legislative agenda. A study[194] conducted for the European Commission focused on due diligence requirements through the supply chain to identify, prevent, mitigate and account for human rights abuses. It identifies market practices and perceptions regarding regulatory options and has shown that voluntary measures have proved to be insufficient, demonstrating the need for a legislative initiative on mandatory human rights and environmental due diligence.

- To provide companies with a framework to make the necessary changes in their behaviour, in 2022 the European Commission published the proposal for a **Corporate Sustainability Due Diligence Directive (CS3D)** which is also key for the S.[195] It would require some larger companies to conduct due diligence on their own activities and those of their suppliers, and take responsibility for human rights abuses (and environmental harm) throughout their global value chains. The directive goes far beyond existing legislation at national level, as in many cases national law has a focus on specific human rights violations (e.g. in the UK where it is specifically aimed at modern slavery[196]). If formally adopted (in 2024), European Member States will have two years to implement the CS3D into national legislation.

Besides legal instruments at the supranational level, each country has its own constitution and legal framework that includes provisions for the protection of human rights. These documents differ among countries but generally incorporate broad human rights standards and may provide additional protections beyond what is guaranteed at the supranational level. It is beyond doubt that there is a real influx of human rights legislation, imposing few, if any, new standards, but rather transparency and reporting obligations.

Enforcement of human rights embedded in various legal instruments is overseen by courts at both national and supranational level. On a supranational level, the European Court of Human Rights, the Court of Justice of the European Union and to a certain extent the EU Global Human Rights Sanction Regime (HRSR) play a significant role in protecting and interpreting human rights issues.

Legal framework for equal pay

The EU has taken substantial steps towards promoting social responsibility and equal pay through the adoption of various legal instruments, such as the **Equal Pay Directive**.[197] However, past non-binding recommendations did not achieve the objective of more effective implementation of the equal pay principle through pay transparency: **women in the EU today still earn (on average) 13% less than their male counterparts**, and little or no progress has been made on this in the past decade.[198] The **EU Pay Transparency Directive**,[199] adopted in 2023, emphasises the need for equal pay practices and for fostering a socially responsible approach to remuneration practices.

The directive aims to implement concrete measures to guarantee equal pay for equal work between women and men, and to eliminate the gender pay gap.

The legislation on equal pay for equal work was initially limited to the principle of non-discrimination on the grounds of gender. While the focus remains on gender pay disparity, employers may now face increased liability if analysis shows that the subjects of pay discrimination are also disproportionately members of other protected classes based on race, ethnicity, religion, etc.

The new directive introduces **minimum standards on pay transparency**, to empower employees and enable them to claim their right to equal pay.

(i) The right to information on the initial pay level or range to be paid to the future worker, provided prior to employment and even prior to the interview, without the employee needing to request it. The employer is prohibited from asking prospective workers about their previous pay history to avoid continuous discrimination (i.e. discrimination carried over from past employment).

(ii) The right for employees to receive information on their individual pay level and the average levels of pay, broken down by gender, for categories of workers doing the same work or work of equal value, and on the – objective and gender-neutral – criteria used to define their pay and career progression.

(iii) Employers with more than 250 employees need to report annually on the gender pay gap and are required to carry out a joint pay assessment with the employee representatives, should the pay gap reporting reflect a difference of min. 5% in average pay levels between female and male employees that cannot be justified by objective, gender-neutral criteria.[200]

If, based on the above (and/or other facts), an employee claims that they have suffered gender pay discrimination, it will be up to the employer to prove that they didn't violate the EU rules on equal pay and pay transparency, rather than up to the employee to prove discrimination (shift of burden of proof). If the employer cannot prove this, the employee can receive compensation, including full recovery of back pay and related bonuses or payments in kind.

Once the Pay Transparency Directive is published in the EU's Official Journal, Member States will have up to three years to transpose the directive and the new rules on pay transparency into their national legislation.

Both at supranational and national level, **equal pay legislation** has immense significance within the framework of ESG legislation, as it **underpins the principles of diversity, equity and inclusion**.

By ensuring fair compensation for all employees, organisations demonstrate their commitment to social responsibility and contribute to a more inclusive society.

Legal framework for well-being at work

Every year, 2.78 million people die as a result of work-related illness. 374 million non-fatal occupational accidents occur.[201] These figures are staggering and prove that there still is a long way to go when it comes to implementing health and safety standards in the workplace.

Meanwhile, the expectations of (potential) employees – and especially Gen Z workers – regarding criteria such as flexible working hours, hybrid work, etc., are notoriously rapidly increasing. A recent survey shows that lack of work-life balance (2nd) and no remote work options (5th) are both in the top five reasons why young talent is leaving their employer.[202]

To provide a legislative framework regarding health and safety standards at the workplace, several directives, guidelines and standards on well-being at work have been published in the past decades.[203] The most important is the **1989 Framework Directive**,[204] which sets out the general principles. This directive aims to establish an equal level of health and safety for the benefit of all workers and obliges employers to take appropriate preventive measures to make work safer and healthier.

Locally specific legislation
Given that broad legislative instruments need to be converted into national legislation, the brunt of the responsibility still lies at national level with the Member States.

Moreover, national legislation often goes beyond what is determined at supranational level. Companies should therefore approach this topic and **implement their well-being policy starting from a local compliance perspective**. For example, whereas the Framework Directive merely states that the employees responsible to carry out activities for the protection and prevention of occupational risks should have *"the necessary capabilities"*[205], it is the national legislation that would explicitly list the conditions that must be met.

Compliance
The fragmented and country specific nature of the legislation on well-being at work may make it more difficult for employers to be fully compliant. However, organisations that invest in compliance with labour standards and a safe and healthy workplace clearly show investors, the public and other stakeholders that they prioritise social responsibility, integrity and risk management — leading to sustainable long-term value creation.

Failure to comply with the local provisions regarding well-being at work can have terrible human consequences. Even minor failures can negatively impact employee satisfaction and potentially damage company reputation. Compliance failures can also result in severe fines and, in very exceptional cases, imprisonment.

The importance of compliance has only increased since the introduction of the aforementioned NFRD and the CSRD. The latter explicitly states that companies' sustainability reporting must include information on:

> *"working conditions, including secure employment, working time, adequate wages, social dialogue, freedom of association, existence of works councils, collective bargaining, including the proportion of workers covered by collective agreements, the information, consultation and participation rights of workers, work-life balance, and health and safety."*[206]

The combination of the newly imposed transparency requirements, together with the ever-increasing expectations of all stakeholders, ensures that well-being at work will become a key element in every company's ESG strategy. It will be crucial, yet not straightforward, to closely monitor all national legislation in this regard and to convert it into a solid well-being policy and appropriate action plan at company level, ideally together with representative bodies within the company.

G from a legal perspective

Within the sustainability context, effective governance serves as **the foundation for ethical conduct, accountability and transparency within** companies, guiding their actions and decisions towards long-term sustainability. By examining the role of law in governance, this section aims to provide companies with the knowledge and tools necessary to build robust governance structures, comply with legal requirements and foster a culture of ethical decision making that aligns with sustainable development goals.

The legal framework for the G in the CSRD

The CSRD principles are supplemented by the so-called ESRS (European Sustainability Reporting Standards) developed by EFRAG, which define on a very detailed legal style level the governance-related reporting requirements under the CSRD. A detailed comment on the G related to ESRS goes beyond the high-level nature of this section; moreover at this time the standards are still in draft and subject to change.[207] The ESRS G1 is a must-read for the responsible legal counsels to understand the legal level of detail of the requested reporting and the impact on, for example, the liability of their boards.

This component of ESRS will require information regarding the supervisory bodies and overall management of the company, including remuneration, and a general description of the risk management and internal control processes and how they enable the directors to exercise their responsibility to oversee the undertaking.

It further aims to disclose anti-competitive behaviour that can limit companies from freely growing (such as fixed prices, lobbying activities and corruption activities).

The importance of G in the Corporate Sustainability Due Diligence Directive

Directors play a pivotal role in overseeing and guiding the organisation's activities, with a fiduciary duty towards shareholders and stakeholders. The concept of director liability, particularly regarding the duty of care, has evolved significantly, reflecting the growing emphasis on responsible business practices and the integration of ESG factors. Other than the duty of care, directors have a duty of loyalty and a duty to act in good faith. Recent cases have shown that **directors are increasingly being held personally liable for not handling climate-related risks well**. The aforementioned Green Claims Directive initiative will naturally weigh in on that trend.

High profile liability cases receive a lot of media attention. In the UK for example, directors of a multinational energy group are being sued, in their personal capacity, by one of their activist minority shareholders, an environmental organisation. The claim alleges that the company's energy transition strategy is *"fundamentally flawed"* and puts the company at risk as the world transitions toward net zero, in breach of the directors' fiduciary duties to the company. It also alleges that its Board is failing to comply with a ruling of another court requiring it to pursue a strategy to arrive at net zero for the company's group-wide carbon emissions by 2050.

This is just one case that is part of a wider movement of shareholder activism on climate and environmental matters, and falls right within the core of good governance practices.

Traditionally, the duty of care imposed on directors was primarily focused on financial performance and the protection of shareholders' interests. Directors were expected to exercise reasonable care, skill and diligence in their decision-making processes, with a primary goal of maximising shareholder value. This duty primarily involved making informed decisions, conducting thorough due diligence and seeking expert advice when necessary.

However, as societal expectations further evolve, the concept of duty of care could over time be expanded to encompass broader responsibilities, including the consideration of ESG factors and stakeholder interests. The current draft of the CS3D (June 2023) states that directors have a duty of care to *"systemically integrate sustainability matters in their decisions."* It introduces duties for the directors of the EU companies covered. These include setting up and overseeing the implementation of the sustainability due diligence processes and integrating due diligence into the corporate strategy. In addition, when fulfilling their duty to act in the best interest of the company, directors must take into account the human rights, climate change and environmental consequences of their decisions.[208]

It remains to be seen how these crucial matters will be dealt with in the final published version.

Such an expansion of responsibilities aligns with the principle that the long-term success of a company is intricately tied to its relationships with stakeholders and society. Directors could be required to exercise care and diligence in understanding and managing these stakeholder relationships, ensuring that the company's activities do not result in harm or negative externalities.

The evolving duty of care presents legal implications and challenges for directors. Non-compliance with ESG regulations, inadequate consideration of stakeholder interests, or failure to manage ESG risks can expose directors to liability, including lawsuits, regulatory enforcement actions and personal financial consequences. The challenge lies in navigating the complex landscape of ESG regulations and understanding the varying legal expectations across jurisdictions. Directors must also grapple with balancing conflicting interests and determining the appropriate trade-offs between short-term profitability and long-term sustainability.

Director liability on ESG issues can be examined from both internal and external perspectives. Internally, directors can face liability arising from their own actions or omissions in fulfilling their fiduciary duties regarding ESG matters. Externally, directors may also face liability stemming from legal obligations and expectations imposed by external stakeholders, such as shareholders, regulatory bodies, or industry standards, which are becoming increasingly proactive.

Expansion of directors' responsibilities

Directors are more and more being required to have a comprehensive understanding of relevant ESG risks and opportunities and to ensure that the company's strategies and operations align with sustainable practices. They are also required to stay informed about evolving ESG regulations, industry best practices and emerging risks associated with environmental and social impacts.

The key role of legal counsels regarding the G

Within a company, different counsels, such as the general counsel, corporate counsel and the commercial counsel, play distinct yet interconnected roles in addressing the legal dimensions of ESG. These counsels work in tandem to ensure compliance, manage risks and guide the company's ESG strategies.

General counsel

The general counsel acts as the primary legal advisor to the company, providing guidance on a wide range of legal matters. In the context of ESG, the general counsel takes a holistic approach, overseeing and coordinating the efforts of both the corporate counsel and the commercial counsel. They serve as the strategic leader, ensuring that the company's legal function aligns with its overall ESG goals and objectives.

The general counsel's role includes monitoring changes in ESG regulations, industry standards and emerging best practices. They stay updated on evolving legal requirements and help the company adapt its policies and practices accordingly. The general counsel also collaborates with external stakeholders, such as regulators, industry associations and NGOs, to stay informed about the latest ESG developments and to participate in shaping regulatory frameworks.

Furthermore, the general counsel plays a critical role in fostering a culture of legal and ethical responsibility within the company. They provide guidance on ethical decision making, ensure transparency and accountability, and foster a culture of integrity throughout the organisation. By integrating ESG considerations into the company's overarching legal strategy, the general counsel helps drive sustainable and responsible practices.

Some examples of questions for the general counsel to consider include:

1. Has your company identified the applicable reporting legislation?

2. Have the responsibilities relating to ESG reporting been established?

3. Does your company have an ESG policy in place?

4. Are there governance controls in place to give the board confidence in signing off on ESG disclosures?

Corporate counsel

The corporate counsel holds an important role in overseeing legal matters related to the company's corporate governance and compliance. In the realm of ESG, the corporate counsel is responsible for ensuring that the company adheres to relevant laws and regulations. They play a key role in developing and implementing – under the supervision of the general counsel – the policies and procedures to ensure the company's compliance with ESG-related legal obligations. Those obligations will also impact any ESG-related group restructurings the company takes part in, as long-term value creation is the ultimate goal.

The corporate counsel also plays a pivotal role in addressing the legal aspects of corporate sustainability and responsible business practices. They collaborate with internal stakeholders, such as the executive team and the board of directors, to establish governance structures that promote ESG integration. This includes developing codes of conduct, overseeing internal controls and facilitating ESG-related training programmes for employees. By working closely with other departments, such as Human Resources and Risk Management, the corporate counsel ensures that ESG considerations are effectively embedded in the company's culture and operations.

More importantly, the corporate counsels should keep oversight on the interconnections between EU, national and other (e.g. the US SEC sustainability standards) ESG-related obligations, and mind their scope of application in time, geography and activity.

Commercial/contract counsel

The commercial/contract counsel focuses on the legal aspects of the company's commercial activities, including contracts, procurement, transactions and relationships with external parties. In the context of ESG, the commercial counsel plays a critical role in negotiating and drafting contracts that reflect the company's commitment to sustainability and responsible business practices. They review and assess supplier agreements, distribution contracts and partnership agreements, to ensure alignment with ESG principles, such as ethical sourcing, environmental standards and social impact. New requirements under the CS3D make it more important than ever for companies to ensure that they are aware of the impact of their operations across the entire supply chain, as embedded in strategic sourcing contracts.

The commercial counsel also evaluates and advises on the legal risks associated with business activities. This includes assessing the potential environmental and social impacts of new ventures, conducting due diligence on suppliers and business partners, and identifying legal risks related to reputational harm or non-compliance with ESG standards. By integrating ESG considerations into commercial contracts and risk assessments, the Commercial Counsel helps mitigate legal and reputational risks, protects the company's interests and strengthens its commitment to sustainable practices.

> Governance in ESG is not limited to its direct legal implications. It permeates the entire organisation, influencing company culture, values and long-term sustainability. Through robust governance structures, companies can foster ethical decision making, stakeholder engagement, and responsible risk management. Within this, the collaboration of the different legal counsels – general, corporate and commercial – is vital to ensure legal compliance, manage risks and guide the company's ESG strategies.

Afterword

7 takeaways on ESG business transformation

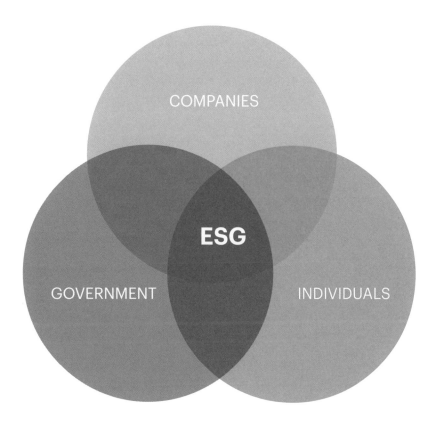

For all of our ESG efforts to be successful we need more symbiosis between what companies are doing, what governments initiate and how individuals try to contribute.

Too often, ESG is seen as a limiting factor that will only make everything more expensive. But – accepting that we need to adapt anyway – when done right, it will be beneficial to all stakeholders and provide us with a more sustainable world to live in.

Unfortunately, many of today's efforts are standalone, either because they are merely local or because they benefit the climate but don't take into account the consequences for local communities (E without S). Our ambition should be to find **solutions that cover all bases and unite all members of society, giving them an inspiring vision for the future**.

We close this book with seven ideas considering what this might mean.

1. A combination of solutions will create more resilient societies

If we want to make real progress, then no single solution will be sufficient. Our ever-increasing knowledge will provide us with multiple options to deal with our environmental, social and governance challenges. If we apply a mix of solutions, then we will be less dependent on the sustainable availability of any single solution. Even if not all solutions are equally 'perfect', it's better to invest in multiple improvements and spread the risks involved.

The traditional example is the gradual replacement of combustion engine vehicles by zero-emissions alternatives. By only investing in electric vehicles, we become dependent on the success of this single option, not knowing whether this is sufficiently scalable to replace the entire existing combustion engine fleet. Therefore, including hydrogen technology and even e-fuels as alternatives puts us in a better position to reduce emissions at full scale in a timely manner.

2. Don't swap one non-sustainable dependency for another one

For many decades, Europe has maintained the illusion of being a welfare region, while it depended on cheap defence (US), cheap energy (Russia, Middle East), cheap labour and products (China) and low inflation (and thus cheap money). A lack of investment has put us in a difficult situation as we arrive at a culmination point where all these cheap resources gradually disappear.

We will therefore need to invest in a more sustainable but also a more self-sufficient future for coming generations. And this includes making choices. If we discover vast reserves of rare earth materials in the north of Sweden, then this may require (polluting) mining activity to access these materials. But not doing so will simply shift our dependency for cheap energy to another dependency on batteries, solar panels or wind turbines. We will therefore need to make choices that combine self sufficiency with staying connected to our partners in the global economy. And yes, that will require making a compromise from time to time.

3. Well-being, flexibility and inclusion can enrich labour gratification

In essence, we are all looking for happiness; being happy with the work we do is an important contributor to that happiness. Fortunately, many employers have found that increased attention to the well-being of their people contributes to their success in the long run. And Covid-19 has taught us that working from anywhere is possible for many activities, increasing the level of flexibility.

Meanwhile, the battle for talent continues. This, however, has an upside, if it facilitates inclusion in the workplace. Where employees may have been reluctant to welcome colleagues perceived as 'outsiders', they are now far more open, understanding that the alternative is that they will have to work harder and enjoy less flexibility.

4. Rules and codes are useless when not properly implemented

Over time, we have seen a lot of new legislation within each of the ESG domains. Lots of new rules related to climate change, labour protection or good governance. And there's no lack of new initiatives on the way. We can expect much more legislative change in the coming years.

But how can all these rules help if they're not properly implemented? It's not because you are compliant in theory that you're compliant in practice. What do all your social regulations achieve if you maintain a toxic company culture? And how does your corporate governance code help you to avoid liability, if your committees fail to pick up on what's actually going on? We often talk about greenwashing in the E space, but the risk is just as real in the S and the G. We should be ready to walk the talk right across the board.

5. A solid data ecosystem prevents ESG reporting becoming a burden

It's clear, as shown in Chapter 9, that non-financial reporting will gain importance, and that being able to collect and use the underlying data is essential. Investing in appropriate processes and systems to map a company's data will therefore be of paramount importance.

Given that complete, timely and insightful reporting is also increasingly being used by rating agencies, investors and the like to assess whether a company is a good investment, there are sufficient incentives to make this happen. Moreover, both clients and suppliers will also be asking for this information, to fulfil their own reporting requirements.

6. Don't let ESG transformation add to disparity

Take a wide view; consider the broader societal consequences of changes. For example, to meet emissions standards, a huge number of houses (and offices) will need to be refurbished to become more energy neutral. This will require significant investment, which not everybody will be able to afford.

There's an increasing risk that only those with more means will still be able to afford their own house, while everyone else is being pushed onto the rental market. A mix of fair government policy and impact investing will be required to ensure a proper balance is found that still allows for equal opportunity in the housing market.

7. Embed and enhance dialogue to counter further polarisation

Communication will be key every step of the way. Policymakers need to make sure they include everyone, explaining the need but also the benefits of proposed or imposed changes. Investing in dialogue to strengthen mutual respect and understanding is much needed in a world where polarisation is at an all-time high.

We maintain that balanced and supported progress will lead to better results than blind and repressive changes, which are forced upon a large group that's already discontented. We will only tackle polarisation if we find and apply ways to reconnect and strengthen the societal tissue. Then and only then will we build a more sustainable society.

Companies have a central role to play in the ESG transition. Given that across the globe they are generally more trusted than governments, companies are in a unique position to lead the way in each of the ESG domains. In doing so, they will not only ensure their own continued relevance for their stakeholders, but also contribute to the sustainability of society as a whole.

We hope this book will contribute, if only in a very small way, to helping companies find and take a road towards a more sustainable future. Much of the content is of course transient and will continue to evolve in the coming years. We therefore plan to update the book from time to time, to ensure its continued relevance.

The journey is far from over, but as the saying goes, *"If you want to go quickly, go alone. If you want to go far, go together."* So join us. Together we can go further...

Acknowledgements

Neither of us would be able to do our jobs, let alone find the time to put together this book, without the continuous support of our respective families. We owe them a debt of gratitude for their patience while we were once again not available to spend time with them, eager as we both were to pursue the journey this book represents. A journey of helping companies navigate the complexities of the many ESG-related challenges they need to overcome in order to have a positive impact on the world in which they operate.

We are also very grateful to our co-authors and contributors, without whom we would not have been able to complete this endeavor successfully. It was their expertise in the wide range of relevant areas that allowed us to put together such a comprehensive guide. Our heartfelt gratitude goes out to all of them (their names can be found at the start of this book). We are privileged to be surrounded by such talented individuals.

We extend our sincere gratitude to Thomas Leysen, whose insightful and inspiring foreword not only captures the urgency of ESG transformation, but also his own unwavering commitment to ethical and sustainable business practices. Thank you, Thomas, for lending your expertise and credibility to this endeavour.

We also owe a special thanks to Fiona McNamara. Although our thoughts on where we wanted to go with this story were clear, and our co-authors and contributors did their utmost to provide valuable content, Fiona was invaluable in turning our initial scribblings into the book we are able to present here. When so many people provide written content, it is essential to have an experienced writer to turn the initial manuscript into a consistent and highly readable publication. Thank you for this, Fiona.

And then there is of course the entire process of chasing the authors, liaising with the publisher, considering the look and feel, and overall ensuring there is a book at the end of the journey. For these efforts, we want to thank Julie Dejonckheere, Leni Smits and Saskia Rademakers.

This book is a powerful reminder of what can be achieved through collaboration and reminds us of the old African proverb *"If you want to go fast, go alone, if you want to go far, go together."*

Appendix 1 — ESG software vendor comparison

Table 8 – ESG software vendor comparison: 'Reporting and Disclosures' and 'Data Management and Analysis'.[209]

	Reporting and Disclosures						Data Management and Analysis			
	Voluntary Frameworks	Regulated & Mandated Frameworks	Materiality assessment	Workflows & Auditability	Industry-Specific Functionality	Engagement Tools	Data Acquisition & Tagging	Performance Management	Industry Benchmarking	Data Quality Enhancement
Alcumus	◑	◑	○	◕	◔	◑	◑	◑	○	◔
APlanet	◕	◕	◑	●	○	◑	◕	◕	○	◑
Archer Integrated Risk Management	◕	◕	◑	●	◔	◕	◕	◑	◔	◑
Assent Compliance	◑	◔	○	◕	◑	◕	◕	◑	◑	◑
Benchmark Gensuite	●	◑	◑	●	○	◑	◕	●	◕	◑
Clarity AI	◑	●	◑	◕	◕	◔	◕	◕	◕	●
Conservice ESG	◑	◔	◔	◔	◕	◔	◑	◑	◔	◔
Cority	●	◑	◕	◕	◔	◑	◑	●	◕	◕
DevonWay	◑	◑	○	◕	○	◑	◕	◑	○	◑
Diginex	●	◔	◔	◕	◔	◔	◑	◑	◔	◑
Diligent Corporation	●	◕	◔	●	◔	◕	◕	◑	◑	◑
DNV	◕	◑	◑	◕	○	◑	◕	◑	◔	◑
Enablon	●	◔	◕	●	◔	◕	◕	●	◕	◕
FigBytes	●	◑	◑	●	◔	●	◕	◕	◑	◕
Greenomy	◔	●	○	●	◕	◕	●	●	◑	◕
Health & Safety Institute (HSI)	◔	○	○	◑	○	◑	◑	◔	○	○
IBM	●	●	◑	●	◑	◑	◕	●	◑	●
Intelex	◕	◔	●	◕	◔	◑	◕	◕	◕	◑
IsoMetrix	●	◑	◑	◕	◔	◑	◕	◕	○	◑
Measurabl	◑	◑	○	◔	◕	◑	◕	◕	◑	◔

MESA (Mesa Cloud)	●	◐	◐	◕	◔	◕	◕	◕	◔	◐
Nasdaq	●	◕	◐	●	◐	●	◕	◕	◔	◐
NAVEX Global	●	◕	◔	◕	◔	◐	●	◕	◐	◐
Novisto	●	●	◔	●	◔	◔	●	◕	◕	●
OneStream	◕	◐	◐	●	○	◐	◕	●	◔	◐
OneTrust	◕	◕	◐	●	○	◐	◕	◐	◔	◕
Ortec Finance	○	◐	○	○	◕	○	◕	●	○	○
Position Green	●	◕	○	●	◐	◐	◕	◕	◔	◐
ProcessMAP	◕	◕	◐	◕	◕	◐	◕	●	◕	◐
Quentic	◕	◐	◕	◕	○	◐	◕	◕	○	◐
SAI360	◕	◕	◐	●	○	◕	◕	◕	◔	◕
Salesforce	◐	◔	○	●	◔	◕	◕	◕	◔	◕
SAP	◕	◕	○	◕	○	◐	◕	●	◔	◕
ServiceNow	◕	◐	◕	●	○	◐	◕	●	◐	◐
Sphera	●	◕	◐	●	◔	◔	●	◕	◕	◕
UL Solutions	●	●	◕	●	◕	◐	◕	◕	◔	◐
VelocityEHS	◕	◐	●	◕	◔	◔	◕	●	◐	●
WayCarbon	◕	◐	○	●	◐	◔	◕	◕	◐	◔
Workiva	●	●	◕	●	◔	◕	●	◕	○	◐

No demonstrated evidence	○
Some product marketing	◔
Some evidence of functionality	◐
OOTB demonstrated functionality	◕
Market-leading functionality, with differentiated offering	●

Appendix 2 — List of relevant sources

Policies

UN 17 SDGs
sdgs.un.org/goals

EU Green Deal
commission.europa.eu/strategy-and-policy/
priorities-2019-2024/european-green-deal_en

Fit for 55
www.consilium.europa.eu/en/policies/green-deal/fit-for-
55-the-eu-plan-for-a-green-transition/

Carbon Border Adjustment Mechanism
taxation-customs.ec.europa.eu/carbon-border-
adjustment-mechanism_en

Circular Economy Action Plan
environment.ec.europa.eu/strategy/circular-economy-
action-plan_en

Corporate Sustainability Due Diligence Directive
ec.europa.eu/commission/presscorner/detail/en/
IP_22_1145

EU Corporate Sustainability Reporting Directive
eur-lex.europa.eu/legal-content/EN/TXT/?uri=
CELEX:32022L2464

EU Taxonomy
finance.ec.europa.eu/sustainable-finance/tools-and-
standards/eu-taxonomy-sustainable-activities_en

Inflation Reduction Act Guidebook
www.whitehouse.gov/cleanenergy/inflation-reduction-
act-guidebook/

Frameworks and data

Global Reporting Initiative
www.globalreporting.org/

Sustainability Accounting Standards Board
sasb.org/

Science Based Targets Initiative
sciencebasedtargets.org/

Task Force on Climate-related Financial Disclosures
www.fsb-tcfd.org/

Greenhouse Gas Protocol
ghgprotocol.org/

Intergovernmental Panel on Climate Change
www.ipcc.ch/

ISO 14001
www.iso.org/iso-14001-environmental-management.html

World Economic Forum
www.weforum.org/

Carbon Disclosure Project
www.cdp.net/en

Ellen MacArthur Foundation
ellenmacarthurfoundation.org/

Our World in Data
ourworldindata.org/

Glossary

Abbreviations

ABAC risk	Anti-Bribery & Corruption risk
CBAM	Carbon Border Adjustment Mechanism
CDP	Carbon Disclosure Project
CEAP	Circular Economy Action Plan
CS3D	Corporate Sustainability Due Diligence Directive
CSR	Corporate social responsibility
CSRD	Corporate Sustainability Reporting Directive
ESRS	European Sustainability Reporting Standards
ETS	EU Emissions Trading System
GAAP	Generally Accepted Accounting Principles
GHG	Greenhouse gas
GRI	Global Reporting Initiative
IFRS	International Financial Reporting Standards
IPCC	Intergovernmental Panel on Climate Change
IRA	US Inflation Reduction Act
NFRD	Non-Financial Reporting Directive
PE	Private equity
SASB	Sustainability Accounting Standards Board
SBTi	Science Based Targets Initiative
SDG	Sustainable development goals
SFDR	Sustainable Finance Disclosure Regulation
TCFD	Task Force on Climate-Related Financial Disclosures

Glossary

Carbon neutral
Having a balance between emitting carbon and absorbing carbon from the atmosphere in carbon sinks — i.e. any system that absorbs more carbon than it emits (soil, forests, oceans).

Climate TRACE
Climate TRACE (Tracking Real-Time Atmospheric Carbon Emissions): an independent group that monitors and publishes GHG emissions.

Digital product passports (DPP)
A tool for collecting and sharing product data throughout its entire lifecycle, used to illustrate a product's sustainability, environmental and recyclability attributes.

Double materiality analysis
Analysis based on the evaluation of both (1) the impact of an organisation's activities – operations, products and/or services – on the environment and society ('inside-out') and (2) the financial impact of sustainability factors on the company ('outside-in').

EU Green Deal
A set of initiatives to set the EU on the path to a green transition, with the ultimate goal of reaching climate neutrality by 2050, by addressing environmental issues such as climate change, biodiversity loss, ozone depletion, water pollution, urban stress, waste production and more.

EU Taxonomy Regulation
A classification system for environmentally sustainable economic activities.

Fit for 55
A package of measures to translate the Green Deal's ambitions into legally binding legislation.

Greenhushing

The practice of concealing climate or sustainability plans from public scrutiny.

Greenwashing

The deceptive or misleading practice of promoting false assertions about environmental credentials, such as claims about eco-friendly products, green investment funds, etc.

Grievance mechanism

A procedure that provides a clear and transparent framework to address complaints in recruitment and the workplace.

Materiality: impact, financial and double

Impact materiality is about the external impacts an organisation's activities have, including impacts on the environment and society ('inside-out').

Financial materiality is about the factors that internally impact a company's financial performance and its ability to create economic value for investors and shareholders ('outside-in').

Financial and impact materiality are interconnected, with both perspectives combined in the concept of *double materiality.*

Net zero

Reduction of absolute emissions across the whole supply chain in order to support the 2015 Paris Agreement goal to limit global temperature increases to 1.5°C.

Paris Agreement

A legally binding international treaty on climate change that was adopted by 196 Parties at the UN Climate Change Conference (COP21) in Paris, France, on 12 December 2015 and entered into force on 4 November 2016. Its overarching goal is to hold *"the increase in the global average temperature to well below 2°C above pre-industrial levels"* and pursue efforts *"to limit the temperature increase to 1.5°C above pre-industrial levels."*

Planetary boundaries

A set of nine limited zones within which humanity can continue to develop and thrive. The further one gets beyond the safe zone, the higher the probability of a change to the functioning of the Earth system, with heavy consequences for the planet and people.

Science Based Targets Initiative (SBTi)

Best practices and guidance in defining emissions reductions and net-zero targets in line with climate science. Companies can define their emission reduction targets and have them validated by SBTi, meaning that approved targets are aligned with the Paris Agreement.

Scope 1 emissions

Direct emissions that a company generates through operating the assets it owns or controls (running buildings, driving vehicles, powering machinery...).

Scope 2 emissions

Indirect emissions: those created by the production of the energy the company buys for power, heating and cooling.

Scope 3 emissions

Everything else: both upstream and downstream indirect emissions. It includes emissions due to the use or disposal of a company's products by their customers and users further down the value chain, right to the end of the product's life cycle, or emissions produced by suppliers that make the products the company uses.

Spiral economy

A concept describing a world *"where the by-products of one organisation or industry not only form a component of another one, but rather become a platform which spawns endlessly unfolding opportunities at varying scales much like the famous Fibonacci sequence."* (See endnote 74.)

Endnotes

1 Witold Henisz, Tim Koller, Robin Nuttall, *Five ways that ESG creates value*, 2019, McKinsey and Co. www.mckinsey.com/capabilities/strategy-and-corporate-finance/our-insights/five-ways-that-esg-creates-value

2 *What is ESG?*, 2023, McKinsey and Co. www.mckinsey.com/featured-insights/mckinsey-explainers/what-is-esg

3 Lucy Pérez, Dame Vivian Hunt, Hamid Samandari, Robin Nuttall, Krysta Biniek, *Does ESG really matter—and why?*, 2022, McKinsey and Co. www.mckinsey.com/capabilities/sustainability/our-insights/does-esg-really-matter-and-why

4 In some circles, the term 'woke' is a buzzword used to refer disparagingly or mockingly to any topic under 'ESG' or 'sustainability'. For obvious reasons, it's not used in this book.

5 commission.europa.eu/strategy-and-policy/priorities-2019-2024/european-green-deal_en

6 www.epa.gov/green-power-markets/summary-inflation-reduction-act-provisions-related-renewable-energy

7 www.edelman.com/trust/trust-barometer

8 Byrne, Dan, *What is the history of ESG?*, Corporate Governance Institute, 21 October 2022. www.thecorporategovernanceinstitute.com/insights/lexicon/what-is-the-history-of-esg/

9 idem

10 *Who Cares Wins, Connecting Financial Markets to a Changing World*, UN Global Compact, 2004. www.unepfi.org/fileadmin/events/2004/stocks/who_cares_wins_global_compact_2004.pdf

11 *26th Annual Global CEO Survey*, PwC, 2023. www.pwc.com/ceosurvey

12 www.ncei.noaa.gov/access/monitoring/monthly-report/global/202206

13 www.visualcapitalist.com/global-temperture-graph-1851-2020/

14 unfccc.int/process-and-meetings/the-paris-agreement

15 *Net Zero Economy Index 2022.* www.pwc.co.uk/sustainability-climate-change/pdf/net-zero-economy-index-2022.pdf

16 www.ipcc.ch/

17 Carbon footprint = the total GHG emissions expressed as carbon dioxide equivalent (CO_2e), from: Laurence A. Wright et al, *Carbon footprinting: towards a universally accepted definition*, Carbon Management, Volume 2, Issue 1 (2011), Future Science Group. www.tandfonline.com/toc/tcmt20/2/1

18 ghgprotocol.org/

19 *What is the difference between Scope 1, 2 and 3 emissions, and what are companies doing to cut all three?*, 2022, World Economic Forum. www.weforum.org/agenda/2022/09/scope-emissions-climate-greenhouse-business/

20 *Corporate Value Chain (Scope 3) Accounting and Reporting Standard*, 2011, Greenhouse Gas Protocol, page 5. ghgprotocol.org/sites/default/files/standards/Corporate-Value-Chain-Accounting-Reporing-Standard_041613_2.pdf

21 Data source: Yearly carbon dioxide peak, Climate Central. www.climatecentral.org/graphic/yearly-carbon-dioxide-peak

22 Data source: *IPCC Sixth Assessment Report*, 2023, IPCC, www.ipcc.ch/report/ar6/wg3/figures/summary-for-policymakers/figure-spm-1

23 Source: Climate Watch, the World Resources Institute (2020). Licensed under CC-BY by Hannah Ritchie (2020). ourworldindata.org/ghg-emissions-by-sector

24 Xu, X., Sharma, P., Shu, S. et al., *Global greenhouse gas emissions from animal-based foods are twice those of plant-based foods*, Nat Food 2, 724–732 (2021). doi.org/10.1038/s43016-021-00358-x

25 Data source: International Energy Agency, May 2023.

26 idem

27 Source: Our World in Data, based on Vaclav Smil (2017) and BP *Statistical Review of World Energy.* ourworldindata.org/fossil-fuels

28 *Fact Sheet | Biogas: Converting Waste to Energy*, 2017, Environmental and Energy Study Institute. www.eesi.org/papers/view/fact-sheet-biogasconverting-waste-to-energy)

29 Energy carriers can exist in a variety of forms and can be converted from one form to another, while energy sources are the original resource from which an energy carrier is produced.

30 Data source: Our World in Data interactive chart, *Statistical Review of World Energy*, BP, 2022. ourworldindata.org/renewable-energy

31 idem

32 www.stockholmresilience.org

33 Designed by Azote for Stockholm Resilience Centre, based on analysis in Persson et al 2022 and Steffen et al 2015. Licenced under CC BY 4.0. www.stockholmresilience.org/research/planetary-boundaries.html

34 *WEF Global Risk Report*, 2023, World Economic Forum. www.weforum.org/reports/global-risks-report-2023/

35 *Carbon Border Adjustment Mechanism*, taxation-customs.ec.europa.eu/carbon-border-adjustment-mechanism_en

36 ec.europa.eu/commission/presscorner/detail/en/qanda_21_3661

37 *PwC Global Survey: ESG Empowered Value Chains 2025*, PwC, www.pwc.de/en/strategy-organisation-processes-systems/operations/global-esg-in-operations-survey.html

38 *The ESG Global Survey 2021*, BNP Paribas. securities.cib.bnpparibas/esg-global-survey-2021/

39 Saul, Jason, *Fixing the S in ESG. How to move from net zero to net impact*, Stanford Social Innovation Review, February 2022.

40 tonyschocolonely.com/nl/en/our-mission

41 www.statista.com/statistics/942628/revenue-market-share-of-tony-s-chocolonely-in-the-netherlands/

42 Photographs by Sebastian Koppehel. commons.wikimedia.org/wiki/File:Tony%27s_Chocolonely_01.jpg and upload.wikimedia.org/wikipedia/commons/1/15/Tony%27s_Chocolonely_03.jpg

43 www.ecgi.global/content/codes

44 corporategovernancecommittee.be/en/about-committee/european-corporate-governance-codes-network

45 Leo E. Strine, Jr., Justin L. Brooke, Kyle M. Diamond, and Derrick L. Parker Jr., *It's time to focus on the "G" in ESG*, Harvard Business Review, 18 November 2022. hbr.org/2022/11/its-time-to-focus-on-the-g-in-esg

46 idem

47   Who Cares Wins, Recommendations by the financial industry to better integrate environmental, social and governance issues in analysis, asset management and securities brokerage. Report to the United Nations, 2004, page ii. www.unepfi.org/fileadmin/events/2004/stocks/who_cares_wins_global_compact_2004.pdf

48   corporategovernancecommittee.be/en/about-2020-code/2020-belgian-code-corporate-governance

49   What Are the Belgian and International References on Corporate Governance? economie.fgov.be/en/themes/enterprises/develop-and-manage-business/responsible-business-conduct/corporate-governance/what-are-belgian-and

50   Source: PwC

51   Paul Polman, Andrew Winston, Net Positive. How courageous companies thrive by giving more than they take, 2021, Harvard Business Review Press

52   Rochelle March, The ESG Explainer: Why ESG Data Is Valuable for Supply Management, 2021, Dun&Bradstreet. www.dnb.co.uk/perspectives/supply-chain/esg-data-valuable-for-supply-management-procurement.html

53   www.un.org/sustainabledevelopment/news/communications-material/

54   The Sustainable Development Goals Report 2022, United Nations. unstats.un.org/sdgs/report/2022/

55   www.pwc.com/gx/en/sustainability/SDG/sdg-2019.pdf

56   Creating a strategy for a better world, SDG Challenge 2019, PwC, www.pwc.com/gx/en/sustainability/SDG/sdg-2019.pdf

57   idem

58   SDG Impact Standards for Enterprises, UNDP. sdgimpact.undp.org/enterprise.html

59   idem

60   Screening of websites for 'greenwashing': half of green claims lack evidence, Press release, 28 January 2021, European Commission. ec.europa.eu/commission/presscorner/detail/en/ip_21_269

61   Integrity Matters: Net Zero Commitments by Businesses, Financial Institutions, Cities and Regions, 2022, United Nations. www.un.org/sites/un2.un.org/files/high-level_expert_group_n7b.pdf

62   Going green, then going dark – One in four companies are keeping quiet on science-based targets, Press release, 18 October 2022, South Pole. www.southpole.com/news/going-green-then-going-dark#

63   Data source: www.visualcapitalist.com/forecast-when-well-run-out-of-each-metal/

64   Sydney Hollingsworth, Will the Earth ever run out of resources?, 2021, InterSTEM. www.interstem.us/2021/07/10/will-the-earth-ever-run-out-of-resources

65   Living in the EU: Circular economy, 2021, European Parliament. www.europarl.europa.eu/RegData/etudes/ATAG/2021/659391/EPRS_ATA(2021)659391_EN.pdf

66   The butterfly diagram: visualising the circular economy, Ellen Mac Arthur Foundation. ellenmacarthurfoundation.org/circular-economy-diagram

67   idem

68   Some sources state that the term was coined in a blog post by Ronald Harwood.

69   Luis M. Jiménez Herrero, Elena Pérez Lagüela, Economía Circular-Espiral: Transición hacia un metabolismo económico cerrado, Ecobook, 2019. Citation translation from: www.unescosost.org/post/unescosost-is-co-author-of-the-new-publication

70   Towards A Spiral Economy, 100open. www.100open.com/towards-a-spiral-economy/

71   PwC Global Survey: ESG Empowered Value Chains 2025, PwC, www.pwc.de/en/strategy-organisation-processes-systems/operations/global-esg-in-operations-survey.html

72   www.naturabrasil.fr/en-us/our-values/sustainable-development

73   www.bcorporation.net/en-us/

74   www2.hm.com/en_ie/sustainability-at-hm/our-work/close-the-loop.html

75   www.thredup.com and www.vinted.com

76   www.inter.ikea.com/en/-/media/InterIKEA/IGI/Financial%20Reports/English_The_testament_of_a_dealer_2018.pdf

77   Transforming into a circular business, IKEA Group. about.ikea.com/en/sustainability/a-world-without-waste

78   Commission.environment.ec.europa.eu/strategy/circular-economy-action-plan_en

79   Paul Leinwand, Cesare R. Mainardi, Strategy That Works. How Winning Companies Close the Strategy-to-Execution Gap, 2016, Harvard Business Review Press

80   Data source: Gunnar Friede et al, ESG and financial performance: Aggregated evidence from more than 2000 empirical studies, Journal of Sustainable Finance & Investment, October 2015, Volume 5, Number 4, pp. 210-33; www.tandfonline.com/doi/full/10.1080/20430795.2015.1118917

81   Data from PwC Annual Corporate Directors Surveys, 2019, 2020 and 2021.

82   PwC Annual Corporate Directors Survey, 2022. www.pwc.com/us/en/services/governance-insights-center/library/annual-corporate-directors-survey.html

83   Vision and mission statements are closely linked: the terms are often used interchangeably.

84   www.beyondmeat.com/en-US/mission

85   John Goddard, Why Companies Aren't Living Up to Their Climate Pledges, 2022, Harvard Business Review. hbr.org/2022/08/why-companies-arent-living-up-to-their-climate-pledges

86   Corporate Climate Responsibility Monitor 2023, New Climate Institute. newclimate.org/resources/publications/corporate-climate-responsibility-monitor-2023

87   Climate change: Top companies exaggerating their progress – study, BBC News 7 February 2022. www.bbc.com/news/science-environment-60248830

88   On climate, most corporations more talk than action, Press release, Agence France Presse, 13 February 2023. www.france24.com/en/live-news/20230213-on-climate-most-corporations-more-talk-than-action

89 Kate Mackenzie, *Too Many Companies Are Banking on Carbon Capture to Reach Net Zero*, 15 January 2021, Bloomberg. www.bloomberg.com/news/articles/2021-01-15/too-many-companies-are-banking-on-carbon-capture-to-reach-net-zero#xj4y7vzkg (paywall content)

90 *'Net zero' carbon targets are dangerous distractions from the priority of cutting emissions says new Oxfam report*, Press release, Oxfam International, 3 August 2021. www.oxfam.org/en/press-releases/net-zero-carbon-targets-are-dangerous-distractions-priority-cutting-emissions-says

91 W. Chan Kim and Renée Mauborgne, *Blue Ocean Strategy, Expanded Edition: How to Create Uncontested Market Space and Make the Competition Irrelevant*, 2015, Harvard Business Review Press. blueoceanstrategy.com/what-is-blue-ocean-strategy

92 *ESG Empowered Value Chains 2025*. PwC, 2023. www.pwc.de/en/strategy-organisation-processes-systems/operations/global-esg-in-operations-survey.html

93 idem

94 idem

95 idem

96 idem

97 idem

98 idem

99 www.globalreporting.org

100 www.sasb.org

101 sdgs.un.org/goals

102 www.cdp.net

103 www.fsb-tcfd.org

104 sciencebasedtargets.org

105 www.onetrust.com/blog/esg-reporting/

106 commission.europa.eu/strategy-and-policy/priorities-2019-2024/european-green-deal/delivering-european-green-deal_en

107 *The European Green Deal*, COM(2019) 640 final, European Commission.eur-lex.europa.eu/resource.html?uri=cellar:b828d165-1c22-11ea-8c1f-01aa75ed71a1.0002.02/DOC_1&format=PDF

108 idem

109 eur-lex.europa.eu/eli/reg/2019/2088/oj

110 finance.ec.europa.eu/sustainable-finance/tools-and-standards/eu-taxonomy-sustainable-activities_en

111 eur-lex.europa.eu/legal-content/EN/TXT/?uri=CELEX:32022L2464

112 Data sources: PwC and Hazell Ransome, Benjamin Taylor, *CSRD and ESRS: how EU corporate sustainability reporting is evolving*, 2022, PRI. www.unpri.org/pri-blog/csrd-and-esrs-how-eu-corporate-sustainability-reporting-is-evolving/10539.article

113 Ryno Rouxn Cedric Bodart, Aidan Geel, *How to prepare and progress towards EU Taxonomy alignment in 2023*, Sustainalize. www.sustainalize.com/news/eu-taxonomy-alignment/

114 *The Enhancement and Standardization of Climate-Related Disclosures for Investors*, Proposed rule, 21 March 2022, Securities and Exchange Commission. www.sec.gov/rules/proposed/2022/33-11042.pdf

115 *Ninety One survey finds European fund industry overly reliant on ESG scores*, 22 May 2022, Ninety One. ninetyone.com/en/united-states/newsroom/ninety-one-survey-finds-european-fund-industry-overly-reliant-on-esg-scores

116 Brian Tayan, ESG Ratings: *A Compass without Direction*, 24 August 2022, Harvard Law School Forum on Corporate Governance. corpgov.law.harvard.edu/2022/08/24/esg-ratings-a-compass-without-direction/

117 *The ESG Mirage*, 10 December 2021, Bloomberg. www.bloomberg.com/news/audio/2021-12-10/the-esg-mirage-podcast

118 *Draft European Sustainability Reporting Standards, ESRS 1 – General Requirements*, 2022, EFRAG. efrag.org/Assets/Download?assetUrl=%2Fsites%2Fwebpublishing%2FsiteAssets%2F06%2520Draft%2520ESRS%25201%2520General%2520requirements%2520November%25202022.pdf

119 *Yale CELI List of Companies Leaving and Staying in Russia*, www.yalerussianbusinessretreat.com/

120 climatetrace.org/

121 Paul Polman, Andrew Winston, *Net Positive. How courageous companies thrive by giving more than they take*, 2021, Harvard Business Review Press

122 Jessica Pransky, Kim Knickle, *Best Practices: Creating An RFP For ESG Reporting And Data Management Software*, 2023, Verdantix. www.verdantix.com/report/best-practices-creating-an-rfp-for-esg-reporting-and-data-management-software

123 idem endnotes 1, 2 and 3

124 *Sustainability Report 2021*, DEME. www.deme-group.com/sites/default/files/2022-05/Sustainability_Report_2021%20%281%29.pdf
www.deme-group.com/sites/default/files/2023-02/DEME%20FY2022%20Results%2027.02.2023.pdf

125 trendsimpactawards.be/en/home_en/

126 www.bekaert.com/en/sustainability/reports
www.bekaert.com/en/sustainability/protect-the-planet

127 *Bekaert included in BEL ESG index of Euronext Brussels*, Press release, 15 February 2023. www.bekaert.com/en/about-us/news-room/news/bekaert-included-in-bel-esg-index-of-euronext-brussels

128 *Sustainable Business Transformation Playbook*, 2022, PwC

129 *Sustainable Corporate Governance Position Paper*, 2023, PwC

130 *Sustainable Business Transformation Playbook*, 2022, PwC

131 Jeff Waller, Adrien Couton, *Three Stages Of Integration: How The CFO Can Drive Sustainability Transformation*, Engie Impact. www.engieimpact.com/insights/sustainable-finance

132 *Sustainability Integration Framework*, 2023, Global Sustainability, Allianz. www.allianz.com/content/dam/onemarketing/azcom/Allianz_com/responsibility/documents/Allianz_ESG_Integration_Framework.pdf
www.allianz.com/content/dam/onemarketing/azcom/Allianz_com/sustainability/documents/Allianz_Group_Sustainability_Report_2020-web.pdf
www.allianz.com/en/sustainability/ratings.html#tabpar_6716_8Tab

133 Mehdi Miremadi, Christopher Musso, Ulrich Weihe, *How much will consumers pay to go green?*, 2012, McKinsey Sustainability. www.mckinsey.com/capabilities/sustainability/our-insights/how-much-will-consumers-pay-to-go-green

134 *SDG Industry Matrix*, 2015, UN Global Compact and KPMG. unglobalcompact.org/library/3111

135 *Creating Shared Value and Sustainability Report 2021*, Nestlé. www.nestle.com/sites/default/files/2022-03/creating-shared-value-sustainability-report-2021-en.pdf

136 carbonpricingdashboard.worldbank.org/

137 *PwC Global Survey: ESG Empowered Value Chains 2025*, PwC, www.pwc.de/en/strategy-organisation-processes-systems/operations/global-esg-in-operations-survey.html

138 Jean-Charles van den Branden, Piet de Paepe, Magali Deryckere, Jelle Dhaen, *Belgian Companies Use ESG to Create Value and Differentiate*, 2023, Bain & Co. www.bain.com/insights/Belgian-companies-use-esg-to-create-value-and-differentiate/

139 idem

140 www.aspiravi.be/en/ and brochure.aspiravi.be/en/growth-of-the-aspiravi-group

141 eu.patagonia.com and www.patagoniaworks.com/press/2022/6/24/patagonia-supports-choice

142 www.fairlabor.org/

143 apparelcoalition.org/

144 www.bcorporation.net/en-us/

145 *Blockchain for Supply Chain: Driving Transparency and Traceability*, 2020, World Economic Forum. www3.weforum.org/docs/WEF_IBC_White_Paper_Blockchain_for_Supply_Chain.pdf

146 *Communication: A Green Deal Industrial Plan for the Net-Zero Age*, 2023, European Commission. commission.europa.eu/document/41514677-9598-4d89-a572-abe21cb037f4_en

147 *European Social Fund Plus*, European Commission, ec.europa.eu/european-social-fund-plus/en

148 Interreg, interreg.eu/

149 F&T Portal, European Commission, ec.europa.eu/info/funding-tenders/opportunities/portal/screen/home

150 *Summary of Inflation Reduction Act provisions related to renewable energy*, US Environmental Protection Agency. www.epa.gov/green-power-markets/summary-inflation-reduction-act-provisions-related-renewable-energy

151 *Facilitating the Green Transition for ASEAN SMEs*, 2021, OECD. www.oecd.org/southeast-asia/regional-programme/networks/OECD-Facilitating-the-green-transition-for-ASEAN-SMEs.pdf

152 Commonly referred to as Sharia compliant bonds: en.wikipedia.org/wiki/Sukuk

153 Aarti Nagraj, *Strong pipeline of green bonds likely from Middle East in 2023, S&P says*, The National News, 8 February 2023

154 Yousef Saba, Yoruk Bahceli, *Saudi wealth fund to raise $5.5 billion with second green bond sale*, 7 February 2023, Reuters. www.reuters.com/markets/rates-bonds/saudi-arabias-pif-selling-three-tranche-dollar-green-bonds-2023-02-07/

155 Source: analysis of data in an internal PwC system.

156 www.netzeroassetmanagers.org/

157 *Global Private Equity Responsible Investment Survey 2021*, PwC

158 idem 2021 and 2013

159 Miriam Pozza, *Will ESG factors create or destroy value in your next deal? Six orange flags for dealmakers*, 27 February 2023, s+b, a PwC Publication. Extract reproduced with the permission of the author.

160 Proposal for a Directive of the European Parliament and of the Council on Corporate Sustainability Due Diligence and amending Directive (EU) 2019/1937

161 Overview of current ESG related proposals: *Legislative Train Schedule*, European Parliament. www.europarl.europa.eu/legislative-train/

162 commission.europa.eu/strategy-and-policy/priorities-2019-2024/european-green-deal/delivering-european-green-deal_en

163 Directive (EU) 2018/2001 of the European Parliament and of the Council of 11 December 2018 on the promotion of the use of energy from renewable sources

164 Directive (EU) 2018/2002 of the European Parliament and of the Council of 11 December 2018 amending Directive 2012/27/EU on energy efficiency

165 Council Directive 2003/96/EC of 27 October 2003 restructuring the Community framework for the taxation of energy products and electricity

166 Directive 2010/31/EU of the European Parliament and of the Council of 19 May 2010 on the energy performance of buildings

167 Regulation (EU) 2019/631 of the European Parliament and of the Council of 17 April 2019 setting CO_2 emission performance standards for new passenger cars and for new light commercial vehicles

168 *European Green Deal: ambitious new law agreed to deploy sufficient alternative fuels infrastructure*, 2023, European Commission. ec.europa.eu/commission/presscorner/detail/en/IP_23_1867

169 *Sustainable aviation fuels – ReFuelEU Aviation*, European Commission. ec.europa.eu/info/law/better-regulation/have-your-say/initiatives/12303-Sustainable-aviation-fuels-ReFuelEU-Aviation_en

170 *FuelEU Maritime initiative: Provisional agreement to decarbonise the maritime sector*, Press release, 23 March 2023, European Council. www.consilium.europa.eu/en/press/press-releases/2023/03/23/fueleu-maritime-initiative-provisional-agreement-to-decarbonise-the-maritime-sector/

171 *Carbon Border Adjustment Mechanism.* taxation-customs.ec.europa.eu/carbon-border-adjustment-mechanism_en

172 Directive 2003/87/EC of the European Parliament and of the Council of 13 October 2003 establishing a system for greenhouse gas emission allowance trading within the Union

173 Regulation (EU) 2023/956 of the European Parliament and of the Council of 10 May 2023 establishing a carbon border adjustment mechanism

174 *Circular economy action plan*, European Commission. environment.ec.europa.eu/strategy/circular-economy-action-plan_en

175 Directive 2008/98/EC of the European Parliament and of the Council of 19 November 2008 on waste

176 Directive (EU) 2019/904 of the European Parliament and of the Council of 5 June 2019 on the reduction of the impact of certain plastic products on the environment

177 European Parliament and Council Directive 94/62/EC of 20 December 1994 on packaging and packaging waste

178 Proposal for a Regulation of the European Parliament and of the Council concerning batteries and waste batteries, repealing Directive 2006/66/EC and amending Regulation (EU) No 2019/1020. data.consilium.europa.eu/doc/document/ST-5469-2023-INIT/en/pdf

179 *Rules promoting the repair of goods*, European Commission. commission.europa.eu/law/law-topic/consumer-protection-law/consumer-contract-law/rules-promoting-repair-goods_en

180 *Ecodesign for Sustainable Products Regulation*, European Commission. commission.europa.eu/energy-climate-change-environment/standards-tools-and-labels/products-labelling-rules-and-requirements/sustainable-products/ecodesign-sustainable-products_en

181 *Proposal for a Directive on empowering consumers for the green transition and annex*, 2022, European Commission. commission.europa.eu/publications/proposal-directive-empowering-consumers-green-transition-and-annex_en

182 *Proposal for a Directive on green claims*, 2022, European Commission. environment.ec.europa.eu/publications/proposal-directive-green-claims_en

183 Directive 2009/125/EC of the European Parliament and of the Council of 21 October 2009 establishing a framework for the setting of ecodesign requirements for energy-related products

184 *Nature restoration law*, European Commission. environment.ec.europa.eu/topics/nature-and-biodiversity/nature-restoration-law_en

185 *EU passes nature restoration law in knife-edge vote*, 12 July 2023, The Guardian. www.theguardian.com/world/2023/jul/12/eu-passes-nature-restoration-law-vote-meps

186 Regulation (EU) 2018/841 of the European Parliament and of the Council of 30 May 2018 on the inclusion of greenhouse gas emissions and removals from land use, land use change and forestry in the 2030 climate

187 files.mutualcdn.com/ituc/files/2022-ITUC-Rights-Index-Exec-Summ-EN.pdf

188 *The relationship between European Union law and the European Social Charter*, 15 July 2014, Council of Europe, rm.coe.int/CoERMPublicCommonSearchServices/DisplayDCTMContent?documentId=09000016806544ec

189 European Convention for the Protection of Human Rights and Fundamental Freedoms, as amended by Protocols Nos. 11 and 14, 4 November 1950, ETS 5, Council of Europe

190 European Social Charter, 18 October 1961, ETS 35, Council of Europe

191 Charter of Fundamental Rights of the European Union, 26 October 2012, 2012/C 326/02, European Union

192 Regulation (EU) 2019/2088 of the European Parliament and of the Council of 27 November 2019 on sustainability-related disclosures in the financial services sector.

193 Directive (EU) 2022/2464 of the European Parliament and of the Council of 14 December 2022 amending Regulation (EU) No 537/2014, Directive 2004/109/EC, Directive 2006/43/EC and Directive 2013/34/EU, as regards corporate sustainability reporting

194 Francisca Torres-Cortés, et al, *Study on due diligence requirements through the supply chain – Final report*, 2020, European Commission. data.europa.eu/doi/10.2838/39830.

195 Proposal for a Directive of the European Parliament and of the Council on Corporate Sustainability Due Diligence and amending Directive (EU) 2019/1937.

196 Modern Slavery Act 2015, www.legislation.gov.uk/ukpga/2015/30/contents/enacted

197 Directive (EU) 2006/54/EC of the European Parliament and of the Council of 5 July 2006 on the implementation of the principle of equal opportunities and equal treatment of men and women in matters of employment and occupation.

198 *Gender pay gap: Council adopts new rules on pay transparency*, Press release, 24 April 2023, European Council. www.consilium.europa.eu/en/press/press-releases/2023/04/24/gender-pay-gap-council-adopts-new-rules-on-pay-transparency/

199 idem

200 Articles 8 and 9 of Directive (EU) of the European Parliament and of the Council to strengthen the application of the principle of equal pay for equal work or work of equal value between men and women through pay transparency and enforcement mechanisms. Not yet published in the EU Official Journal.

201 *A Safe and Healthy Working Environment*, UN Global Compact. unglobalcompact.org/take-action/safety-andhealth

202 *Gen Z in The Workplace*, Survey by TalentLMS and BamboolHR. www.talentlms.com/research/gen-z-workplace-statistics#what-matters-to-Gen-Z

203 osha.europa.eu/en/safety-and-health-legislation

204 Council Directive 89/391/EEC of 12 June 1989 on the introduction of measures to encourage improvements in the safety and health of workers at work.

205 Art. 7, 5., Council Directive 89/391/EEC of 12 June 1989 on the introduction of measures to encourage improvements in the safety and health of workers at work.

206 Chapter 6a, article 29b, 2,b,ii, Directive (EU) 2022/2464 of the European Parliament and of the Council of 14 December 2022 amending Regulation (EU) No 537/2014, Directive 2004/109/EC, Directive 2006/43/EC and Directive 2013/34/EU, as regards corporate sustainability reporting.

207 viewpoint.pwc.com/dt/gx/en/pwc/in_briefs/in_briefs_INT/in_briefs_INT/the-revised-draft-european-sustainability-reporting-standards-have-been-released-for-feedback.html

208 *Corporate sustainability due diligence, What are the obligations for companies and their directors?*, European Commission. commission.europa.eu/business-economy-euro/doing-business-eu/corporate-sustainability-due-diligence_en#what-are-the-obligations-for-companies-and-their-directors

209 Jessica Pransky, Kim Knickle, *Smart Innovators: ESG Reporting and Data Management Software*, 2023, Verdantix. www.verdantix.com/report/smart-innovators-esg-reporting-and-data-management-software